BLEU
1

McDOUGAL LITTELL

Discovering
FRENCH
Nouveau!

Unit 3 Resource Book

Components authored by Jean-Paul Valette and Rebecca M. Valette:

- Workbook
- Communipak
- Assessment Program
- Video Program
- Audio Program

Components authored by Sloane Publications:

- Family Letter, *Patricia Smith*
- Absent Student Copymasters, *E. Kristina Baer*
- Family Involvement, *Patricia Smith*
- Multiple Choice Test Items, *Nicole Dicop-Hineline*

Other Components

- Video Activities, *T. Jeffrey Richards, Philip D. Korfe, Consultant*
- Comprehensive (Semester) Tests, *T. Jeffrey Richards*
- Activités pour tous, *Patricia L. Ménard*

ISBN-13: 978-0-618-29828-0   ISBN-10: 0 - 618 - 29828 - 2

8 9 10 — BHV — 09 08 07 06

Discovering
FRENCH
Nouveau!

BLEU

Unité 3

Table of Contents

Table of Contents
Unité 3. Qu'est-ce qu'on fait?

LEÇON 8 Un concert de musique africaine 93

URB
p. iv

To the Teacher

The Unit Resource Books that accompany each unit of *Discovering French, Nouveau!–Bleu* provide a wide variety of materials to practice, expand on, and assess the material in the *Discovering French, Nouveau!–Bleu* student text.

Components

Following is a list of components included in each Unit Resource Book, correlated to each **Leçon:**
• Workbook, Teacher's Edition
• *Activités pour tous*, Teacher's Edition
• Lesson Plans
• Block Scheduling Lesson Plans
• Family Letter
• Absent Student Copymasters
• Family Involvement
• Video Activities
• Videoscripts
• Audioscripts
• Lesson Quizzes

Unit Resources include the following materials:
• Communipak
• *Activités pour tous* Reading, Teacher's Edition
• Workbook Reading and Culture Activities, Teacher's Edition
• Lesson Plans for *Images*
• Block Scheduling Lesson Plans for *Images*
• Assessment
    Unit Test
    Listening Comprehension Performance Test
    Speaking Performance Test
    Reading Comprehension Performance Test
    Writing Performance Test
    Multiple Choice Test Items
    Comprehensive Test
    Test Scoring Tools

• Audioscripts
• Videoscripts for *Images*
• Answer Key

Component Description

Workbook, Teacher's Edition

The *Discovering French, Nouveau!–Bleu* Workbook directly references the student text. It provides additional practice to allow students to build their control of French and develop French proficiency. The activities provide guided communicative practice in meaningful contexts and frequent opportunity for self-expression.

Listening Activities give students the opportunity to demonstrate comprehension of spoken French in a variety of realistic contexts. Students listen to excerpts from the CD that accompanies the *Discovering French, Nouveau!–Bleu* program while working through listening activities to improve both general and discrete comprehension skills.

Writing Activities give students the chance to develop their writing skills and put into practice what they have learned in class. The last activity is called *Communication* and encourages students to express themselves in various additional communicative situations.

The Reading and Culture Activities contain realia (illustrations and objects from real life) from French-speaking countries and various kinds of cultural activities. Each unit includes one set of Reading and Culture Activities.

Activités pour tous, Teacher's Edition

The activities in *Activités pour tous* include vocabulary, grammar, and reading practice at varying levels of difficulty. Each practice section is three pages long, with each page corresponding to a level of difficulty (A, B, and C). A is the easiest and C is the most challenging.

Lesson Plans

These lesson plans follow the general sequence of a *Discovering French, Nouveau!–Bleu* lesson. Teachers using these plans should become familiar with both the overall structure of a *Discovering French, Nouveau!–Bleu* lesson and with the format of the lesson plans and available ancillaries before translating these plans to a daily sequence.

Block Scheduling Lesson Plans

These plans are structured to help teachers maximize the advantages of block scheduling, while minimizing the challenges of longer periods.

Family Letter and Family Involvement

This section offers strategies and activities to increase family support for students' study of French language and culture.

Absent Student Copymasters

The Absent Student Copymasters enable students who miss part of a **Leçon** to go over the material on their own. The Absent Student Copymasters also offer strategies and techniques to help students understand new or challenging information. If possible, make a copy of the CD, video, or DVD available, either as a loan to an absent student or for use in the school library or language lab.

Video Activities and Videoscript

The Video Activities that accompany the Video or DVD for each module focus students' attention on each video section and reinforce the material presented in the module. A transcript of the Videoscript is included for each **Leçon.**

Audioscripts

This section provides scripts for the Audio Program and includes vocabulary presentations, dialogues, readings and reading summaries, audio for Workbook and Student Text activities, and audio for Lesson Quizzes.

Communipak

The Communipak section contains five types of oral communication activities introduced sequentially by level of challenge or difficulty. Designed to encourage students to use French for communication in conversational exchanges, they include *Interviews*, *Tu as la parole*, *Conversations*, *Échanges*, and *Tête à tête* activities.

Assessment

Lesson Quizzes

The Lesson Quizzes provide short accuracy-based vocabulary and structure assessments. They measure how well students have mastered the new conversational phrases, structures, and vocabulary in the lesson. Also designed to encourage students to review material in a given lesson before continuing further in the unit, the quizzes provide an opportunity for focused cyclical re-entry and review.

Unit Tests

The Unit Tests are intended to be administered upon completion of each unit. They may be given in the language laboratory or in the classroom. The total possible score for each test is 100 points. Scoring suggestions for each section appear on the test sheets. The Answer Key for the Unit Tests appears at the end of the Unit Resource Book.

There is one Unit Test for each of the eight units in *Discovering French, Nouveau!–Bleu*. Each test is available in two versions: Form A and Form B. A complete Audioscript is given for the listening portion of the tests; the recordings of these sections appear on CD 14.

Speaking Performance Test

These tests enable teachers to evaluate students' comprehension, ability to respond in French, and overall fluency. Designed to be administered to students individually, each test consists of two sections, *Conversations* and *Tu as la parole*.

Reading Comprehension Performance Test

These tests allow for evaluation of students' ability to understand material written in French. The Reading Comprehension Performance Test is designed for group administration. Each test contains several reading selections, in a variety of styles. Each selection is accompanied by one to four related multiple-choice questions in English.

Listening Comprehension Performance Test

The Listening Comprehension Test is designed for group administration. Each test contains ten short listening items, each accompanied by a multiple-choice question. The test is divided into two parts, *Conversations* and *Questions et réponses*. The listening selections are recorded on CD, and the full script is also provided so that the teacher can administer the test either by playing the CD or by reading the selections aloud.

Writing Performance Test

The Writing Performance Test gives students the opportunity to demonstrate how well they can use the material in the unit for self-expression. The emphasis is not on the production of specific grammar forms, but rather on the communication of meaning. Each test contains several guided writing activities, which vary in format from unit to unit.

Multiple Choice Test Items

These are the print version of the multiple choice questions from the Test Generator. They are contextualized and focus on vocabulary, grammar, reading, writing, and cultural knowledge.

Answer Key

The Answer Key includes answers that correspond to the following material:

- Video Activities
- Lesson Quizzes
- Communipak Activities
- Unit Tests
- Comprehensive Tests
- Performance Tests
- Multiple Choice Test Items

Discovering
FRENCH *Nouveau!*

B L E U

Unité 3
Leçon 5

Workbook TE

Unité 3. Qu'est-ce qu'on fait?

LEÇON 5   Le français pratique: Mes activités

LISTENING ACTIVITIES

Section 1. J'aime . . . Je n'aime pas . . .

A. Compréhension orale

M = Marc   C = Caroline

1. M _____

2. M _____

3. C, M _____

4. C _____

5. C _____

6. M _____

7. C _____

8. C _____

9. M _____

10. M, C _____

11. C _____

12. C, M _____

Unité 3
Leçon 5

Workbook TE

Nom _____

Classe _____ Date _____

Discovering
FRENCH
Nouveau!

B L E U

B. Parlez.

Modèle: J'aime écouter la radio.
(Je n'aime pas écouter la radio.)

1. J'aime regarder la télé.
(Je n'aime pas regarder la télé.)

2. J'aime jouer au foot.
(Je n'aime pas jouer au foot.)

3. J'aime jouer au tennis.
(Je n'aime pas jouer au tennis.)

4. J'aime manger.
(Je n'aime pas manger.)

5. J'aime téléphoner.
(Je n'aime pas téléphoner.)

6. J'aime nager.
(Je n'aime pas nager.)

7. J'aime voyager.
(Je n'aime pas voyager.)

Section 2. Invitations

C. Compréhension orale

1. At a party.   a. ✓ accepts   b. ____ declines

2. By the tennis courts.   a. ✓ accepts   b. ____ declines

3. At home.   a. ____ accepts   b. ✓ declines

Est-ce que vous allez aller
au cinéma?

Nom _____

Classe _____ Date _____ _____

Discovering
FRENCH
Nouveau!

B L E U

Unité 3
Leçon 5
Workbook TE

D. Parlez.

Modèle: Est-ce que tu veux jouer au foot avec moi?

1. Est-ce que tu veux jouer
au basket avec moi?

2. ... regarder la télé ...?

3. ... nager ...?

4. ... chanter ...?

5. ... voyager ...?

Section 3. Dictée

E. Écoutez et écrivez.

— Dis, Stéphanie, est-ce que tu *veux* jouer au tennis *avec* moi?

— Je regrette, mais je ne *peux* pas.

— Pourquoi? *(Why?)*

— Je *dois* étudier.

Discovering
FRENCH
Nouveau

BLEU

WRITING ACTIVITIES

A* 1. Qu'est-ce qu'ils aiment faire? *(What do they like to do?)*

The following people are saying what they like to do. Complete the bubbles, as in the model.

2. Et toi?

Say whether or not you like to do the activities suggested by the pictures.

 1. J'aime (je n'aime pas) regarder la télé. _____

 2. J'aime (je n'aime pas) manger. _____

 3. J'aime (je n'aime pas) travailler. _____

 4. J'aime (je n'aime pas) parler français. _____

 5. J'aime (je n'aime pas) parler espagnol. _____

 6. J'aime (je n'aime pas) écouter la radio. _____

 7. J'aime (je n'aime pas) jouer aux jeux vidéo. _____

 8. J'aime (je n'aime pas) chanter. _____

*NOTE: Beginning with this unit, activities are coded to <u>sections</u> in your textbook (Ex: Leçon 5, Section A) for your reference.

Nom _____

Classe _____ Date _____

Discovering
FRENCH *Nouveau!*

B L E U

Unité 3
Leçon 5

Workbook TE

B/C 3.  Communication: En français!

1. You are spending your vacation in a French summer camp.

   Ask your friend Patrick . . .

   • *if he likes to swim*

   Est-ce que tu aimes nager?

   • *if he likes to play basketball*

   Est-ce que tu aimes jouer au basket?

   • *if he wants to play soccer with you*

   Est-ce que tu veux jouer au foot avec moi?

2. Your friend Cécile is phoning to invite you to go to a restaurant. Unfortunately you have an English exam tomorrow.

   Tell Cécile . . .

   • *that you are sorry*

   Je regrette.

   • *that you cannot have dinner at the restaurant with her*

   Je ne peux pas dîner au restaurant avec toi.

   • *that you have to study*

   Je dois étudier.

3. At the tennis court, you meet your friend Jean-Claude.

   • *Tell him that you would like to play tennis.*

   Je voudrais jouer au tennis.

   • *Ask him if he wants to play with you.*

   Est-ce que tu veux jouer avec moi?

TENNIS

Nom _____

Classe _____ Date _____ _____

Discovering
FRENCH
Nouveau!

B L E U

Unité 3
Leçon 5

Activités pour tous TE

Unité 3. Qu'est-ce qu'on fait?

LEÇON 5 Le français pratique: Mes activités

A

Activité 1   J'aime . . . Je n'aime pas . . .

Fill in the blanks using the visual cues and either **j'aime** or **je n'aime pas**.

| j'aime | | je n'aime pas |

1. —Moi, _j'aime_____ étudier le français!

2. —Moi, _j'aime_____ jouer au foot avec mes copains.

3. —Moi, _je n'aime pas_____ toujours jouer aux jeux vidéo.

4. —Moi, _j'aime_____ dîner au restaurant.

5. —Moi, _je n'aime pas_____ toujours travailler.

Activité 2   Je veux . . . Je ne veux pas . . .

First fill in the blanks using the visual cues and either **je veux** or **je ne veux pas.** Then match the statement to the person most likely to have made it.

| Je veux | | Je ne veux pas |

_b_ 1. _Je veux_____ parler bien anglais.   a. Venus Williams

_d_ 2. _Je veux_____ parler avec le président.   b. Penelope Cruz

_e_ 3. _Je ne veux pas_ nager.   c. Céline Dion

_a_ 4. _Je veux_____ jouer au tennis avec ma sœur. d. Barbara Walters

_c_ 5. _Je veux_____ chanter mes chansons.   e. Silvestre, le chat

Activité 3   Invitations

Are the following people accepting or declining an invitation?

1. Je voudrais bien jouer avec toi, mais je ne peux pas aujourd'hui.   accepting   (declining)

2. Oui, bien sûr. Merci pour l'invitation.   (accepting)   declining

3. Merci, mais je dois travailler vendredi soir.   accepting   (declining)

4. D'accord. Je veux bien.   (accepting)   declining

5. Je regrette, mais je ne peux pas.   accepting   (declining)

Nom _____

Classe _____ Date _____

B

Activité 1 J'aime . . . Je n'aime pas . . .

First fill in the blanks with **J'aime** or **Je n'aime pas,** using the cues. Then match the beginning of each sentence with its logical conclusion.

☺ _c_ 1. __J'aime__ parler français . . .   a. parce que mes amis sont là.

☺ _d_ 2. __J'aime__ dîner au restaurant . . . b. parce que je ne danse pas.

☹ _b_ 3. __Je n'aime pas__ les boums . . .   c. parce que mon copain parle français.

☹ _e_ 4. __Je n'aime pas__ voyager . . .   d. parce que j'aime manger.

☺ _a_ 5. __J'aime__ aller au lycée . . .   e. parce que j'ai un chat à la maison.

Activité 2 Je veux . . . Je ne veux pas . . .

First fill in the blanks using the cues and either **je veux** or **je ne veux pas.** Then respond in complete sentences to the question: **Et toi?**

1. —Moi, _je ne veux pas_ étudier ce soir.   Et toi?

— _Moi, je ne veux pas étudier ce soir._

2. —Moi, _je veux_ jouer au foot samedi.   Et toi?

— _____

3. —Moi, _je veux_ voyager en France.   Et toi?

— _____

4. —Moi, _je veux_ jouer au tennis avec toi.   Et toi?

— _____

5. —Moi, _je ne veux pas_ travailler samedi après-midi.   Et toi?

— _____

Activité 3 Invitations

Taking your cue from the smile or the pout, choose the best response to each question.

1. Est-ce que tu veux jouer aux jeux vidéo? ☺
   a. Oui, bien sûr.   b. Oui, mais je ne peux pas.

2. Est-ce que tu peux aller au café avec nous? ☹
   a. D'accord. À tout à l'heure!   b. Non, je ne peux pas.

3. Est-ce que tu peux dîner au restaurant samedi soir? ☹
   a. Je regrette, mais je ne peux pas.   b. Je veux bien, merci.

4. Est-ce que tu veux regarder la télé avec moi? ☺
   a. Oui, je veux bien, mais je dois travailler.   b. Oui, d'accord.

Nom _____

Classe _____ Date _____

Discovering
FRENCH *Nouveau!*

B L E U

Unité 3
Leçon 5   Activités pour tous TE

C

Activité 1   J'aime . . . . Je n'aime pas . . .   (sample answers)

Using the cues, write complete sentences about activities that you like or don't like to do.

1. ☺ À l'école, j'aime parler français.

2. ☺ Avec mes copains, j'aime jouer au basket.

3. ☹ En hiver, je n'aime pas nager.

4. ☹ À la maison, je n'aime pas faire la vaisselle.

5. ☹ En été, je n'aime pas étudier.

Activité 2   Je veux . . . Je ne veux pas . . .

Fill in the first blank with the correct verb for the activity shown. Then, using the cues, write sentences stating that you want or do not want to do the activities.

1. jouer au basket   ☺   Je veux jouer au basket

2. jouer aux jeux vidéo   ☺   Je veux jouer aux jeux vidéo.

3. danser   ☹   Je ne veux pas danser.

4. écouter la radio   ☹   Je ne veux pas écouter la radio.

5. dîner au restaurant   ☺   Je veux dîner au restaurant.

Activité 3   Invitations

Invite the following people to do certain activities. They either accept or decline the invitation.

1. Sylvie: danser avec toi

   —— Est-ce que tu veux danser avec moi ?

   —Oui, je veux bien .

2. Michel: parler espagnol avec toi

   —— Est-ce que tu peux parler espagnol avec moi ?

   —Je regrette, mais je ne peux pas .

3. Caroline: jouer aux jeux vidéo

   —— Est-ce que tu veux jouer aux jeux vidéo ?

   —Oui, mais je ne peux pas .

4. Frédéric: voyager avec toi

   —— Est-ce que tu veux voyager avec moi ?

   —Oui, d'accord !

LEÇON 5 Le français pratique: Mes activités, page 72

Objectives

Communicative Functions and Topics To describe daily activities
To say what people do and don't do
To talk about what you want, would like, and do not want or like to do
To invite a friend, accept an invitation, and turn down an invitation

Linguistic Goals To use *je (veux)* and *je ne (veux) pas*

Cultural Goals To learn about daily activities of French young people

Motivation and Focus

❏ Have students look at the picture on page 70–71 and tell where the people in the photo are and what they are doing. Discuss similarities and differences between French and American activities. Read *Thème et Objectifs* to preview the content of the unit.

Presentation and Explanation

❏ *Lesson Opener:* Have students look at the pictures on pages 72–73 and read *Accent sur…*. Ask them to point out which of these activities they enjoy doing. Help them read the captions for the photos.

❏ *Vocabulary A:* To introduce talking about preferences, play **Audio** CD 2, Track 1 or **Video** 5.1–2, or model the expressions in *Préférences*, pages 74–75, using **Overhead Transparencies** 14a and b to clarify meanings. Point out the *Préférences* box on pages 74–75. Have students talk about their own likes and dislikes using the expressions.

❏ *Vocabulary B:* Present *Souhaits*, page 77. After modeling the expressions, have students repeat. Point out the verb forms in the box. Ask students to complete the expressions with their own wishes.

❏ *Vocabulary C:* As you model *Invitations*, page 78, use gestures and intonation to help clarify meanings of expressions for accepting and turning down an invitation. Play **Video** 5.3. Have students repeat the questions and expressions.

❏ Introduce information about the French telephone system by playing **Video** 5.5 or reading that section in the **Videoscript**, page 26. Students can comment on similarities and differences in public telephones in France and in the U.S.

Guided Practice and Checking Understanding

❏ Have students practice expressing preferences, wishes, and invitations with **Overhead Transparencies** S9 and 14a and b, using the activities on pages A14 and A60–A61.

❏ To check listening comprehension, use the **Audio** CD 7, Tracks 1–5 or read from the **Audioscript** as students do **Workbook** Listening Activities A–E on pages 59–61.

❏ Play the **Video** or read from the **Videoscript** and have students do **Video Activities** 1–6, pages 21–24.

❏ Use the COMPREHENSION Activity on page 74 of the TE for practice talking about everyday activities.

Independent Practice

❏ Model the Activities on pages 74–78. For activity 1, follow the suggestions in ORAL INTRODUCTION, page 75 of the TE, and GROUP PRACTICE, page 75 of the TE. Activities 2, 5, 6, and 7 can be completed for homework. Activities 3, 4, 8, and 9 can be done in pairs.

❏ Have pairs of students do **Communipak** *Interview* 3, *Tu as la parole* 1–3, *Échange* 1, or

Tête à tête 1 (pages 129–137), or **Video Activities** Activité 7, page 24.

❏ Have students do the activities in **Activités pour tous,** pages 33–35.

Monitoring and Adjusting

❏ Have students complete the Writing Activities on **Workbook** pages 62–63.

❏ As students work on the Activities on pages 74–78, monitor language used for preferences, wishes, and invitations. Refer them back to the boxes on pages 74–75, 77, and 78 as needed. The suggestions for the VARIATION and CHALLENGE Activities on pages 76–78 of the TE can be used to meet all students' needs.

Assessment

❏ Administer Quiz 5 on pages 31–32 after completing the lesson's activities. Adjust lesson quizzes to the class's specific needs by using the **Test Generator**.

Reteaching

❏ Redo any appropriate activities from the **Workbook**.

❏ Students can use the **Video** to review portions of the lesson.

Summary and Closure

❏ Have students prepare the role plays described in the Goal 1 Activity on page A14 of **Overhead Transparencies**, using Transparency S9. As they present their role plays, ask others to summarize the communicative functions that they have heard in this lesson.

❏ You may wish to have students prepare Activity 5 on page 95 for inclusion in their *Written Portfolios.*

End-of-Lesson Activities

❏ *À votre tour!:* Arrange students in pairs to practice Activities 2, 3, and 4 on pages 80–81. Use Audio CD 2, Tracks 2–5 with Activities 1–4. Assign any or all of activities 5–6 for homework. Follow the suggestions in the TE margin for GROUP READING PRACTICE.

LEÇON 5 Le français pratique: Mes activités, page 72

Block Schedule (3 Days to Complete)

Objectives

Communicative Functions and Topics
To describe daily activities
To say what people do and don't do
To talk about what you want, would like, and do not want or like to do
To invite a friend, accept an invitation, and turn down an invitation

Linguistic Goals
To use *je (veux)* and *je ne (veux) pas*

Cultural Goals
To learn about daily activities of French young people

Block Schedule

Gather and Sort Have students generate a list of sports. Have them predict which sport will be the most popular. Then have students ask each other what sport they prefer (using *préférer*). Have them tabulate their results and compare them to their predictions. ■

Day 1

Motivation and Focus

❏ Have students look at the picture on pages 70–71 and tell where the people in the photo are and what they are doing. Discuss similarities and differences between French and American activities. Read *Thème et Objectifs* to preview the content of the unit.

Presentation and Explanation

❏ *Lesson Opener:* Have students look at the pictures on pages 72–73 and read *Accent sur…*. Ask them to point out which of these activities they enjoy doing. Help them read the captions for the photos.
❏ *Vocabulary A:* To introduce talking about preferences, play **Audio** CD 2, Track 1 or **Video** 5.1–2, or model the expressions in PRÉFÉRENCES, pages 74–75, using **Overhead Transparencies** 14a and b to clarify meanings. Point out the PRÉFÉRENCES box on pages 74–75. Have students talk about their own likes and dislikes using the expressions.
❏ *Vocabulary B:* Present *Souhaits*, page 77. After modeling the expressions, have students repeat. Point out the verb forms. Ask them to complete the expressions with their own wishes.
❏ *Vocabulary C:* As you model *Invitations*, page 78, use gestures and intonation to help clarify meanings of expressions for accepting and turning down an invitation. Play **Video** 5.3 or **Audio** 5.3–4. Have students repeat the questions and expressions.
❏ Introduce information about the French telephone system by playing **Video** 5.5 or reading that section in the **Videoscript**, page 26. Students can comment on similarities and differences in public telephones in France and in the U.S.

Guided Practice and Checking Understanding

❏ Have students practice expressing preferences, wishes, and invitations with **Overhead Transparencies** S9 and 14a and b, using the activities on pages A14 and A60–A61.
❏ To check listening comprehension, use the **Audio** CD 7, Tracks 1–5 or read from the **Audioscript** as students do **Workbook** Listening Activities A–E on pages 59–61.

Discovering
FRENCH *Nouveau!*

BLEU

Unité 3
Leçon 5
Block Scheduling
Lesson Plans

Day 2

Motivation and Focus

❏ Play the **Video** or read from the **Videoscript** and have students do **Video Activities** 1–6, pages 21–24.

❏ Use the COMPREHENSION activity on page 74 of the TE for practice talking about everyday activities.

Independent Practice

❏ Model the activities on pages 74–78. For activity 1, follow the suggestions in ORAL INTRODUCTION, page 75 of the TE, and GROUP PRACTICE, page 75 of the TE. Activities 2, 5, 6, and 7 can be completed for homework. Activities 3, 4, 8, and 9 can be done in pairs.

❏ Have pairs of students do **Communipak** *Interview* 3, *Tu as la parole* 1–3, *Échange* 1, or *Tête à tête* 1 (pages 129–137), or **Video Activities** Activité 7, page 24.

Monitoring and Adjusting

❏ Have students complete the Writing Activities on **Workbook** pages 62–63.

❏ As students work on the Activities on pages 74–78, monitor language used for preferences, wishes, and invitations. Refer them back to the boxes on pages 74–75, 77, and 78 as needed. The suggestions for the VARIATION and CHALLENGE Activities on pages 76–78 of the TE can be used to meet all students' needs.

Day 3

End-of-Lesson Activities

❏ *À votre tour!:* Arrange students in pairs to practice Activities 2, 3, and 4 on pages 80–81. Use **Audio** CD 2, Tracks 2–5 with Activities 1–4. Assign any or all of Activities 5–6 for homework. Follow the suggestions in the TE margin for GROUP READING PRACTICE.

❏ Have students do the **Block Schedule Activity** on the previous page.

❏ Use **Block Scheduling Copymasters** pages 33–40.

Reteaching (as needed)

❏ Redo any appropriate activities from the **Workbook**.

❏ Students can use the **Video** to review portions of the lesson.

Extension and Enrichment (as desired)

❏ For expansion activities, direct students to www.classzone.com.

Summary and Closure

❏ Have students prepare the role plays described in the Goal 1 activity on page A14 of **Overhead Transparencies**, using Transparency S9. As they present their role plays, ask others to summarize the communicative functions that they have heard in this lesson.

Assessment

❏ Administer Quiz 5 on pages 31–32 after completing the lesson's activities. Adjust lesson quizzes to the class's specific needs by using the **Test Generator**.

BLEU

Date:

Dear Family,

We are currently working on Unit 3 of the *Discovering French, Nouveau!–Bleu* program. It focuses on authentic culture and real-life communication in French. It practices reading, writing, listening, and speaking, and introduces students to culture typical of France. By comparing French language and culture with their own community, students employ their critical thinking skills.

In this unit, students are learning to describe daily activities, express likes and dislikes, ask and answer questions, invite friends to do something, and accept or turn down an invitation. In addition, they are also learning about grammar—how to conjugate and use regular **–er** verbs and the irregular verbs **être** and **faire** in both the affirmative and negative.

Please feel free to call me with any questions or concerns you might have as your student practices reading, writing, listening, and speaking in French.

Sincerely,

Nom _____

Classe _____ Date _____ _____

Discovering
FRENCH
Nouveau!

BLEU

Unité 3
Leçon 5

Absent Student
Copymasters

LEÇON 5 Le français pratique: Mes activités, pages 70–73

Materials Checklist

• **Student Text**

Steps to Follow

• Unit Opener: Look at the photograph on pages 70–71. What sports do these students play? What other activities can you identify in the photograph? Which of these sports or activities do you enjoy?
• Read *Accent sur . . . Les activités de la semaine* (p. 72).
• Look at the photos on pages 72–73 and read the captions.
• Write the captions on a separate sheet of paper. Underline all the words you recognize.

If You Don't Understand . . .

• Look at the pictures carefully to see if there are clues that help you with the words you do not understand.
• Write down questions so that you can ask your partner or your teacher later.

Self-Check

Answer the following questions on a separate sheet of paper. Write complete sentences.

1. Où (*where*) est Mélanie?
2. Est-ce que Marc, Élodie et David jouent au tennis?
3. Est-ce qu'Olivier est à la maison (*at home*)?
4. Est-ce que Zaïna joue au tennis?

Answers

1. Mélanie est à la maison. 2. Marc, Élodie et David jouent au foot. 3. Olivier est en ville. 4. Zaïna joue aux jeux vidéo.

Nom _____

Classe _____ Date _____

A. Vocabulaire: Préférences, pages 74–76

Materials Checklist

- **Student Text**
- **Audio CD** 2, Track 1; **CD** 7, Tracks 1–2
- **Video** 2 or **DVD** 1; Counter 6:44–8:30
- **Workbook**

Steps to Follow

- Study *Vocabulaire: Préférences* (p. 74). Copy the new expressions on a separate sheet of paper. Check meanings.
- Watch **Video** 2 or **DVD** 1; Counter 6:44–8:30. Listen to **Audio CD** 2, Track 1 *Vocabulaire: Préférences* (p. 75). Say everything aloud.
- Do Activities 1 and 2 in the text (pp. 74–76). Write the answers in complete sentences on a separate sheet of paper. Look at the captions as necessary to refresh your memory.
- Do Activities 3 and 4 in the text (p. 76). On a separate sheet of paper, write the questions and answers for both speakers in complete sentences.
- Do **Writing Activities** 1, 2 A in the **Workbook** (p. 62)
- Do **Listening Activities** A–B in the **Workbook** (pp. 59–60). Use **Audio CD** 7, Tracks 1–2.

If You Don't Understand . . .

- Watch the **Video** or **DVD** in a quiet place. Try to stay focused. If you get lost, stop the **Video** or **DVD.** Replay it and find your place.
- Listen to the **CDs** in a quiet place. Try to stay focused. If you get lost, stop the **CDs**. Replay them and find your place.
- Repeat aloud with the audio. Try to sound like the people on the recording.
- On a separate sheet of paper, write down the words that are underlined in the text. Check for meaning.
- Reread the activity directions. Put the directions in your own words.
- Say aloud everything that you write. Be sure you understand what you are saying.
- Write down questions so that you can ask your partner or your teacher later.

Self-Check

Answer the following questions on a separate sheet of paper. Use the appropriate pronoun, and write complete sentences.

1. Est-ce que tu aimes parler espagnol? (oui / préférer parler français)
2. Est-ce que Jean aime téléphoner? (non / préférer jouer aux jeux vidéo)
3. Est-ce que Nathalie aime voyager? (oui / préférer rester à la maison)
4. Est-ce que vous aimez danser? (oui / préférer jouer au basket)
5. Est-ce que Jean et Éric aiment chanter? (non / préférer danser)

Answers

1. Oui, j'aime parler espagnol mais je préfère parler français.   2. Non, il n'aime pas téléphoner. Il préfère jouer aux jeux vidéo.   3. Oui, elle aime voyager mais elle préfère rester à la maison.   4. Oui, nous aimons danser mais nous préférons jouer au basket. / Oui, j'aime danser mais je préfère jouer au basket.   5. Non, ils n'aiment pas chanter. Ils préfèrent danser.

Discovering
FRENCH
Nouveau!

BLEU

Unité 3
Leçon 5

Absent Student
Copymasters

B. Vocabulaire: Souhaits, page 77

Materials Checklist

- **Student Text**
- **Workbook**

Steps to Follow

- Study *Vocabulaire: Souhaits* (p. 77). Copy the new expressions on a separate sheet of paper.
- Do Activities 5, 6, and 7 in the text (p. 77). Write the answers in complete sentences.
- Do **Writing Activities** B/C 3 in the **Workbook** (p. 63).

If You Don't Understand . . .

- Reread the activity directions. Put the directions in your own words.
- Say aloud everything that you write. Be sure you understand what you are saying.
- Write down questions so that you can ask your partner or your teacher later.

Self-Check

Say whether or not you would like to do the following activities this weekend. Write complete sentences on a separate sheet of paper.

1. travailler
2. jouer aux jeux vidéo
3. danser
4. téléphoner à une copine
5. regarder la télé

Answers

1. Non, je ne veux pas (ne voudrais pas) travailler. / Oui, je veux (voudrais) travailler.   2. Non, je ne veux pas (ne voudrais pas) jouer aux jeux vidéo. / Oui, je veux (voudrais) jouer aux jeux vidéo.   3. Non, je ne veux pas (ne voudrais pas) danser. / Oui, je veux (voudrais) danser.   4. Non, je ne veux pas (ne voudrais pas) téléphoner à une copine. / Oui, je veux (voudrais) téléphoner à une copine.   5. Non, je ne veux pas (ne voudrais pas) regarder la télé. / Oui, je veux (voudrais) regarder la télé.

Nom _____

Classe _____ Date _____

C. Vocabulaire: Invitations, pages 78–79

- **Student Text**
- **Audio CD** 2, Tracks 2–5; **CD** 7, Tracks 3–5
- **Video** 2 or **DVD** 1; Counter 8:31–11:49
- **Workbook**

Steps to Follow

- Study *Vocabulaire: Invitations* (p. 78). Write the expressions on a separate sheet of paper.
- Watch **Video** 2 or **DVD** 1; Counter 8:31–11:49. Repeat everything you hear.
- Do Activities 8 and 9 in the text (p. 78). On a separate sheet of paper write the questions and answers for both speakers in complete sentences.
- Read the *Note culturelle* (p. 79). Answer the questions in *Comparaisons culturelles* (p. 79) on a separate sheet of paper.
- Do **Writing Activities** B/C 3 in the **Workbook** (p. 63).
- Do **Listening Activities** C–E in the **Workbook** (pp. 2–3). Use **Audio CD** 7, Tracks 3–5.
- Do Activities 1–6 of *À votre tour!* in the text (pp. 80–81). Use **Audio CD** 2, Tracks 2–5 with Activities 1–4.

If You Don't Understand . . .

- Watch the **Video** or **DVD** in a quiet place. Try to stay focused. If you get lost, stop the **Video** or **DVD**. Replay it and find your place.
- Reread the activity directions. Put the directions in your own words.
- Say aloud everything that you write. Be sure you understand what you are saying.
- Write down questions so that you can ask your partner or your teacher later.

Self-Check

Answer the following questions in complete sentences on a separate sheet of paper. Use the appropriate expression to accept or decline the invitation.

1. Est-ce que tu peux aller au cinéma avec moi? (oui)
2. Est-ce que tu peux dîner au restaurant avec nous? (non)
3. Est-ce que tu veux jouer au ping-pong? (oui)
4. Est-ce que tu peux étudier avec moi? (non)
5. Est-ce que tu veux jouer aux jeux vidéo? (oui)

Answers

1. Oui, bien sûr, je veux bien. / Oui, merci, je veux bien. / Oui, d'accord, je veux bien.   2. Je regrette, mais je ne peux pas.   3. Oui, bien sûr, je veux bien. / Oui, merci, je veux bien. / Oui, d'accord, je veux bien.   4. Je regrette, mais je ne peux pas.   5. Oui, bien sûr, je veux bien. / Oui, merci, je veux bien. / Oui, d'accord, je veux bien.

Nom _____

Classe _____ Date _____ _____

Discovering FRENCH *Nouveau!*

BLEU

Unité 3
Leçon 5 Family Involvement

LEÇON 5 Le français pratique: Mes activités

J'aime . . .

Interview a family member about what activities he or she likes to do.

- First, explain your assignment.
- Help him or her pronounce the words correctly by modeling the pronunciation of possible answers: **J'aime . . .** and the words under each picture. Point to the picture as you model each answer.
- Then, ask him or her the question under each picture.
- After you get an answer, complete the sentence at the bottom of the page.

Tu aimes manger?　　**Tu aimes voyager?**　　　**Tu aimes regarder la télé?**　　**Tu aimes danser?**

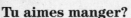

Family member: **J'aime** _____.

Nom _____

Classe _____ Date _____

Tu veux . . . ?

Invite a family member to do something with you. Have the family member choose from the activities shown below.

- First, explain your assignment.
- Model the pronunciation of the words below each picture. Point to the words as you say them. Model the pronunciation of the possible answers: **Je veux** _____.
- Then, ask the question: **Tu veux** _____ **avec moi?**
- After you get an answer, complete the sentence at the bottom of the page.

nager

dîner au restaurant

jouer au tennis

jouer aux jeux vidéo

Family member: **Oui, je veux** _____.

Nom _____

Classe _____ Date _____

Discovering FRENCH *Nouveau!*

BLEU

MODULE 5 Le français pratique: Mes activités

Video 2, DVD 1

5.1 Activité 1. J'aime . . .   Counter 6:44–7:28

What do French young people like to do? Watch the
video and number the activities (1–13) in the order
you hear them. (*Note:* Two activities are used twice.
Number each only the first time it is mentioned.)

a. _____   b. _____   c. _____   d. _____

e. _____   f. _____   g. _____   h. _____

i. _____   j. _____   k. _____   l. _____

m. _____

Nom _____

Classe _____ Date _____

5.2 Activité 2. Tu aimes écouter la radio?

Counter 7:29–8:30

After watching the video segment about activities, fill in the blank under each picture with the appropriate word or phrase from the box.

jouer au tennis	jouer au foot	manger	voyager
regarder la télé	écouter la radio	nager	téléphoner

1. Tu aimes _____ ?

2. Tu aimes _____ ?

3. Tu aimes _____ ?

4. Tu aimes _____ ?

5. Tu aimes _____ ?

6. Tu aimes _____ ?

7. Tu aimes _____ ?

8. Tu aimes _____ ?

Nom _____

Classe _____ Date _____ _____

Discovering FRENCH *Nouveau!*

BLEU

Unité 3
Leçon 5   Video Activities

 5.3 Activité 3. Invitations

Counter 8:31–8:52

Do the people in the video accept or decline their friends' invitations? Listen to the scenes and then mark an **X** in front of the correct answer.

1.
> **Est-ce que tu veux danser?**

_____ Oui, je veux bien.

_____ Je regrette, mais je ne peux pas.

2.
> **Tu veux jouer aux jeux vidéo avec moi?**

_____ Oui, je veux bien.

_____ Non, merci, je regarde la télé.

3.
> **Tu veux jouer au tennis avec moi?**

_____ Oui, je veux bien.

_____ Non, merci, je dois étudier.

4.
> **Tu veux dîner au restaurant?**

_____ Oui, bien sûr. J'ai faim!

_____ Non, merci, je n'ai pas faim.

5.4 Activité 4. Tennis?

Counter 8:53–10:00

Who will be Nicolas' tennis partner? Watch the video and see. If the people listed below are able to play, circle **oui.** If not, circle **non.**

1. Jean-Claude   **oui   non**

2. Nathalie   **oui   non**

3. Marie   **oui   non**

 5.5 Activité 5. Le téléphone

Counter 10:01–11:49

As you watch the **Vignette culturelle**, answer the questions below about the French phone system.

1. What is a **portable**? _____

2. Where and when can you not use a **portable**? _____

Nom _____

Classe _____ Date _____

 5.5 Activité 6. Pour téléphoner . . .

Listen and watch the phone etiquette rules.
Samantha is trying to call her friend Thomas. What
does she say if Thomas answers the phone? What
does she say if his mother answers the phone? Place
the letters below in the correct order. One letter will
be used twice.

THOMAS   Responses

1. _____   a. Bonjour. Ça va . . .

2. _____   b. Allô!

3. _____   c. Bonjour Madame.

THOMAS' MOTHER

4. _____   d. Ici Samantha.

5. _____   e. Ici Samantha Phillips.

6. _____   f. Est-ce que je pourrais parler à Thomas?

7. _____

 Activité 7. Une conversation téléphonique
(A telephone conversation)

Pretend to call a classmate on the telephone (in French) and
invite him or her to do something. Your classmate will accept
or decline your invitation. (If your friend declines, he or she
should give a reason!)

Phrases utiles
Allô?
Ça va?
Je veux bien …
Je regrette, mais je dois …
Au revoir.

Discovering
FRENCH
Nouveau!

BLEU

Unité 3
Leçon 5
Videoscripts

MODULE 5 Le français pratique: Mes activités

Video 2, DVD 1

What do you like to do when you have some free time? It probably all depends on where you are, what day of the week it is, and what the weather is like. On weekends, some French teenagers like to go shopping downtown or to the movies. They might meet their friends at a café or, if the weather is nice, many play sports. In the summer, some teenagers like to go swimming or to the beach. Many young people enjoy roller-blading. And, of course, they simply may prefer to stay at home and watch TV or listen to music.

5.1 Mini-scenes: Listening—J'aime téléphoner
Counter: 6:44–7:28

Let's ask a few people what they like to do.

Qu'est-ce que tu aimes faire?

—J'aime téléphoner.
—J'aime jouer au tennis.
—J'aime jouer au volley.
—J'aime nager.

—J'aime parler anglais. I like to speak English. How are you, my friends?

—J'aime manger.

—J'aime danser.
—Et moi, j'aime manger.

—J'aime regarder la télé.

—J'aime écouter la musique.

—J'aime jouer aux jeux vidéo.

—J'aime voyager.

—Qu'est-ce que tu aimes faire?
—J'aime jouer au foot.
—Tu aimes étudier?
—Ah, non, je n'aime pas étudier.

5.2 Mini-scenes: Speaking—Tu aimes écouter la radio?
Counter: 7:29–8:30

Now it's your turn. You'll see pictures of various activities. Ask your classmates if they like to do these things.

—Tu aimes écouter la radio? [screen card]
—Oui, j'aime écouter la radio.
—Et toi, tu aimes écouter la radio?
—Non, je n'aime pas écouter la radio.

—Tu aimes jouer au tennis? [screen card]
[Oui, j'aime jouer au tennis. / Non, je n'aime pas jouer au tennis.]

—Tu aimes jouer au foot? [screen card]
[Oui, j'aime jouer au foot. / Non, je n'aime pas jouer au foot.]

—Tu aimes regarder la télé? [screen card]
[Oui, j'aime regarder la télé. / Non, je n'aime pas regarder la télé.]

—Tu aimes manger? [screen card]
[Oui, j'aime manger. / Non, je n'aime pas manger.]

—Tu aimes téléphoner? [screen card]
[Oui, j'aime téléphoner. / Non, je n'aime pas téléphoner.]

—Tu aimes nager? [screen card]
[Oui, j'aime nager. / Non, je n'aime pas nager.]

—Tu aimes voyager? [screen card]
[Oui, j'aime voyager. / Non, je n'aime pas voyager.]

5.3 Mini-scenes: Listening— Invitations
Counter: 8:31–8:52

Now you'll see French people asking their friends to join in various activities. Watch.

—Est-ce que tu veux danser?
—Oui, je veux bien.

—Tu veux jouer aux jeux vidéo avec moi?
—Oui, je veux bien.

—Tu veux jouer au tennis avec moi?
—Oui, je veux bien.

—Tu veux dîner au restaurant?
—Non, merci, je n'ai pas faim.

5.4 Dialogue: Tennis Counter: 8:53–10:00

It's a beautiful day and Nicolas is looking for a tennis partner. First he calls his classmate, Jean-Claude.

JEAN-CLAUDE: Allô!

NICOLAS: Allô, Jean-Claude? Bonjour, ça va?

JEAN-CLAUDE: Euh, oui, ça va.

NICOLAS: Dis, est-ce que tu veux jouer au tennis avec moi?

JEAN-CLAUDE: Ah, je regrette, mais je ne peux pas jouer au tennis avec toi aujourd'hui.

Now Nicolas is phoning his girlfriend Nathalie.

NICOLAS: Allô, Nathalie.

NATHALIE: Allô, Nicolas, ça va?

NICOLAS: Oui, ça va. Dis, est-ce que tu veux jouer au tennis?

NATHALIE: À quelle heure?

NICOLAS: À quatre heures.

NATHALIE: Je regrette, mais je ne peux pas. Je dois étudier. Au revoir.

Finally, Nicolas decides to call his cousin, Marie.

MARIE: Allô.

NICOLAS: Allô, Marie! Ça va?

MARIE: Oui, ça va.

NICOLAS: Dis, est-ce que tu veux jouer au tennis?

MARIE: Oui, bien sûr.

NICOLAS: À quelle heure?

MARIE: À quatre heures.

5.5 Vignette culturelle: Le téléphone
Counter: 10:01–11:49

—Allô, Anne? Salut. Ça va? C'est Jean-Claude.

*Do you like to call your friends on the phone? Like their American counterparts, French teenagers love to spend hours talking on the phone. When you're not at home, you can make calls from public telephones. But now, more and more French people use cell phones which they call **un téléphone portable** or **un portable.** Young people like cell phones because they can call their friends any time and from any place. Using cell phones can, however, be distracting, or even dangerous. This is why French students cannot take their cell phones to school. French people cannot use their cell phones when driving. And it is considered impolite to use a cell phone in a café or restaurant. Now we will learn some phone etiquette. Watch.*

—Allô! Ici Samantha. Bonjour, ça va . . .

Always introduce yourself when you make a phone call. Listen again.

—Allô! Ici Samantha. Bonjour, ça va . . .

Now listen to what to say if your friend is not home and a parent answers.

—Allô! Ici Samantha Philippe. Bonjour, Madame. Est-ce que je pourrais parler à Thomas?

Introduce yourself, giving your full name. Then ask if you can speak to your friend. Listen again.

—Allô! Ici Samantha Philippe. Bonjour, Madame. Est-ce que je pourrais parler à Thomas?

Discovering
FRENCH
Nouveau!

BLEU

Unité 3
Leçon 5
Audioscripts

LEÇON 5 Le français pratique: Mes activités

PE AUDIO

CD 2, Track 1

Vocabulaire: Préférences, p. 74

How to talk about what you like and don't like to do. Écoutez et répétez.

Est-ce que tu aimes . . . ? #   Est-ce que tu aimes parler français? #

J'aime . . . #   Oui, j'aime parler français. #
Je n'aime pas . . . #   Non, je n'aime pas parler français.
Je préfère . . . #   Je préfère parler anglais. #

Now practice the names of the activities.

téléphoner #   J'aime téléphoner. #
parler français #   J'aime parler français. #
parler anglais #   J'aime parler anglais. #
parler espagnol #   J'aime parler espagnol. #
manger #   J'aime manger. #
chanter #   J'aime chanter. #
danser #   J'aime danser. #
nager #   J'aime nager. #

jouer au tennis #   J'aime aussi jouer au tennis. #
jouer au basket #   J'aime aussi jouer au basket. #
jouer au basket #   J'aime jouer au basket. #
jouer au foot #   J'aime jouer au foot. #
jouer aux jeux vidéo #   J'aime jouer aux jeux vidéo. #
regarder la télé #   Mais je préfère regarder la télé. #
écouter la radio #   Mais je préfère écouter la radio. #
dîner au restaurant #   Mais je préfère dîner au restaurant. #
voyager #   Mais je préfère voyager. #

étudier #   Je n'aime pas toujours étudier. #
travailler #   Je n'aime pas toujours travailler. #

À votre tour

CD 2, Track 2

1. Écoutez bien!, p. 80

You will hear French young people telling you what they like to do. Listen carefully to each activity. If it is illustrated in the picture on the left, mark A. If it is illustrated in the picture on the right, mark B.

1. J'aime écouter la radio.
2. J'aime téléphoner.
3. J'aime manger.
4. J'aime jouer au tennis.
5. J'aime nager.
6. J'aime regarder la télé.
7. J'aime étudier.
8. J'aime voyager.
9. J'aime jouer aux jeux vidéo.
10. J'aime jouer au foot.

CD 2, Track 3

2. Communication, p. 80

Listen to the following conversation.

—Est-ce que tu aimes regarder la télé?
—Oui, j'aime regarder la télé.

—Est-ce que tu veux jouer aux jeux vidéo?
—Oui, je veux jouer aux jeux vidéo. (Non, je ne veux pas jouer aux jeux vidéo.)

—Est-ce que tu aimes écouter la radio?
—Oui, j'aime écouter la radio. (Non, je n'aime pas écouter la radio.)

—Est-ce que tu veux manger une pizza?
—Oui, je veux manger un pizza. (Non, je ne veux pas manger de pizza.)

Nom _____

Classe _____ Date _____

CD 2, Track 4

3. Conversation dirigée, p. 80

Écoutez la conversation entre Trinh et Céline.

TRINH: Salut, Céline. Ça va?
CÉLINE: Oui, ça va, merci.
TRINH: Tu veux dîner au restaurant?
CÉLINE: À quelle heure?
TRINH: À 8 heures.
CÉLINE: Je regrette, mais je dois étudier.
TRINH: Dommage!

CD 2, Track 5

4. Créa-dialogue, p. 81

Listen to the following dialogues and match the invitations with the excuses.

Modèle: —Est-ce que tu veux jouer au tennis avec moi?
—Non, je ne peux pas. Je dois travailler.

You should draw a line from the model to "b":

Je dois travailler in the Excuses column.

1. —Est-ce que tu veux jouer au basket avec moi?
   —Non, je ne peux pas. Je dois téléphoner à une copine. #

2. —Est-ce que tu veux manger une pizza?
   —Non, je ne peux pas. Je dois dîner avec ma cousine. #

3. —Est-ce que tu veux regarder la télé?
   —Non, je ne peux pas. Je dois parler avec ma mère. #

4. —Est-ce que tu veux jouer au ping-pong?
   —Non, je ne peux pas. Je dois étudier. #

5. —Est-ce que tu veux dîner au retaurant?
   —Non, je ne peux pas. Je dois chanter avec la chorale. #

WORKBOOK AUDIO

Section 1. J'aime . . . Je n'aime pas . . .

CD 7, Track 1

A. Compréhension orale, p. 59

Look at the activities illustrated in your Workbook. Listen as Marc and Caroline tell you what they like to do. When you hear an activity that Marc likes to do, write an "M" under the picture of that activity. When you hear an activity that Caroline likes to do, write a "C" under the corresponding picture. Note that some activities may be liked by both Marc and Caroline. You will hear each statement twice.

Listen to the model.

Modèle:
—Je m'appelle Caroline. J'aime jouer au foot. J'aime jouer au foot.

Caroline likes to play soccer.

You should write the letter "C" under Picture 3, soccer.

Commençons. Let's begin.

—Je m'appelle Marc. J'aime écouter la radio. J'aime écouter la radio. #
—J'aime nager. (repeat) #
—J'aime téléphoner. #
—J'aime regarder la télé. #
—J'aime manger. #
—J'aime jouer aux jeux vidéo. #
—J'aime jouer au basket. #
—J'aime danser. #
—J'aime jouer au foot. #
—J'aime voyager. #
—J'aime chanter. #
—J'aime dîner au restaurant. #
—J'aime nager. #
—J'aime chanter. #

Now check your answers.

Discovering
FRENCH
Nouveau!

B L E U

Unité 3
Leçon 5

Audioscripts

Activity 1: Marc; Activity 2: Marc; Activity 3: Caroline and Marc; Activity 4: Caroline; Activity 5: Caroline; Activity 6: Marc; Activity 7: Caroline; Activity 8: Caroline; Activity 9: Marc; Activity 10: Marc and Caroline; Activity 11: Caroline; Activity 12: Caroline and Marc.

CD 7, Track 2

B. Parlez., p. 60

Now look at the numbered illustrations in your activity. As you hear the number of each activity, say whether or not you like that activity.

First, listen to the model.

Modèle. #
        —J'aime écouter la radio.
        or:
        —Je n'aime pas écouter la radio.

Commençons. Let's begin.
 1. # —J'aime regarder la télé.
    —Je n'aime pas regarder la télé.
 2. # —J'aime jouer au foot.
    —Je n'aime pas jouer au foot.
 3. # —J'aime jouer au tennis.
    —Je n'aime pas jouer au tennis.
 4. # —J'aime manger.
    —Je n'aime pas manger.
 5. # —J'aime téléphoner.
    —Je n'aime pas téléphoner.
 6. # —J'aime nager.
    —Je n'aime pas nager
 7. # —J'aime voyager.
    —Je n'aime pas voyager.

Section 2. Invitations

CD 7, Track 3

C. Compréhension orale, p. 60

Now you will hear people inviting friends to do something. Listen carefully to determine whether the friend accepts or declines the invitation and mark your answer in your Workbook.

Écoutez.

 1. At a party
    —Est-ce que tu veux danser?
    —Oui, je veux bien. #

2. By the tennis courts
    —Est-ce que tu veux jouer au tennis avec moi?
    —Oui, je veux bien. #

3. At home
    —Est-ce que tu veux dîner au restaurant?
    —Non, merci, je n'ai pas faim. #

Now check your answers. You should have marked 1-a, 2-a and 3-b.

CD 7, Track 4

D. Parlez., p. 61

Now it is your turn to invite a French friend to join you. Look at the illustrations and ask your friend if he or she wants to do the activities shown.

Look at the model.

This picture shows someone playing soccer. You would say:

Est-ce que tu veux jouer au foot avec moi? #

Commençons. Let's begin.

 1. # Est-ce que tu veux jouer au basket avec moi? #
 2. # Est-ce que tu veux regarder la télé avec moi? #
 3. # Est-ce que tu veux nager avec moi? #
 4. # Est-ce que tu veux chanter avec moi? #
 5. # Est-ce que tu veux voyager avec moi? #

Section 3. Dictée

CD 7, Track 5

E. Écoutez et écrivez., p. 61

You will hear a short dialogue spoken twice. First listen carefully to what the people are

saying. The second time you hear the dialogue, fill in the missing words.

Écoutez.

—Dis, Stéphanie, est-ce que tu veux jouer au tennis avec moi?

—Je regrette, mais je ne peux pas.
—Pourquoi?
—Je dois étudier.

Listen again and fill in the missing words.

....

LESSON 5 QUIZ

Part I: Listening

CD 14, Track 1

A. Conversations

You will hear a series of short conversations between Marc and Caroline. Listen to each conversation carefully. Then answer the corresponding questions on your answer sheet by circling the appropriate letter (a, b, or c). You will hear each conversation twice.

Let's begin.

1. CAROLINE: Est-ce que tu aimes jouer aux jeux vidéo?
   MARC: Non, je n'aime pas jouer aux jeux vidéo.

2. MARC: Est-ce que tu aimes parler espagnol?

   CAROLINE: Oui, mais je préfère parler anglais.

3. MARC: Est-ce que tu veux dîner avec moi?
   CAROLINE: Oui, je veux bien. À quelle heure?
   MARC: À sept heures et demie.
   CAROLINE: D'accord!

4. CAROLINE: Est-ce que tu veux jouer au basket avec moi samedi?
   MARC: Je regrette, mais je ne peux pas. Je dois étudier.

5. MARC: Est-ce que tu veux jouer au tennis avec moi?
   CAROLINE: À quelle heure?
   MARC: À cinq heures.
   CAROLINE: Je ne peux pas. J'ai un rendez-vous avec une copine.

Nom _____

Classe _____ Date _____

Discovering FRENCH *Nouveau!*

BLEU

Unité 3
Leçon 5
Lesson Quiz

QUIZ 5

Part I: Listening

A. Conversations (40 points)

You will hear a series of short conversations between Marc and Caroline. Listen to each conversation carefully. Then answer the corresponding questions on your answer sheet by circling the appropriate letter (a, b, or c). You will hear each conversation twice.

1. What activity does Marc dislike?
   a. Swimming.
   b. Playing video games.
   c. Dancing.

2. What language does Caroline prefer to speak?
   a. English.
   b. Italian.
   c. Spanish.

3. What are Caroline and Marc going to do at seven-thirty?
   a. Have dinner.
   b. Watch TV.
   c. Study.

4. What is Marc going to do on Saturday?
   a. Work.
   b. Study.
   c. Travel.

5. Why is Caroline not going to play tennis with Marc?
   a. She is tired.
   b. She does not like to play tennis with him.
   c. She has other plans.

Part II: Writing

B. Activités (30 points)

Complete each of the following sentences with the appropriate activity.

1. J'aime _____ la radio.

2. Je préfère _____ la télé.

3. Je regrette, mais je ne peux pas _____ au foot avec toi.

4. Est-ce que tu veux _____ une pizza?

5. Mais oui! Je veux bien _____ espagnol avec toi.

Nom _____

Classe _____ Date _____

C. Expression personnelle (30 points)

Describe two things that you LIKE to do when you are on vacation and one you DO NOT LIKE to do.

- _____
- _____

- _____

Nom _____

Classe _____ Date _____

Discovering
FRENCH
Nouveau!

BLEU

Unité 3
Leçon 6

Workbook TE

LEÇON 6 Une invitation

LISTENING ACTIVITIES

Section 1. Le verbe être

A. Écoutez et parlez.

Modèle: Paris   **Vous êtes de Paris.**

1. Québec   Il est de Québec.
2. Lille   Elle est de Lille.
3. New York   Ils sont de New York.
4. Montréal   Elles sont de Montréal.

5. Los Angeles   Je suis de Los Angeles.
6. Manchester   Tu es de Manchester.
7. Lyon   Vous êtes de Lyon.
8. Boston   Nous sommes de Boston.

Section 2. Tu ou vous?

B. Écoutez et parlez.

Modèle: Stéphanie   **Tu es française?**
           Monsieur Lambert   **Vous êtes français?**

Commençons.

1. Philippe   Tu es français?
2. Mélanie   Tu es française?
3. Madame Dubois   Vous êtes française?
4. Mademoiselle Masson   Vous êtes française?
5. Thomas   Tu es français?
6. Monsieur Dorval   Vous êtes français?

Section 3. Où sont-ils?

C. Compréhension orale

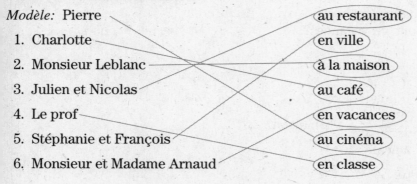

Modèle: Pierre   au restaurant

1. Charlotte   en ville

2. Monsieur Leblanc   à la maison

3. Julien et Nicolas   au café

4. Le prof   en vacances

5. Stéphanie et François   au cinéma

6. Monsieur et Madame Arnaud   en classe

URB
p. 33

Unité 3
Leçon 6

Workbook TE

Nom _____

Classe _____ Date _____

Discovering
FRENCH
Nouveau!

B L E U

D. Questions et réponses

▶ —Est-ce qu'il est à la maison ou au restaurant?
—**Il est au restaurant.**

▶

 Elle est au café.

 Ils sont en vacances.

 Ils sont au cinéma.

 Il est à la maison.

 Elles sont en ville.

 Ils sont en classe.

Elle est à Paris.

Section 4. Non!

E. Écoutez et parlez.

Modèle: Kevin: français?
Non, il n'est pas français.

1. Stéphanie: canadienne?   Non, elle n'est pas canadienne.
2. Jean-Paul: à la maison?   Non, il n'est pas à la maison.
3. Juliette: au cinéma?   Non, elle n'est pas au cinéma.
4. Thomas: en classe?   Non, il n'est pas en classe.

Modèle: Éric et Nicolas: en ville?
Non, ils ne sont pas en ville.

5. Anne et Claire: à la maison?   Non, elles ne sont pas à la maison.
6. Monsieur et Madame Moreau: à Québec?   Non, ils ne sont pas à Québec.
7. Monsieur et Madame Dupont: en vacances?   Non, ils ne sont pas en vacances.

Section 5. Dictée

F. Écoutez et écrivez.

—Salut Thomas! Tu es _____ à la maison?

—Non, je suis _____ au café.

—Est-ce que ta soeur est avec toi?

—Non, elle n'est pas _____ avec moi.

Elle est en ville _____ avec une copine.

Elles sont _____ au cinéma.

Nom _____

Classe _____ Date _____

Discovering
FRENCH *Nouveau!*

B L E U

Unité 3
Leçon 6
Workbook TE

WRITING ACTIVITIES

A 1. Mots croisés *(Crossword puzzle)*

Complete the crossword puzzle with the forms of **être**. Then write the corresponding subject pronoun in front of each form.

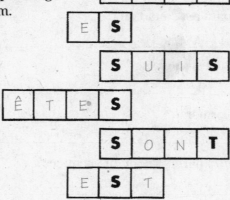

▶ nous _____

1. tu _____
2. je _____
3. vous _____
4. ils/elles _____
5. il/elle _____

2. En vacances

The people in parentheses are on vacation. Say where they are, using the appropriate pronouns: **il, elle, ils,** or **elles**.

▶ (Cécile) — Elle est à Québec.

1. (Jean-Marc) — Il est à Tours.
2. (Catherine et Sophie) — Elles sont à Nice.
3. (Mademoiselle Simon) — Elle est à Montréal.
4. (Jérôme et Philippe) — Ils sont en Italie.
5. (Isabelle, Thomas et Anne) — Ils sont au Mexique.
6. (Monsieur et Madame Dupin) — Ils sont au Japon.

3. Où sont-ils?

Complete the following sentences, saying where the people are.

Nous sommes en classe.

Vous êtes au cinéma.

M. Bernard est à la maison.

Éric et Claire sont au restaurant.

Nom _____

Classe _____ Date _____

B/C 4. Non!

Answer the following questions in the negative, using pronouns in your answers.

1. Est-ce que tu es français (française)?

    Non, je ne suis pas français(e).

2. Est-ce que ton copain est canadien?

    Non, il n'est pas canadien.

3. Est-ce que ta copine est anglaise?

    Non, elle n'est pas anglaise.

4. Est-ce que tu es au cinéma?

    Non, je ne suis pas au cinéma.

5. Est-ce que tes (*your*) parents sont en vacances?

    Non, ils ne sont pas en vacances.

5. Communication: En français!

1. The phone rings. It is your French friend Caroline who wants to talk to your brother.

    Tell Caroline that he is not home.
    Il n'est pas à la maison.

    Tell her that he is downtown with a friend.
    Il est en ville avec un copain (un ami).

2. You are phoning your friend Marc. His mother answers.

    Ask her if Marc is there.
    Est-ce que Marc est là?

    Ask her if you can please speak with Marc.
    Est-ce que je peux parler avec Marc, s'il vous plaît?

Nom _____

Classe _____ Date _____ _____

Discovering
FRENCH
Nouveau!

B L E U

Unité 3
Leçon 6

Activités pour tous TE

LEÇON 6   Une invitation

A

Activité 1   Être ou ne pas être?

Circle the word that correctly completes each sentence.

1. Jean-Michel n'*es* / *est* pas en classe.
2. Je *suis* / *sommes* en ville.
3. Vous n'*êtes* / *es* pas d'accord avec moi?
4. Mes amies *est* / *sont* au cinéma.
5. Tu *es* / *suis* en vacances maintenant?
6. Ils ne *sommes* / *sont* pas à la maison.

Activité 2   Opinions (sample answers)

Circle the term that best describes how you feel about each question.

1. Janet Jackson chante bien, non?   Mais oui!   Mais non!   Comme ci, comme ça.
2. Est-ce que tu aimes la classe de français?   Mais oui!   Mais non!   Comme ci, comme ça.
3. Est-ce que tu danses bien?   Oui!   Non!   Comme ci, comme ça.
4. Est-ce que ton père joue bien au basket?   Mais oui!   Non!   Comme ci, comme ça.

Activité 3   Oui ou non?

Using the cues, fill in the blanks with the affirmative or negative form of the verbs.

1. Est-ce que Nicole est de Boston?

   Oui, elle _est_ de Boston.

2. Est-ce que le copain de Nicole est là?

   Mais _non_, il _n'est pas_ là.

3. Est-ce que Pierre aime danser?

   Non, il _n'aime pas_ danser.

4. Est-ce que Pierre aime travailler?

   Non, il _n'aime pas_ travailler.

B

Activité 1   Où sont-ils?

Fill in the blanks with the correct form of **être**.

1. Le prof _est_ en classe.
2. Mes cousins _sont_ à Québec.
3. Nous _sommes_ au cinéma.
4. Est-ce que vous _êtes_ ici?
5. Moi, je _suis_ en vacances.
6. Tu _es_ au café avec les copains?

Nom _____

Classe _____ Date _____

Discovering
FRENCH
Nouveau!

B L E U

Activité 2 Oui ou non?

Match each question with the most logical answer.

_d___ 1. Est-ce qu'elles sont en ville?   a. Mais oui, à huit heures.

_c___ 2. Tu es à la maison, n'est-ce pas?   b. Oui, j'aime Paris et New York!

_e___ 3. Est-ce que je peux téléphoner à mon copain? c. Oui, je regarde la télé.

_a___ 4. Ils dînent au restaurant, n'est-ce pas?   d. Mais oui, elles sont au café.

_b___ 5. Est-ce que tu aimes voyager?   e. Oui, si tu veux.

Activité 3 Questions et réponses

Choose the most logical answer to each question.

1. Est-ce que vous jouez au foot?
   a. Oui, elles jouent au foot.   b. Non, nous ne jouons pas au foot.

2. Est-ce qu'elle étudie?
   a. Oui, elle travaille à la maison.   b. Non, elle n'aime pas voyager.

3. Tu es de Paris, n'est-ce pas?
   a. Oui, je suis de Dallas.   b. Non, je ne suis pas français.

C

Activité 1 Où sont-ils?

Using the visual cues, write a sentence explaining where people are.

1. Je suis en ville.   3. Vous êtes au café.

2. Ils sont en classe.   4. Tu es en vacances.

Activité 2 Questions

Write questions that would produce the following responses.

1. —Où est Caroline?   3. —Est-ce que tu veux jouer au basket avec moi?

   —Caroline? Elle est à la maison.   —Oui, je veux bien jouer au basket avec toi.

2. —Est-ce qu'il travaille là-bas?   4. —Est-ce que tu aimes parler français?

   —Mais non, il ne travaille pas là-bas.   —Mais oui, j'aime parler français.

Activité 3 Mais non . . .

Answer the following questions negatively.

1. Est-ce que vous êtes en vacances? Mais non, nous ne sommes pas en vacances.

2. Est-ce que la prof de français est anglaise? Mais non, elle n'est pas anglaise.

3. Est-ce que tu écoutes souvent la radio? Mais non, pas souvent.

Discovering
FRENCH
Nouveau!

BLEU

Unité 3
Leçon 6

Lesson Plans

LEÇON 6   Une invitation, page 82

Objectives

Communicative Functions and Topics
To talk about where people are
To ask and answer yes/no questions
To express negation

Linguistic Goals
To use subject pronouns
To use the verb *être* and the negative *ne ... pas*
To use yes/no questions with *est-ce que*
To pronounce the vowel /a/

Cultural Goals
To talk about where French young people spend their free time

Motivation and Focus

❑ Have students look at the photos on page 83. Ask where the students in the photos are and what they are doing. Talk about places students like to go after school or on weekends. You might play the **Video** for Module 6 as an introduction to the lesson.

Presentation and Explanation

❑ *Lesson Opener:* Use the SETTING THE STAGE activity, page 82 of the TE. Check understanding with the *Compréhension* activity on page 82. Have students read the conversation and discuss what they think it is about. Play **Audio** CD 2, Tracks 6–7 to present the dialog.

❑ *Note culturelle:* Read *Le mercredi après-midi*, page 83. Do the CROSS-CULTURAL OBSERVATION on page 83 of the TE after students view **Video** 6.4, *Au café*, or after you read that section in the **Videoscript**, page 53–54.

❑ *Grammar A:* Use **Overhead Transparency** 16 to present and explain subject pronouns and the verb *être*, as presented in the grammar box on page 84. Point out forms students have already practiced. See the notes in the TE margin. Introduce questions with *où* using **Overhead Transparency** 15. Point out location expressions in the vocabulary box, page 85.

❑ *Grammar B:* Present yes/no questions with *est-ce que* and expressions to answer them, pages 86–87. Give statements; have students respond with a yes/no question.

❑ *Grammar C:* Present negatives and useful words, pages 88–89. Practice using these forms with SPEAKING PRACTICE, page 88 of the TE, and **Overhead Transparency** 15.

❑ *Prononciation:* Have students read the box on page 89. Play **Audio** CD 2, Track 8, or model the words and have students repeat.

Guided Practice and Checking Understanding

❑ Practice affirmative and negative verb forms and where and yes/no questions with **Overhead Transparencies** 14a and b and 15.

❑ Play the **Audio** CD 7, Tracks 6–11 or read the **Audioscript** and have students do **Workbook** Listening Activities A–F on pages 65–66.

❑ Have students complete **Video Activities** 1–4, pages 49–52, as they watch the **Video** or listen to you read the **Videoscript**.

❑ Check understanding of places and questions with *où* using the COMPREHENSION activity, page 85 of the TE.

Independent Practice

❏ Do Activities 1–10, pages 85–88. Students can work alone or for homework on 1, 2, 5, 7, 9, and 10. Do 3, 4, 6, and 8 on text pages 86–88 as PAIR PRACTICE.

❏ Use **Communipak** *Tête à tête* 1, pages 136–137, or **Video Activities** Activity 5, page 52, for pair or group practice.

❏ Have students do the activities in **Activités pour tous,** pages 37–38.

Monitoring and Adjusting

❏ Monitor students' writing as they work with **Workbook** Writing Activities 1–5 on pages 67–68.

❏ Point out and discuss the grammar explanations on pages 84–89. Help with pronunciation and tag questions using the TEACHING NOTES on pages 86–87 of the TE.

Assessment

❏ After students have completed the lesson's activities, administer Quiz 6 on pages 59–60. Use the **Test Generator** to adapt questions to your class's needs.

Reteaching

❏ If students have difficulty with any of the activities in the **Workbook**, reteach the content and have them redo the activity.

❏ Individual students can use the **Video** to review portions of the lesson.

❏ Use **Teacher to Teacher**, pages 7 and 8, to reteach *être*.

Extension and Enrichment

❏ Play the LISTENING GAME on page 89 of the TE.

Summary and Closure

❏ Have pairs of students present role plays as described in the activity at the top of **Overhead Transparencies** page A61. Other students can summarize linguistic and communicative goals demonstrated in the role plays.

❏ Do PORTFOLIO ASSESSMENT as suggested on page 91 of the TE.

End-of-Lesson Activities

❏ *À votre tour!:* Do the Activities on pages 90–91. Students can work individually on Activities 2 and 4. Use **Audio** CD 2, Tracks 9–10 with Activities 1 and 3. Have students work in small groups to practice and present to the class the *Créa-dialogue* Activity on page 91.

Discovering
FRENCH *Nouveau!*

BLEU

Unité 3
Leçon 6
Block Scheduling
Lesson Plans

LEÇON 6 Une invitation, page 82

Block schedule (3 days to complete)

Objectives

Communicative Functions and Topics	To talk about where people are
	To ask and answer yes/no questions
	To express negation
Linguistic Goals	To use subject pronouns
	To use the verb *être* and the negative *ne ... pas*
	To use yes/no questions with *est-ce que*
	To pronounce the vowel /a/
Cultural Goals	To talk about where French young people spend their free time

Block Schedule

Change of Pace Before class, write a list of clue sentences for cities in France, the U.S., and other countries (for example, "*Paul is in the city they call 'The Big Apple.'*"). Divide the class into two teams. Place an object, such as a tennis ball, on a table and have a student from each team stand by it. Read one of the clue sentences. The student who grabs the object gets to guess the city. The student must answer in French, using a form of the verb *être* ("*Paul est à New York.*"), to win a point. If the student responds incorrectly, the other student can try to answer. Play to a designated number of points. ■

Day 1

Motivation and Focus

❏ Have students look at the photos on page 83. Ask where the students in the photos are and what they are doing. Talk about places students like to go after school or on weekends. You might play the **Video** for Module 6 as an introduction to the lesson.

Presentation and Explanation

❏ *Lesson Opener:* Use the SETTING THE STAGE activity, page 82 of the TE. Check understanding with the *Compréhension* activity on page 82. Have students read the conversation and discuss what they think it is about. Play **Audio** CD 2, Tracks 6–7 to present the dialog.

❏ *Note culturelle:* Read *Le mercredi après-midi*, page 83. Do the CROSS-CULTURAL OBSERVATION on page 83 of the TE after students view **Video** 6.4, *Au café*, or after you read that section in the **Videoscript**, page 53–54.

❏ *Grammar A:* Use **Overhead Transparency** 16 to present and explain subject pronouns and the verb *être*, as presented in the grammar box on page 84. Point out forms students have already practiced. See the notes in the TE margin. Introduce questions with *où* using **Overhead Transparency** 15. Point out location expressions in the vocabulary box, page 85.

❏ *Grammar B:* Present yes/no questions with *est-ce que* and expressions to answer them, pages 86–87. Give statements; have students respond with a yes/no question.

❏ *Grammar C:* Present negatives and useful words, pages 88–89. Practice using these forms with SPEAKING PRACTICE, page 88 of the TE, and **Overhead Transparency** 15.

❏ *Prononciation:* Have students read the box on page 89. Play **Audio** CD 2, Track 8, or model the words and have students repeat.

Guided Practice and Checking Understanding

❑ Practice affirmative and negative verb forms and where and yes/no questions with **Overhead Transparencies** 14a and b and 15.

❑ Play the **Audio** CD 7, Tracks 6–11 or read the **Audioscript** and have students do **Workbook** Listening Activities A–F on pages 65–66.

Day 2

Motivation and Focus

❑ Have students complete **Video Activities** 1–4, pages 49–52, as they watch the **Video** or listen to you read the **Videoscript**.

❑ Check understanding of places and questions with *où* using the COMPREHENSION activity, page 85 of the TE.

Independent Practice

❑ Do Activities 1–10, pages 85–89. Students can work alone or for homework on 1, 2, 5, 7, 9, and 10. Do 3, 4, 6, and 8 on text pages 86–88 as PAIR PRACTICE.

❑ Use **Communipak** *Tête à tête* 1, pages 136–137, or **Video Activities** Activity 5, page 52, for pair or group practice.

❑ Have students do the activities in **Activités pour tous,** pages 37–38.

Monitoring and Adjusting

❑ Monitor students' writing as they do **Workbook** Writing Activities 1–5 on pages 67–68.

❑ Point out and discuss the grammar explanations on pages 84–89. Help with pronunciation and tag questions using the TEACHING NOTES on pages 86–87 of the TE.

Day 3

End-of-Lesson Activities

❑ *À votre tour!:* Do the activities on pages 90–91. Students can work alone on Activities 2 and 4. Use **Audio** CD 2, Tracks 9–10 with Activities 1 and 3. Students can work in pairs to present Activity 3 on page 91.

❑ Have students do the **Block Schedule Activity** on the previous page.

❑ Use **Block Scheduling Copymasters** pages 41–48.

Reteaching (as needed)

❑ Reteach and redo any of the activities in the **Workbook.**

❑ Individual students can use the **Video** to review portions of the lesson.

❑ Use **Teacher to Teacher**, pages 7 and 8, to reteach *être.*

Extension and Enrichment (as desired)

❑ Play the LISTENING GAME on page 89 of the TE.

❑ For expansion activities, direct students to www.classzone.com.

Assessment

❑ Administer Quiz 6 on pages 59–60. Use the **Test Generator** to adapt questions to your class.

Nom

Classe _____ Date _____

Discovering FRENCH *Nouveau!*

BLEU

Unité 3
Leçon 6

Absent Student Copymasters

LEÇON 6 Une invitation, pages 82–83

Materials Checklist

- **Student Text**
- **Audio CD** 2, Tracks 6–7
- **Video** 2 or **DVD** 1; Counter 11:59–13:28, Counter 15:06–16:42

Steps to Follow

- Read the dialogue *Une invitation* (p. 82). Copy the underlined words and expressions. Check their meanings.
- Read the *Compréhension* questions (p. 82) before you listen to the audio or watch the video or **DVD.** They will help you understand what you hear.
- Listen to **Audio** CD 2, Tracks 6–7 or watch **Video** 2 or **DVD** 1; Counter 12:37–13:28, Counter 15:06–16:42. Say everything aloud.
- Answer the *Compréhension* questions (p. 82) in complete sentences on a separate sheet of paper.
- Read the *Note culturelle* and look at the photos on p. 83.
- Answer the *Comparaisons culturelles* questions in complete sentences on a separate sheet of paper.

If You Don't Understand . . .

- Watch the **Video** or **DVD** in a quiet room. Try to stay focused. If you get lost, stop the **Video** or **DVD.** Replay it and find your place.
- Listen to the **CD** in a quiet place. Try to stay focused. If you get lost, stop the **CD.** Replay it and find your place.
- Repeat aloud with the audio. Try to sound like the people on the recording.
- On a separate sheet of paper, write down the words that are underlined in the text. Check for meaning.
- Write down questions so that you can ask your partner or your teacher later.

Self-Check

1. Où est Léa?
2. Où sont Stéphanie et Julie?
3. Où est Mathieu?
4. Où est Antoine?

Answers

1. Léa est à la maison. 2. Stéphanie et Julie sont au restaurant. 3. Mathieu est en ville. 4. Antoine est au café.

Nom _____

Classe _____ Date _____

A. Le verbe *être* et les pronoms sujets, pages 84–85
Vocabulaire: *Où?*, pages 85–86

Materials Checklist

- **Student Text**
- **Audio CD** 7, Tracks 6–7
- **Video** 2 or **DVD** 1; Counter 13:29–15:05
- **Workbook**

Steps to Follow

- Study *Le verbe être et les pronoms sujets* (p. 84). Write the conjugation of **être** on a separate sheet of paper. Circle the subject pronouns.
- Study *Tu or vous?* (p. 84). When do you use **tu**? When do you use **vous**?
- Study *Ils or elles?* (p. 85). When do you use **ils**? When do you use **elles**?
- Watch **Video** 2 or **DVD** 1; Counter 13:29–15:05. Repeat everything you hear.
- Study *Vocabulaire: Où?* (p. 85). Copy the new expressions on a separate sheet of paper.
- Complete Activities 1–4 in the text (pp. 85–86). Write your answers in complete sentences.
- Do Activity 5 (p. 86). Write the parts for both speakers on a separate sheet of paper.
- Do **Writing Activities** A 1, 2 in the **Workbook** (p. 67).
- Do **Listening Activities** A–B in the **Workbook** (p. 65). Use **Audio CD** 7, Tracks 6–7.

If You Don't Understand . . .

- Watch the **Video** or **DVD** in a quiet place. Try to stay focused. If you get lost, stop the **Video** or **DVD**. Replay it and find your place.
- Reread the activity directions. Put the directions in your own words.
- Say aloud everything that you write. Be sure you understand what you are saying.
- Write down questions so that you can ask your partner or your teacher later.
- When writing a sentence, ask yourself, "What do I mean? What am I trying to say?"

Self-Check

Answer the following questions on a separate sheet of paper. Use the appropriate pronoun, and write in complete sentences.

1. Où est Céline? (à Chicago)
2. Où sont Thomas et Annette? (en vacances)
3. Où es-tu? (à la maison)
4. Où sont Anne et Jeanette? (en ville)
5. Où est Martin? (au restaurant)
6. Où sont Jean et Pierre? (là)

Answers

1. Elle est à Chicago. 2. Ils sont en vacances. 3. Je suis à la maison. 4. Elles sont en ville. 5. Il est au restaurant. 6. Ils sont là.

Nom _____

Classe _____ Date _____

Discovering
FRENCH
Nouveau!

BLEU

Unité 3
Leçon 6

Absent Student
Copymasters

B. Les questions à réponse affirmative ou négative, pages 86–87
Vocabulaire: Expressions pour la conversation, page 89

Materials Checklist

- **Student Text**
- **Audio CD** 7, Tracks 8–9
- **Video** 2 or **DVD** 1; Counter 13:52–15:05
- **Workbook**

Steps to Follow

- Study *Les questions à réponse affirmative ou négative* (pp. 86–87).
- Watch **Video** 2 or **DVD** 1; Counter 13:52–15:05. Repeat what you hear.
- Study *Vocabulaire: Expressions pour la conversation* (p. 87). Write the expressions on a separate sheet of paper.
- Do Activities 5 and 6 in the text (p. 87). For Activity 6, write the parts for both speakers.
- Do **Writing Activities** B/C 4 in the **Workbook** (p. 68).
- Do **Listening Activities** C–D in the **Workbook** (pp. 65–66). Use **Audio CD** 7, Tracks 8–9.

If You Don't Understand . . .

- Watch the **Video** or **DVD** in a quiet place. Try to stay focused. If you get lost, stop the **Video** or **DVD**. Replay it and find your place.
- Reread the activity directions. Put the directions in your own words.
- Read the model several times. Be sure you understand it. Underline new question expressions, for example, **Est-ce que Jim est américain?**
- Say aloud everything that you write. Be sure you understand what you are saying.
- Write down questions so that you can ask your partner or your teacher later.
- When writing a sentence, ask yourself, "What do I mean? What am I trying to say?"

Self-Check

Answer the following questions affirmatively on a separate sheet of paper. Use the appropriate pronoun, and write complete sentences.

1. Tu es américain(e), n'est-ce pas?
2. Est-ce que Joëlle est française?
3. Anne et Thomas sont canadiens, n'est-ce pas?
4. Est-ce que Marie-Jacques et Annique sont suisses (*Swiss*)?
5. Nous sommes d'accord, n'est-ce pas?

Answers

1. Oui, je suis américain(e). 2. Oui, elle est française. 3. Oui, ils sont canadiens. 4. Oui, elles sont suisses. 5. Oui, nous sommes d'accord.

URB
p. 45

Nom _____

Classe _____ Date _____

Discovering
FRENCH
Nouveau

B L E U

Unité 3
Leçon 6

Absent Student Copymasters

C. La négation, page 88
Vocabulaire: Mots utiles, page 89

Materials Checklist

- **Student Text**
- **Audio CD** 2, Tracks 8–10; **CD** 7, Tracks 10–11
- **Video** 2 or **DVD** 1; Counter 12:37–13:28
- **Workbook**

Steps to Follow

- Study *La négation* (p. 88). Write out negative sentences for **vous**, **ils**, and **elles** with the appropriate form of **être**.
- Watch **Video** 2 or **DVD** 1; Counter 12:37–13:28. Repeat what you hear.
- Do Activities 7 and 8 in the text (p. 88). Write the answers in complete sentences.
- Study *Vocabulaire: Mots utiles* (p. 89). Say the expressions and the model sentences aloud.
- Do Activities 9 and 10 in the text (p. 89). Write the answers in complete sentences.
- Listen to *Prononciation: La voyelle /a/* on **Audio** CD 2, Track 8. Repeat what you hear. Try to sound like the people in the recording.
- Do **Writing Activities** B/C 5 in the **Workbook** (p. 68).
- Do **Listening Activities** E–F in the **Workbook** (p. 66). Use **Audio CD** 7, Tracks 10–11.
- Do Activities 1–4 of *À votre tour!* in the text (pp. 90–91). Use **Audio CD** 2, Tracks 9–10 with Activities 1 and 3.

If You Don't Understand . . .

- Reread the activity directions. Put the directions in your own words.
- Read the model several times before beginning so you are certain what to do. Copy the model. Underline the negative expressions, for example, **Anne n'est pas ici.**
- Say aloud everything that you write. Listen and be sure you understand what you are saying.
- Write down any questions so that you can ask your teacher or your partner later.
- Watch the **Video** or **DVD** in a quiet place. Try to stay focused. If you get lost, stop the **Video** or **DVD**. Replay it and find your place.
- Listen to the **CDs** in a quiet place. Try to stay focused. If you get lost, stop the **CDs**. Replay them and find your place.
- Repeat aloud with the audio. Try to sound like the people on the recording.

Self-Check

Answer the following questions negatively on a separate sheet of paper. Use the appropriate pronoun, and write in complete sentences.

1. Est-ce que tu es de Chicago?
2. Est-ce que Jean est à la maison?
3. Est-ce que Marie et Jeanne sont en classe?

Answers

1. Non, je ne suis pas de Chicago. 2. Non, il n'est pas à la maison. 3. Non, elles ne sont pas en classe. 4. Non, je ne suis pas de Paris. / Non, nous ne sommes pas de Paris. 5. Non, nous ne sommes pas en retard.

Nom _____

Classe _____ Date _____

Discovering FRENCH Nouveau!

B L E U

Unité 3
Leçon 6

Family Involvement

LEÇON 6 Une invitation

Où est Cécile?

Ask a family member to indicate where Cécile is. Have him or her point to the phrase indicated by each drawing.

- First, explain your assignment.
- Model the pronunciation of the words. Point to the words as you say them and then provide the English equivalent for each one.
- Then, ask the question: **Où est Cécile?**
- Have the family member draw a line to the sentence that matches each drawing.

Elle est au café.

Elle est au cinéma.

Elle est à la maison.

Elle est en classe.

Nom _____

Classe _____ Date _____

Discovering
FRENCH
Nouveau!

B L E U

Les préférences

Interview a family member about his or her preferences.

- First, explain your assignment.
- Model the pronunciation of possible answers: **Je préfère** _____ and the words under each drawing. Point to the picture as you model each answer.
- Ask the question, **Tu préfères** _____ **ou** _____?
- Choose among the possible answers to complete the sentence at the bottom of the page.

manger à la maison   ou   **dîner au restaurant?**

regarder la télé   ou   **regarder le film au cinéma?**

travailler   ou   **parler avec moi?**

_____ aime _____ et _____,

mais _____ préfère _____.

MODULE 6   Une invitation

Video 2, DVD 1

6.1 Activité 1. Où sont les copains?

Counter 11:59–13:28

Antoine is having trouble finding his friends. He sees Céline in a café and asks her where everyone is. Circle the letter of the correct completion to each sentence below as you watch the video.

1. Léa est . . .   a. à la maison   b. au restaurant
2. Mathieu est . . .   a. au restaurant   b. en ville
3. Il est avec . . .   a. un copain   b. une copine
4. Julie et Stéphanie sont . . . a. au restaurant   b. au cinéma

Nom _____

Classe _____ Date _____

6.2 Activité 2. Où est tout le monde? (everyone)

Counter 13:29–13:51

Where is everyone today? Listen and watch as eleven people in the video tell you where they are. Place a check mark after each place each time it is mentioned in the video. Then record the number of check marks for each item in the TOTAL column.

		Total
à la maison		
à Paris		
au café		
en classe		
en France		
en vacances		
en ville		

Nom _____

Classe _____ Date _____

Discovering FRENCH
Nouveau!

B L E U

6.3 Activité 3. Où sont-ils?

Counter 13:52–15:05

Where are the people in the pictures below? After watching the video segment, draw a line from each sentence to the corresponding picture.

a.

1. Elle est à Paris.

2. Elles sont en ville.

e.

b.

3. Il est à la maison.

4. Il est au restaurant.

f.

c.

5. Elle est au café.

6. Ils sont en vacances.

g.

d.

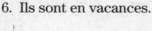

7. Ils sont en classe.

8. Ils sont au cinéma.

h.

BLEU

6.4 Activité 4. Au café

Counter 15:06–16:42

As you watch the **Vignette culturelle,** answer the questions below.

1. What is the main reason French teenagers go to a café? _____

2. What section of the café is **la terrasse?** _____

3. Why do people enjoy eating on **la terrasse?** _____

4. What section of the café is **l'intérieur?** _____

5. What is **le babyfoot?** _____

 Question personnelle: If you lived in France, would you prefer to go to a typical café or a fast-food place? Why?

Réponse: _____

Activité 5. Un jeu: Où es-tu?

Form a group with three or four classmates. One of you copies each place listed below onto a separate slip of paper. Put the slips of paper into a pile, face down. One of you draws a place from the pile and the others try to guess it. When the place has been correctly identified, another student continues. As you go, keep track of the students who guess correctly. The student with the most correct guesses is the winner.

à Québec	en classe	en ville
en vacances	en France	au café
au restaurant	au cinéma	à la maison

▶ ÉLÈVE 2: Est-ce que tu es en classe?

ÉLÈVE 1: Non, je ne suis pas en classe.

ÉLÈVE 3: Tu es au cinéma?

ÉLÈVE 1: Oui, je suis au cinéma.

Discovering
FRENCH
Nouveau!

BLEU

Unité 3
Leçon 6

Videoscripts

MODULE 6   Une invitation

Video 2, DVD 1

Where are you now? Probably at school. And where are you on the weekends? Possibly at home? or maybe downtown or at the mall? What do you do when you go out with your friends? Do you go shopping? or to the movies? Do you stop for something to eat?

6.1 Dialogue: Une invitation

Counter: 12:37–13:28

It is Wednesday afternoon. Antoine is looking for his friends but cannot find anyone. Finally he sees Céline at the Café Le Bercy and asks her where everyone is.

ANTOINE: Où est Léa?
CÉLINE: Elle est à la maison.
ANTOINE: Et Mathieu? Il est là?
CÉLINE: Non, il n'est pas là.
ANTOINE: Où est-il?
CÉLINE: Il est en ville avec une copine.
ANTOINE: Et Julie et Stéphanie? Est-ce qu'elles sont ici?
CÉLINE: Non, elles sont au restaurant.
ANTOINE: Alors, qui est là?
CÉLINE: Moi, je suis ici.
ANTOINE: C'est vrai, tu es ici! Eh bien, puisque tu es là, je t'invite au cinéma. D'accord?
CÉLINE: Super! Antoine, tu es un vrai copain!

6.2 Mini-scenes: Listening—Je suis en classe

Counter: 13:29–13:51

Watch the following scenes and listen as people tell you where they are.

—Je suis en classe.
—Nous sommes en classe.
—Je suis à la maison.
—Nous sommes en ville.
—Nous sommes en vacances.
—Je suis au café.
—Je suis au café avec un copain.
—Nous sommes en vacances.
—Nous sommes en France.
—Nous sommes à Paris.

6.3 Mini-scenes: Speaking— Où sont-ils?

Counter: 13:52–15:05

Now it's your turn. You'll see a series of pictures showing people in various places. Answer by saying where these people are.

—Est-ce qu'il est à la maison ou au restaurant? [screen card]
—Il est au restaurant.

—Est-ce qu'elle est au café ou à la maison? [screen card]
—Elle est au café.

—Est-ce qu'ils sont en classe ou en vacances? [screen card]
—Ils sont en vacances.

—Est-ce qu'ils sont au cinéma ou au restaurant? [screen card]
—Ils sont au cinéma.

—Est-ce qu'il est en ville ou à la maison? [screen card]
—Il est à la maison.

—Est-ce qu'elles sont en ville ou à la maison? [screen card]
—Elles sont en ville.

—Est-ce qu'ils sont en classe ou au café? [screen card]
—Ils sont en classe.

—Est-ce qu'elle est à Paris ou à New York? [screen card]
—Elle est à Paris.

6.4 Vignette culturelle: Au café

Counter: 15:06–16:42

The café is a favorite gathering place for French young people. They go there to have something to eat or drink, or listen to music, or even to study. But the main reason French teenagers go to a café is to meet their friends and talk. A French café has two sections. The outside is called **la terrasse**. **La terrasse** is simply an extension of the café onto the sidewalk. In the spring and summer, **la terrasse** is the ideal spot to enjoy the sun and watch people passing by. The indoor section is called **l'intérieur**. In cafés located in student areas, the **intérieur** may have games such as **le flipper** or **le babyfoot**, a table-top soccer game.

Let's ask these students which part of the café they prefer and why.

—Tu préfères être à l'intérieur ou à la terrasse?
—Je préfère être à l'intérieur.
—Pourquoi?
—Parce que j'aime jouer au flipper.

—Et toi?
—Aujourd'hui, je préfère être à la terrasse.
—Pourquoi?
—Parce qu'il fait beau.

Discovering
FRENCH
Nouveau!
BLEU

Unité 3
Leçon 6
Audioscripts

LEÇON 6 Une invitation

PE AUDIO

CD 2, Track 6
Compréhension orale, p. 82

It is Wednesday afternoon. Antoine is looking for his friends but cannot find anyone. Finally he sees Céline at the Café Le Bercy and asks her where everyone is.

ANTOINE: Où est Léa?
CÉLINE: Elle est à la maison.
ANTOINE: Et Mathieu? Il est là?
CÉLINE: Non, il n'est pas là.
ANTOINE: Où est-il?
CÉLINE: Il est en ville avec une copine.
ANTOINE: Et Julie et Stéphanie? Est-ce qu'elles sont ici?
CÉLINE: Non, elles sont au restaurant.
ANTOINE: Alors, qui est là?
CÉLINE: Moi, je suis ici.
ANTOINE: C'est vrai, tu es ici! Eh bien, puisque tu es là, je t'invite au cinéma. D'accord?
CÉLINE: Super! Antoine, tu es un vrai copain!

CD 2, Track 7
Écoutez et répétez, p. 82

You will now hear a paused version of the dialog. Listen to the speaker and repeat right after he or she has completed the sentence.

Prononciation, p. 89

CD 2, Track 8
La voyelle /a/

Écoutez: chat

The letter "a" alone always represents the sound /a/ as in the English word *ah*. It never has the sound of "*a*" as in English words like *class*, *date*, or *cinema*.

Répétez: chat # ça va # à # la # là-bas # avec # ami # voilà #
classe # café # salade # dame # date # Madame # Canada #
Anne est au Canada avec Madame Laval. #

À votre tour!

CD 2, Track 9
1. Allô!, p. 90

Jacques is phoning some friends. Match his questions on the left with his friends' answers on the right.

1. Où es-tu?
Je suis à la maison.

2. Où est ta soeur?
Elle est en classe.

3. Est-ce que ton frère est à la maison?
Non, il est au cinéma.

4. Tes parents sont en vacances, n'est-ce pas?
Oui! Ils sont à Paris.

5. Ta soeur est avec une copine?
Oui, elles sont au restaurant.

CD 2, Track 10
3. Créa-dialogue, p. 91

Listen to some sample *Créa-dialogues.*
Écoutez les conversations.

Modèle: —Bonjour. Vous êtes anglaise?
—Oui, je suis anglaise.
—Est-ce que vous êtes de Londres?
—Mais non, je ne suis pas de Londres. Je suis de Liverpool.

Maintenant, écoutez le dialogue numéro 1.

—Bonjour. Vous êtes américaine?
—Oui, je suis américaine.
—Est-ce que vous êtes de New York?
—Mais non, je ne suis pas de New York. Je suis de Washington.

Unité 3
Leçon 6

Audioscripts

Discovering
FRENCH
Nouveau

BLEU

WORKBOOK AUDIO

Section 1. Le verbe *être*

CD 7, Track 6

A. Écoutez et parlez., p. 65

You will hear what nationalities certain people are, and then you will hear the name of a city. Say that these people are from that city.

Listen to the model.

Modèle: Vous êtes français. # Paris # Vous êtes de Paris. #

Commençons. Let's begin.

1. Il est canadien. # Québec # Il est de Québec.
2. Elle est française. # Lille # Elle est de Lille.
3. Ils sont américains. # New York # Ils sont de New York.
4. Elles sont canadiennes. # Montréal # Elles sont de Montréal.
5. Je suis américain. # Los Angeles # Je suis de Los Angeles.
6. Tu es anglais. # Manchester # Tu es de Manchester.
7. Vous êtes français. # Lyon # Vous êtes de Lyon.
8. Nous sommes américaines. # Boston # Nous sommes de Boston.

Section 2. Tu ou vous?

CD 7, Track 7

B. Écoutez et parlez., p. 65

You will hear the names of different people. Ask each person whether he or she is French. Remember to address young people as "tu" and adults as "vous". Listen to the models.

Modèle: Stéphanie Tu es française? #
Monsieur Lambert Vous êtes français? #

Commençons.

1. Philippe # Tu es français?
2. Mélanie # Tu es française?
3. Madame Dubois # Vous êtes française?
4. Mademoiselle Masson # Vous êtes française?
5. Thomas # Tu es français?
6. Monsieur Dorval # Vous êtes français?

Section 3. Où sont-ils?

CD 7, Track 8

C. Compréhension orale, p. 65

You will hear where certain people are. In your Workbook, draw a line connecting the name of each person to the corresponding location. You will hear the statements twice.

Modèle: Pierre est au cinéma.

You should draw a line from Pierre to the movie theater.

Commençons.

1. Charlotte est au café. #
2. Monsieur Leblanc est à la maison. #
3. Julien et Nicolas sont au restaurant. #
4. Le prof est en classe. #
5. Stéphanie et François sont en ville. #
6. Monsieur et Madame Arnaud sont en vacances. #

CD 7, Track 9

D. Questions et réponses, p. 66

You will see series of pictures showing people in various places. Answer the questions, saying where the people are. After you have given your answer, listen to the confirmation.

Modèle: Est-ce qu'il est à la maison ou au restaurant?
(response) Il est au restaurant.

1. Est-ce qu'elle est au café ou à la maison? #
   Elle est au café.

2. Est-ce qu'ils sont en classe ou en vacances? #
   Ils sont en vacances.

3. Est-ce qu'ils sont au cinéma ou au restaurant? #
   Ils sont au cinéma.

4. Est-ce qu'il est en ville ou à la maison? #
   Il est à la maison.

5. Est-ce qu'elles sont en ville ou à la maison? #
   Elles sont en ville.

6. Est-ce qu'ils sont en classe ou au café? #
   Ils sont en classe.

7. Est-ce qu'elle est à Paris ou à New York? #
   Elle est à Paris.

Section 4. Non!

CD 7, Track 10

E. Écoutez et parlez., p. 66

You will hear a series of questions about individuals. Answer them negatively using **il** or **elle** as appropriate. Listen to the model.

Modèle: Kevin est français? # Non, il n'est pas français.

Commençons.

1. Stéphanie est canadienne? # Non, elle n'est pas canadienne.

2. Jean-Paul est à la maison? # Non, il n'est pas à la maison.

3. Juliette est au cinéma? # Non, elle n'est

pas au cinéma.

4. Thomas est en classe? # Non, il n'est pas en classe.

Now you will hear similar questions about several people. Listen to the model.

Modèle: Éric et Nicolas sont en ville? # Non, ils ne sont pas en ville.

5. Anne et Claire sont à la maison? # Non, elles ne sont pas à la maison.

6. Monsieur et Madame Moreau sont à Québec? # Non, ils ne sont pas à Québec.

7. Monsieur et Madame Dupont sont en vacances? # Non, ils ne sont pas en vacances.

Section 5. Dictée

CD 7, Track 11

F. Écoutez et écrivez., p. 66

You will hear a short phone conversation spoken twice. First listen carefully to what the people are saying. The second time you hear the dialogue, fill in the missing words.

Écoutez.

—Salut Thomas! Tu es à la maison?
—Non, je suis au café.
—Est-ce que ta soeur est avec toi?
—Non, elle n'est pas avec moi. Elle est en ville avec une copine. Elles sont au cinéma.

Listen again and fill in the missing words.

Unité 3
Leçon 6

Audioscripts

Discovering
FRENCH
Nouveau

BLEU

LESSON 6 QUIZ

Part 1: Listening

CD 14, Track 2

A. Conversations

You will hear a series of short conversations between Philippe and Juliette. Listen to each conversation carefully. Then answer the corresponding questions on your answer sheet by circling the appropriate letter (a, b, or c). You will hear each conversation twice.

Let's begin.

1. PHILIPPE: Ton copain est canadien?
   JULIETTE: Non, il est français. Il est de Marseille.

2. JULIETTE: Ta soeur est à la maison?
   PHILIPPE: Non, elle est en ville.

3. PHILIPPE: Où est Caroline?
   JULIETTE: Elle est en vacances.
   PHILIPPE: Où?
   JULIETTE: À Chicago. Elle aime voyager!

4. PHILIPPE: Où est Nathalie?
   JULIETTE: Avec un copain.
   PHILIPPE: Où sont-ils?
   JULIETTE: Ils sont au cinéma.

5. JULIETTE: Allô, Philippe!
   PHILIPPE: Allô, Juliette! Ça va?
   JULIETTE: Oui, ça va! Dis, est-ce que tu veux dîner avec moi?
   PHILIPPE: Oui, d'accord! Où es-tu?
   JULIETTE: Je suis à la maison.

Nom _____

Classe _____ Date _____ _____

Discovering FRENCH *Nouveau!*

B L E U

Unité 3 Leçon 6

Lesson Quiz

QUIZ 6

Part I: Listening

A. Conversations (25 points)

You will hear a series of short conversations between Philippe and Juliette. Listen to each conversation carefully. Then answer the corresponding questions on your answer sheet by circling the appropriate letter (a, b, or c). You will hear each conversation twice.

1. What do we know about Juliette's friend?
   a. He is Canadian.
   b. He is in Marseille.
   c. He is from Marseille.

2. Where is Philippe's sister?
   a. At home.
   b. Downtown.
   c. In class.

3. Why is Caroline in Chicago?
   a. She is on vacation there.
   b. She studies there.
   c. She is visiting a cousin.

4. Where is Nathalie?
   a. At the movies.
   b. On vacation.
   c. At a friend's house.

5. Where is Juliette?
   a. At a café.
   b. In a restaurant.
   c. At home.

Part II: Writing

B. Oui et non (40 points)

Complete the following conversations with the appropriate form of **être**.
NOTE: In conversations 3 and 4 the answers are in the NEGATIVE.

OUI

1. —Céline _____ avec Alice?

   —Oui, elles _____ en ville.

2. —Vous _____ en vacances?

   —Oui, nous _____ en vacances.

NON

3. —Nathalie _____ à la maison?

   —Non, elle _____ à la maison.

4. —Tu _____ français?

   —Non, je _____ français.

Discovering
FRENCH
Nouveau

BLEU

C. Le mot juste *(The right word)* **(15 points)**

Complete each sentence with the word in parentheses that fits logically.

1. (ou / mais)   Qui est-ce? Roger _____ Julien?

2. (à / de)   M. Leclerc est en France. Aujourd'hui il est _____ Paris.

3. (avec / et)   Julie _____ Nicolas sont à Tours.

4. (pour / de)   Je voudrais travailler _____ Mme Duroc.

5. (mais / avec)   J'aime jouer au ping-pong, _____ je ne veux pas jouer avec Bernard.

D. Expression personnelle **(20 points)**

Give the following information in French. Use complete sentences.

- Say where you are now.

_____

- Choose a person you know and say where he or she is.

_____

Discovering French, Nouveau! Bleu

Nom _____

Classe _____ Date _____

Discovering FRENCH *Nouveau!*

BLEU

Unité 3
Leçon 7

Workbook TE

LEÇON 7   Une boum

LISTENING ACTIVITIES

Section 1. Je parle français.

A. Questions et réponses

Modèle: Tu parles français.
Oui, je parle français.

B. Regardez et parlez . . .

Modèle: [Pauline}   **Elle joue au foot.**

Pauline

1. Thomas
Il joue au basket.

2. Stéphanie
Elle nage.

3. Marc
Il mange.

4. Isabelle
Elle regarde la télé.

5. Frédéric
Il téléphone.

6. Mélanie
Elle chante.

7. M. Rémi
Il travaille.

8. Mme Dupin
Elle voyage.

Section 2. Nous parlons français.

C. Questions et réponses

Modèle: Vous parlez français ?
Oui, nous parlons français.

Nom _____

Classe _____ Date _____

D. Compréhension orale

	Modèle	1	2	3	4	5	6	7	8
A. oui		✓		✓			✓	✓	
B. non	✓		✓		✓	✓			✓

E. Questions et réponses

▶—Est-ce qu'il travaille?
—**Non, il ne travaille pas.**

Non, ils ne travaillent pas.   Oui, il voyage.   Non, ils ne visitent pas New Yor

Non, ils ne jouent pas   Non, elle ne chante pas bien.   Oui, elle nage bien.
au tennis.

Section 4. Dictée

F. Écoutez et écrivez.

—Est-ce que tu <u>aimes</u> jouer au basket?

—Oui, je joue <u>souvent</u> avec ma cousine.

—Est-ce qu'elle joue <u>bien</u> ?

—Non, elle <u>ne joue pas</u> très bien, mais elle <u>aime</u> jouer!

Nom _____

Classe _____ Date _____

Discovering FRENCH *Nouveau!*

BLEU

Unité 3
Leçon 7

Workbook TE

WRITING ACTIVITIES

A/B 1. Tourisme

The following people are traveling abroad. Complete the
sentences with the appropriate forms of **visiter.**

1. Nous visitons Québec.

2. Tu visites Fort-de-France.

3. Jean et Thomas visitent Paris.

4. Vous visitez Genève.

5. Hélène visite San Francisco.

6. Je visite La Nouvelle Orléans.

7. Marc visite Tokyo.

8. Monsieur et Madame Dupont visitent Mexico.

2. Qu'est-ce qu'ils font?

Describe what people are doing by completing the sentences with the appropriate verbs. First
write the infinitive in the box, and then fill in the correct form in the sentence. Be logical.

manger	écouter	regarder	dîner
jouer	organiser	parler	

▶	dîner	Nous dînons au restaurant.
1.	jouer	Christine et Claire jouent au tennis.
2.	regarder	Vous regardez la télé.
3.	écouter	J' écoute la radio.
4.	parler	Tu parles français avec le professeur.
5.	manger	Jérôme mange un sandwich.
6.	organiser	Nous organisons une boum.

Nom _____

Classe _____ Date _____

Discovering
FRENCH
Nouveau

BLEU

3. Descriptions

Look carefully at the following scenes and describe what the different people are doing.

▶ Mélanie _nage_ .

Éric et Vincent _jouent au foot_ .

Monsieur Boulot _travaille_ .

Claire et Philippe _regardent_ .

Le professeur _parle_ .

Hélène et Marc _écoutent_ .

Diane _chante_ .

Jean-Paul et Bernard _écoutent_ .

Nom _____

Classe _____ Date _____

Discovering
FRENCH
Nouveau!

BLEU

Unité 3
Leçon 7

Workbook TE

C 4. Et toi?

Your French friend Caroline wants to know more about you. Answer her questions, affirmatively or negatively.

1. Tu parles anglais?

   Oui, je parle anglais.

2. Tu parles souvent français?

   Non, je ne parle pas souvent français. (Oui, je parle souvent français.)

3. Tu habites à New York?

   Oui, j'habite à New York. (Non, je n'habite pas à New York.)

4. Tu étudies l'espagnol?

   Oui, j'étudie l'espagnol. (Non, je n'étudie pas l'espagnol.)

5. Tu joues aux jeux vidéo?

   Oui, je joue aux jeux vidéo. (Non, je ne joue pas aux jeux vidéo.)

6. Tu dînes souvent au restaurant?

   Oui, je dîne souvent au restaurant. (Non, je ne dîne pas souvent . . .)

RESTAURANT GRILL

Le Boeuf Jardinier

5. Dimanche

For many people, Sunday is a day of rest. Say that the following people are not doing the activities in parentheses.

▶ (étudier)   Tu *n'étudies pas* .

1. (étudier)   Nous *n'étudions pas* .

2. (travailler)   Vous *ne travaillez pas* .

3. (parler)   Mon copain *ne parle pas* français.

4. (téléphoner)   La secrétaire *ne téléphone pas* .

5. (jouer)   Paul et Thomas *ne jouent pas* au foot.

6. (voyager)   Tu *ne voyages pas* .

Unité 3
Leçon 7

Workbook TE

Discovering
FRENCH
Nouveau!

BLEU

Nom _____

Classe _____ Date _____

6. 👥 Communication (sample answer)

You have a new French pen pal
named Isabelle. Write her a short
letter introducing yourself.

Date your letter.

- *Tell Isabelle your name.*

- *Tell her in which city you live.*

- *Tell her at what school you study.*

- *Tell her whether or not you often
  speak French.*

- *Tell her what sports you play.*

- *Tell her two things you like to do.*

- *Tell her one thing you do not like
  to do.*

Sign your letter.

le 3 novembre

Chère Isabelle,

- Je m'appelle Harriet.
- J'habite à Jacksonville.
- J'étudie à Central High School.
- Je ne parle pas souvent français.

- Je joue au basket et au foot.
- J'aime écouter la radio et jouer aux
  jeux vidéo.
- Je n'aime pas voyager.

Amitiés,

Harriet

Nom _____

Classe _____ Date _____

LEÇON 7 Une boum

A

Activité 1 Verbes

Circle the verb form that correctly completes each sentence.

1. Je *visite* / visites souvent Paris.
2. Marc ne regardes / *regarde* pas la télé.
3. Ils joue / *jouent* bien aux jeux vidéo.
4. Nous n'*habitons* / habitez pas à Boston.
5. Tu *aimes* / aimez mon cousin?
6. Karine et Anna invite / *invitent* des amis à la boum.

Activité 2 Adverbes

Circle the adverb that fits logically.

1. Alan Iverson joue rarement / *très bien* au basket.
2. Whitney Houston chante aussi / *bien*.
3. Le président américain parle *un peu* / beaucoup français.
4. Ma grand-mère écoute souvent / *rarement* la musique hip-hop.
5. Willie Nelson joue *bien* / un peu de la guitare.

Activité 3 Préférences

Fill in the blanks with the correct verbs.

1. Je voudrais jouer aux jeux vidéo, mais je dois _étudier_____.

2. Je dois travailler, mais je voudrais _danser_____.

3. J'aime le français, mais je préfère _parler_____ anglais.

4. Je voudrais _voyager_____ mais je dois aller à l'école.

5. J'aime le basket, mais je préfère _jouer_____ au tennis.

Discovering French, Nouveau! Bleu

Unité 3, Leçon 7
Activités pour tous 39

Unité 3
Leçon 7

Activités pour tous TE

Nom _____

Classe _____ Date _____

Discovering
FRENCH
Nouveau

BLEU

B

Activité 1 Questions

You are new in town. Circle the correct answers to the following questions about yourself and your family.

1. —Tu parles français?
   —*Oui, je parle français.* / Oui, nous parlons français.

2. —Vous habitez ici maintenant?
   —*Oui, j'habite ici maintenant.* / *Oui, nous habitons ici maintenant.*

3. —Tu nages bien?
   —*Oui, je nage bien.* / Oui, nous nageons bien.

4. —Tu joues beaucoup au tennis?
   —*Non, je ne joue pas beaucoup au tennis.* / Non, nous ne jouons pas beaucoup au tennis.

Activité 2 Adverbes

Choose the adverb that best describes the situation. Use each only once.

souvent	beaucoup	peu	très bien	mal

1. Je joue au basket tous les jours. Je joue _souvent_.

2. Paul joue au tennis comme un professionnel. Il joue _très bien_.

3. Mme Leclerc aime parler. Elle parle _beaucoup_!

4. Les Dupont voyagent cinq jours en été. Ils voyagent _peu_.

5. Je ne joue pas beaucoup du piano, parce que je joue _mal_.

Activité 3 Préférences

Using the visual cues and words from the box, write sentences stating your wishes (**je veux**) and obligations (**je dois**).

je veux ☺	je dois ☹

1. _Je veux jouer au tennis_ mais _je dois étudier._!

2. _Je dois travailler_ parce que _je veux voyager._!

3. _Je veux téléphoner_ parce que _je veux parler._!

Nom _____

Classe _____ Date _____

Discovering FRENCH *Nouveau!*

B L E U

Unité 3
Leçon 7
Activités pour tous TE

C

Activité 1 Beaucoup ou peu? (sample answers)

Write how much or how little people do the things pictured, using **beaucoup, peu, souvent,** or **rarement.**

1. Ma mère *joue peu au tennis.*

2. Mes amis *n'étudient pas beaucoup.*

3. Mon père *ne voyage pas beaucoup.*

4. Mon frère *joue beaucoup aux jeux vidéo.*

5. Nous *ne mangeons pas beaucoup.*

6. Est-ce que vous *regardez beaucoup la télévision?*

Activité 2 Mes activités (sample answers)

Write how well you do the following activities, using **très bien, bien, comme ci, comme ça,** or **mal.**

1. *Je joue bien au basket.*   3. *Je danse très bien.*

2. *Je ne nage pas très bien.*   4. *Je chante comme ci, comme ça.*

Activité 3 Préférences (sample answers)

Write sentences stating contrasts as in the example. Use the visual cues and expressions like **j'aime / je n'aime pas, je veux, je ne peux pas, je dois,** and **je ne . . . pas beaucoup.**

Modèle: J'aime danser mais je ne danse pas beaucoup.

1. *J'aime dîner au restaurant mais je ne dîne pas beaucoup au restaurant.*

2. *J'aime nager mais je ne nage pas souvent.*

3. *Je voudrais jouer au tennis mais je dois étudier.*

4. *J'aime jouer aux jeux vidéo mais je ne joue pas bien.*

5. *Je voudrais voyager mais je ne peux pas.*

Unité 3
Leçon 7

Lesson Plans

Discovering
FRENCH *Nouveau*

BLEU

LEÇON 7 Une boum, page 92

Objectives

Communicative Functions and Topics
To describe what one person or several people are doing or are not doing
To talk about what people like and don't like to do
To express approval or regret

Linguistic Goals
To use verb + infinitive
To use regular *-er* verbs
To pronounce vowels /i/ and /u/

Cultural Goals
To become familiar with French party customs

Motivation and Focus

❏ Have students look at the pictures on page 93 and discuss what is happening. Discuss party organization with SETTING THE STAGE on page 92 of the TE. You may show the **Video** to preview the lesson. Have students comment on the activities mentioned.

Presentation and Explanation

❏ *Lesson Opener:* Read the introductory paragraph on page 92 and invite students to guess what Jean-Marc is going to say to Béatrice and Valérie. Play **Video** 7.4 or **Audio** CD 2, Tracks 11–12, the opening conversation. Ask students to read and summarize the conversation.

❏ *Note culturelle:* Have students read *Une boum*, page 93. Encourage them to compare French and American parties by playing the **Video** or reading the **Videoscript** for 7.5.

❏ *Grammar A, B,* and *C:* Present *-er* verbs with **Overhead Transparencies** 14a and b and 17. Explain verb conjugations, pointing out the grammar boxes and information on pages 94 and 96. Practice verb endings using Transparency 16. Introduce affirmative and negative forms on page 98.

❏ *Vocabulaire:* Model and explain the words and expressions in the boxes on page 100. Point out examples of verb + infinitive that students have already practiced. Have students read the grammar explanation on page 101.

❏ *Prononciation:* Model pronunciation of the vowels /i/ and /u/, page 101, and have students repeat the words. Practice pronunciation with **Audio** CD 2, Track 14.

Guided Practice and Checking Understanding

❏ Use **Overhead Transparency** 17 and suggestions on page A64 for practice with *-er* verbs. To practice expressions for how often and how well, have students ask and answer questions about the pictures on Transparencies 14a and b.

❏ Check listening skills with the **Audio** CD 7, Tracks 12–17 or the **Audioscript** and **Workbook** Listening Activities A–F, pages 69–70.

❏ Have students do **Video Activities** pages 81–83 as they view the **Video** or listen while you read the **Videoscript**.

❏ Use the COMPREHENSION Activities on pages 95 and 96 of the TE to check students' understanding of verbs and subject pronouns.

Independent Practice

❏ Practice with the Activities on pages 94–101. Assign Activities 3, 5, 7, and 9, 11–12 for homework. Use the **Audio** CD 2, Track 13 with Activity 10. Use any or all of Activities 1, 2,

Discovering
FRENCH
Nouveau!

BLEU

Unité 3
Leçon 7
Lesson Plans

4, 6, 8, 13, or 14 for PAIR PRACTICE. Follow the suggestions for CLASSROOM MANAGEMENT WRITING PRACTICE, Page 97 of the TE, for Activity 8.

❑ Have pairs of students choose one of the following **Communipak** activities: *Interviews* 1, 2; *Tu as la parole* 4, 5, 6; *Conversations* 1, 2; *Échange* 2; *Tête à tête* 1 (pages 128–137). They may also do page 84 of the **Video Activities**.

❑ Have students do the activities in **Activités pour tous,** pages 39–41.

Monitoring and Adjusting

❑ Have students do the Writing Activities on **Workbook** pages 71–74.

❑ Monitor students' work on the Activities on pages 94–101. Have them review the grammar and vocabulary boxes as needed. Use the TEACHING TIPS and TEACHING NOTES, and explain the PRONUNCIATION and LANGUAGE NOTES, on pages 94–101 of the TE.

Assessment

❑ Administer Quiz 7 on pages 91–92 after completing the lesson. Use the **Test Generator** to adapt the quiz questions to your class's needs.

Reteaching

❑ Redo any appropriate activities from the **Workbook**.

❑ Use the **Video** to reteach portions of the lesson.

❑ Follow the suggestions for VARIATIONS of Activities 4 and 6, pages 96–97 of the TE. **Teacher to Teacher**, page 9, can also be used for additional practice of verb forms.

Extension and Enrichment

❑ Play the GAME described on page 99 of the TE. Students can also do the CHALLENGE Activity on page 103 of the TE to prepare their own illustrated messages.

Summary and Closure

❑ Use **Overhead Transparency** S10, with the Goal 1 Activity on page A15 and the Goal 1 Activity on page A16, to have students summarize the communicative and cultural goals of the lesson.

❑ Do PORTFOLIO ASSESSMENT on page T117.

End-of-Lesson Activities

❑ *À votre tour!*: Have students work in small groups to do activities 1, 2, 3, and 4 on pages 102–103. Use **Audio** CD 2, Tracks 15–16 to check answers to Activities 1–2. Have students write their personal responses to Activity 5 and share them with the class.

Unité 3
Leçon 7

Block Scheduling
Lesson Plans

Discovering
FRENCH *Nouveau*

BLEU

LEÇON 7 Une boum, page 92

Block Schedule (3 Days to Complete)

Objectives

Communicative Functions and Topics	To describe what one person or several people are doing or are not doing
	To talk about what people like and don't like to do
	To express approval or regret
Linguistic Goals	To use verb + infinitive
	To use regular *–er* verbs
	To pronounce vowel /i/ and /u/
Cultural Goals	To become familiar with French party customs

Day 1

Motivation and Focus

❑ Have students look at the pictures on page 93 and discuss what is happening. Discuss party organization with SETTING THE STAGE on page 92 of the TE. You may show the **Video** to preview the lesson. Have students comment on the activities mentioned.

Presentation and Explanation

❑ *Lesson Opener:* Read the introductory paragraph on page 92 and invite students to guess what Jean-Marc is going to say to Béatrice and Valérie. Play **Video** 7.4 or **Audio** CD 2, Tracks 11–12, the opening conversation. Ask students to read and summarize the conversation.

❑ *Note culturelle:* Have students read *Une boum*, page 93. Encourage them to compare French and American parties by playing the **Video** or reading the **Videoscript** for 7.5.

❑ *Grammar A, B,* and *C:* Present *–er* verbs with **Overhead Transparencies** 14a and b and 17. Explain verb conjugations, pointing out the grammar boxes and information on pages 94 and 96. Practice verb endings using Transparency 16. Introduce affirmative and negative forms on page 98.

❑ *Vocabulaire:* Model and explain the words and expressions in the boxes on page 100. Point out examples of verb + infinitive that students have already practiced. Have students read the grammar explanation on page 101.

❑ *Prononciation:* Model pronunciation of the vowels /i/ and /u/, page 101, and have students repeat the words. Practice pronunciation with **Audio** CD 2, Track 14.

Guided Practice and Checking Understanding

❑ Use **Overhead Transparency** 17 and the suggestions on page A64 for practice with *–er* verbs. To practice expressions for how often and how well, have students ask and answer questions about the pictures on Transparencies 14a and b.

❑ Check listening skills with the **Audio** CD 7, Tracks 12–17 or the **Audioscript** and **Workbook** Listening Activities A–F, pages 69–70.

Discovering
FRENCH *Nouveau!*

BLEU

Unité 3
Leçon 7

Block Scheduling
Lesson Plans

Day 2

Motivation and Focus

❏ Have students do **Video Activities** pages 81–83 as they view the **Video** or listen while you read the **Videoscript**.

❏ Use the COMPREHENSION Activities on pages 95 and 96 of the TE to check students' understanding of verbs and subject pronouns.

Independent Practice

❏ Practice with the activities on pages 94–101. Assign activities 3, 5, 7, and 9, 11–12 for homework. Use **Audio** CD 2, Track 13 with activity 10. Use any or all of Activities 1, 2, 4, 6, 8, 13, or 14 for PAIR PRACTICE. Follow the suggestions for CLASSROOM MANAGEMENT WRITING PRACTICE, page 97 of the TE, for activity 8.

❏ Have pairs of students choose one of the following **Communipak** activities: *Interviews* 1, 2; *Tu as la parole* 4, 5, 6; *Conversations* 1, 2; *Échange* 2; *Tête à tête* 1 (pages 128–137). They may also do page 84 of the **Video Activities**.

❏ Have students do activities in **Activités pour tous,** pages 39–41.

Monitoring and Adjusting

❏ Have students do the Writing Activities on **Workbook** pages 71–74.

❏ Monitor students' work on the Activities on pages 94–101. Have them review the grammar and vocabulary boxes as needed. Use the TEACHING TIPS and TEACHING NOTES, and explain the PRONUNCIATION and LANGUAGE NOTES, on pages 94–101 of the TE.

Day 3

End-of-Lesson Activities

❏ *À votre tour!:* Have students work in small groups to do Activities 1, 2, 3, and 4 on pages 102–103. Use Audio CD 2, Tracks 15–16 to check answers to Activities 1–2. Have students write their personal responses to Activity 5.

❏ Use **Block Scheduling Copymasters** pages 49–56.

Reteaching (as needed)

❏ Redo any appropriate activities from the **Workbook.**

❏ Use the **Video** to reteach portions of the lesson.

❏ Follow the suggestions for VARIATIONS of Activities 4 and 6, pages T110–T111. **Teacher to Teacher**, page 9, can also be used for additional practice of verb forms.

Extension and Enrichment (as desired)

❏ For expansion activities, direct students to www.classzone.com.

Summary and Closure

❏ Use **Overhead Transparency** S10, with the Goal 1 Activity on page A15 and the Goal 1 Activity on page A16.

❏ Do PORTFOLIO ASSESSMENT on page T117.

Assessment

❏ Administer Quiz 7 on pages 91–92 after completing the lesson. Use the **Test Generator** to adapt the quiz questions to your class's needs.

Nom _____

Classe _____ Date _____

Discovering
FRENCH
Nouveau

B L E U

LEÇON 7   Une boum, pages 92–93

Materials Checklist

- **Student Text**
- **Audio** CD 2, Tracks 11–12
- **Video** 2 or **DVD** 1; Counter 20:39–21:31

Steps to Follow

- Read the dialogue *Une boum* (p. 92) before you listen to the audio.
- Read the *Compréhension* questions before you listen to the audio. They will help you understand what you hear.
- Watch **Video** 2 or **DVD** 1; Counter 20:39–21:31 or listen to **Audio CD** 2, Tracks 11–12.
- Answer the *Compréhension* questions (p. 92) on a separate sheet of paper.
- Read the *Note culturelle* and look at the photos on p. 93. What are the people in the photographs doing?
- Answer the *Comparaisons culturelles* question (p. 93) on a separate sheet of paper.

If You Don't Understand . . .

- Watch the **Video** or **DVD** in a quiet place. Try to stay focused. If you get lost, stop the **Video** or **DVD**. Replay it and find your place.
- Listen to the **CD** in a quiet place. Try to stay focused. If you get lost, stop the **CD**. Replay it and find your place.
- Repeat aloud with the audio. Try to sound like the people on the recording.
- On a separate sheet of paper, write down the words that are underlined in the text. Check for meaning.

Self-Check

Answer the following questions on a separate sheet of paper. Use the appropriate pronoun, and write in complete sentences.

1. Est-ce que Béatrice aime danser?
2. Est-ce que Béatrice danse bien?
3. Est-ce que Valérie danse bien?
4. Est-ce que Jean-Marc danse bien?
5. Est-ce que Jean-Marc invite Béatrice et Valérie à une boum?

Answers

1. Oui, elle aime danser.   2. Oui, elle danse bien.   3. Non, elle ne danse pas bien.   4. Non, il ne danse pas bien.   5. Oui, il invite Béatrice et Valérie à une boum.

Nom _____

Classe _____ Date _____

Discovering FRENCH *Nouveau!*

BLEU

Unité 3
Leçon 7

Absent Student Copymasters

A. Les verbes en *-er*: le singulier, pages 94–96
Vocabulaire: Les verbes en *-er*, pages 95–96

Materials Checklist

- **Student Text**
- **Audio CD** 7, Tracks 12–13
- **Video** 2 or **DVD** 1; Counter 17:15–18:41
- **Workbook**

Steps to Follow

- Study *Les verbes en –er: le singulier* (p. 94).
- On a separate sheet of paper write the first-, second-, and third-person singular forms for **parler** and **habiter**. Underline the endings.
- Watch **Video** 2 or **DVD** 1; Counter 17:15–18:41. Repeat everything you hear.
- Do Activity 1 in the text (p. 94). On a separate sheet of paper, write the questions and answers for both speakers in complete sentences.
- Study *Vocabulaire: Les verbes en –er* (p. 95). Write the verbs several times.
- Do Activities 2, 3, and 4 in the text (pp. 95–96). Write the answers in complete sentences on a separate sheet of paper.
- Do **Writing Activities** A/B 1, 2 in the **Workbook** (p. 71).
- Do **Listening Activities** A–B in the **Workbook** (p. 69). Use **Audio CD** 7, Tracks 12–13.

If You Don't Understand . . .

- Watch the **Video** or **DVD** in a quiet place. Try to stay focused. If you get lost, stop the **Video** or **DVD**. Replay it and find your place.
- Listen to the **CD** in a quiet place. Try to stay focused. If you get lost, stop the **CD**. Replay it and find your place.
- Reread the activity directions. Put the directions in your own words.
- Say aloud everything that you write. Be sure you understand what you are saying.
- Write down questions so that you can ask your partner or your teacher later.
- When writing a sentence, ask yourself, "What do I mean? What am I trying to say?"

Self-Check

On a separate sheet of paper, write complete sentences using the correct form of the verb given in parentheses.

1. Jacques (habiter / en ville)
2. Tu (parler / au téléphone)
3. Anne (voyager / en France)
4. Je (travailler / en classe)

Answers

1. Jacques habite en ville. 2. Tu parles au téléphone. 3. Anne voyage en France. 4. Je travaille en classe.

Nom _____

Classe _____ Date _____

Discovering
FRENCH
Nouveau

B L E U

B. Les verbes en *-er*: le pluriel, pages 96–97

Materials Checklist

- **Student Text**
- **Audio CD** 7, Track 14
- **Workbook**

Steps to Follow

- Study *Les verbes en –er: le pluriel* (p. 96).
- On a separate sheet of paper, write the first-, second-, and third-person plural forms of **parler** and **habiter**. Circle the endings and underline the liaisons.
- On a separate sheet of paper write the first-, second-, and third-person plural forms of **nager**, **manger**, and **voyager**. Underline the endings.
- Do Activities 5, 7, and 8 in the text (p. 97). Write the answers in complete sentences on a separate sheet of paper.
- Do Activity 6 in the text (p. 97). Write the answers in complete sentences for both speakers.
- Do **Writing Activities** A/B 3 in the **Workbook** (p. 72).
- Do **Listening Activity** C in the **Workbook** (p. 69). Use **Audio CD** 7, Track 14.

If You Don't Understand . . .

- Reread the activity directions. Put the directions in your own words.
- Say aloud everything that you write. Be sure you understand what you are saying.
- Write down questions so that you can ask your partner or your teacher later.
- When writing a sentence, ask yourself, "What do I mean? What am I trying to say?"

Self-Check

Complete the following sentences using **tu**, **elle**, **nous**, or **ils**. Write the complete sentences on a separate sheet of paper.

1. . . . nageons tous les jours (*every day*).
2. . . . habites à Boston.
3. . . . mangeons au restaurant français.
4. . . . parle bien français.
5. . . . étudient l'anglais.
6. . . . voyageons en train.

Answers

1. Nous nageons tous les jours. 2. Tu habites à Boston. 3. Nous mangeons au restaurant français. 4. Elle parle bien français. 5. Ils étudient l'anglais. 6. Nous voyageons en train.

Nom _____

Classe _____ Date _____

Discovering
FRENCH
Nouveau!

B L E U

Unité 3
Leçon 7

Absent Student
Copymasters

C. Le présent des verbes en *-er*: forme affirmative et forme négative, pages 98–99
Vocabulaire: Mots utiles; Expressions pour la conversation, page 100

Materials Checklist

- **Student Text**
- **Audio CD** 2, Track 13; **CD** 7, Tracks 15–16
- **Video** 2 or **DVD** 1; Counter 18:42–19:45
- **Workbook**

Steps to Follow

- Study *Le présent des verbes en –er: forme affirmative et forme négative* (p. 98).
- On a separate sheet of paper, write the negative forms of **parler**, **travailler**, and **chanter** in the singular and plural. Underline the negative expressions.
- Watch **Video** 2 or **DVD** 1; Counter 18:42–19:45. Repeat what you hear.
- Do Activities 9 and 11 in the text (p. 99). Write the answers in complete sentences.
- Do Activity 10 in the text (p. 99). Use **Audio CD** 2, Track 13. Write your answers on a separate sheet of paper.
- Study *Vocabulaire: Mots utiles* (p. 100). Write the words several times.
- Do Activity 12 in the text (p. 100). Write the answers on a separate sheet of paper.
- Do Activity 13 in the text (p. 100). Write the conversation in complete sentences.
- Do **Writing Activities** C 4, 5, 6 in the **Workbook** (p. 73–74).
- Do **Listening Activities** D–E in the **Workbook** (p. 70). use **Audio CD** 7, Tracks 15–16.

If You Don't Understand . . .

- Watch the **Video** or **DVD** in a quiet place. Try to stay focused. If you get lost, stop the **Video** or **DVD**. Replay it and find your place.
- Listen to the **CDs** in a quiet place. Try to stay focused. If you get lost, stop the **CDs**. Replay them and find your place.
- Repeat aloud with the audio. Try to sound like the people on the recording.
- Reread the activity directions. Put the directions in your own words.
- Write down questions so that you can ask your partner or your teacher later.

Self-Check

Answer the following questions using the correct pronoun.

1. Est-ce que Jean joue bien au tennis? (oui)
2. Est-ce qu'Anne et Louise parlent français? (non)
3. Est-ce que vous mangez souvent au restaurant? (oui)
4. Est-ce que Thomas et Jacques voyagent en France? (non)
5. Est-ce que tu étudies maintenant? (oui)
6. Est-ce que Barbara et Alain habitent aussi à Québec? (oui)

Answers

1. Oui, il joue bien au tennis.   2. Non, elles ne parlent pas français.   3. Oui, nous mangeons souvent au restaurant. / Oui, je mange souvent au restaurant.   4. Non, ils ne voyagent pas en France.   5. Oui, j'étudie maintenant.   6. Oui, ils habitent aussi à Québec.

D. La construction: verbe + infinitif, page 101

Materials Checklist

- **Student Text**
- **Audio CD** 2, Tracks 14–16; **CD** 7, Track 17
- **Video** 2 or **DVD** 1; Counter 19:46–20:38

Steps to Follow

- Study *La construction: verbe + infinitif* (p. 101).
- On a separate sheet of paper, write the sample sentences, beginning with **Je préfère travailler.**
- In each sample sentence, underline the verb once and the infinitive twice.
- Watch **Video** 2 or **DVD** 1; Counter 19:46–20:38. Repeat what you hear.
- Do Activity 14 in the text (p. 101). On a separate sheet of paper, write the questions and the answers.
- Do Activity 15 in the text (p. 101).
- Read the list of words in *Pronunciation: Les voyelles /i/ et /u/* (p. 101). Listen to *Pronunciation: Les voyelles /i/ et /u/* on **Audio CD** 2, Track 14. Repeat what you hear.
- Do **Listening Activity** F in the **Workbook** (p. 70). Use **Audio CD** 6, Track 17.
- Do Activities 1–5 of *À votre tour!* in the text (pp. 102–103). Use **Audio CD** 2, Tracks 15–16 with Activities 1–2.

If You Don't Understand . . .

- Reread the activity directions. Put the directions in your own words.
- Say aloud everything that you write. Be sure you understand what you are saying.
- Write down questions so that you can ask your partner or your teacher later.
- When writing a sentence, ask yourself, "What do I mean? What am I trying to say?"
- Listen to the **CDs** in a quiet place. Try to stay focused. If you get lost, stop the **CDs**. Replay them and find your place.
- Repeat aloud with the audio. Try to sound like the people on the recording.

Self-Check

Answer the following questions affirmatively using the appropriate pronoun and saying that the subject prefers to do the activity given in parentheses. Write your answers in complete sentences on a separate sheet of paper.

1. Est-ce que tu aimes nager? (préférer / jouer au tennis)
2. Est-ce que Jean aime voyager? (préférer / travailler)
3. Est-ce que vous aimez dîner au restaurant? (préférer / dîner à la maison)
4. Est-ce que Louise et Anne aiment danser? (préférer / jouer au basket)
5. Est-ce que Jacques et Paul aiment nager? (préférer / jouer au frisbee)

Answers

1. Oui, mais je préfère jouer au tennis. 2. Oui, mais il préfère travailler. 3. Oui, mais nous préférons dîner à la maison. / Oui, mais je préfère dîner à la maison. 4. Oui, mais elles préfèrent jouer au basket. 5. Oui, mais ils préfèrent jouer au frisbee.

Nom _____

Classe _____ Date _____ _____

Discovering
FRENCH
Nouveau!

BLEU

Unité 3
Leçon 7

Unité 3

Family Involvement

LEÇON 7   Une boum

Je n'aime pas

Find out what a family member doesn't like to do. Use the drawings below.

- First, explain your assignment.
- Model the pronunciation of the possible answers: **Je n'aime pas…** using the words below each picture. Point to the picture as you model each answer.
- Then, ask the question, **Qu'est-ce que tu n'aimes pas?**
- After you get the answer, complete the sentence at the bottom of the page.

travailler

étudier

jouer aux
jeux vidéo

parler français

_____ n'aime pas _____.

Nom _____

Classe _____ Date _____

Faire un sondage!

Take a poll of family members. Ask more than one family member, or include the answers for yourself and one family member.

- First, explain your assignment.
- Model the pronunciation of the possible answers along the continuum and give English equivalents.
- Ask each question.
- When you are finished, write up your results. Combine answers using **mais** or **et.**

Tu chantes bien?
mal   bien   trés bien

Tu voyages?
rarement   un peu   souvent   toujours

Tu téléphones?
un peu   beaucoup

(Ma mère) _____.

(Mon frère) _____.

Nom _____

Classe _____ Date _____

Discovering FRENCH Nouveau!

BLEU

Unité 3
Leçon 7

Video Activities

MODULE 7 Une boum

Video 2, DVD 1

7.1 Activité 1. Tout le monde *(Everyone)*

Counter 17:15–18:06

What is everyone doing? As you watch the video, mark an **X** under the name of the person who is speaking—Philippe, Cécile, Antoine, or Yannick.

	Philippe	Cécile	Antoine	Yannick
1. —J'étudie.	❑	❑	❑	❑
2. —Je travaille.	❑	❑	❑	❑
3. —Je regarde la télé.	❑	❑	❑	❑
4. —Je joue à un jeu vidéo.	❑	❑	❑	❑
5. —Je mange un sandwich.	❑	❑	❑	❑
6. —Je mange une pizza.	❑	❑	❑	❑
7. —J'écoute un CD de rock.	❑	❑	❑	❑
8. —Je téléphone.	❑	❑	❑	❑

7.2 Activité 2. D'autres copains *(Other friends)*

Counter 18:07–18:41

Other friends in the video tell you what they are doing. Fill in the missing words below.

1. —Ben oui . . . je _____!

2. —Oui, je _____ le film de science-fiction.

3. —Euh oui, maman . . . je _____.

4. —Non, je _____ avec une copine.

Nom _____

Classe _____ Date _____

7.3 Activité 3. Est-ce qu'il travaille?

What is everyone doing? After you watch the video segment, look at the pictures below and circle **oui** or **non** in response to the questions.

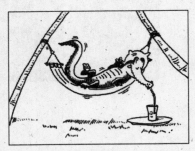

1. Est-ce qu'il travaille?
   oui   non

2. Est-ce qu'ils travaillent?
   oui   non

3. Est-ce qu'il voyage?
   oui   non

4. Est-ce qu'ils visitent Paris?
   oui   non

5. Est-ce qu'ils jouent au tennis
   oui   non

6. Est-ce qu'elle chante bien?
   oui   non

7. Est-ce qu'elle nage bien?
   oui   non

Nom _____

Classe _____ Date _____

Discovering
FRENCH *Nouveau!*

B L E U

Unité 3
Leçon 7

Video Activities

7.4 Activité 4. Comment dansent les copains?

(How do the friends dance?)

Counter 19:46–20:38

On the video, how do Dominique, Jean-Paul, and Nathalie say they dance? If the person dances well, circle **oui**. If not, circle **non**.

1. **oui**   **non**   2. **oui**   **non**   3. **oui**   **non**

7.5 Activité 5. Une boum

Counter 20:39–21:31

A. As you watch the **Vignette culturelle,** take notes in the space provided.
NOTE: the first item has been done for you.

event?	une boum
when?	
where?	
number of guests?	
activities?	

B. What do the two guests shown on the video like to do at a boum? Fill in the bubbles with the appropriate word.

1. J'adore _____ !

2. **Non, je ne danse pas très bien,**
    mais j'aime _____ !

Nom _____

Classe _____ Date _____

BLEU

 Activité 6. Le week-end

What do you like to do on weekends? Write down six activities below. Then ask classmates whether they like these activities. Write your classmate's name on your form if he or she does. (*Attention!* You must get the names of six different classmates.)

▶
TOI: **Est-ce que tu aimes danser?**
NATHALIE: **Non, je n'aime pas danser.**
TOI: **Est-ce que tu aimes danser?**
DOMINIQUE: **Mais oui, j'aime danser!**

Activité	Camarade
▶ danser	Dominique
1.	
2.	
3.	
4.	
5.	
6.	

MODULE 7 Une boum

Video 2, DVD 1

There are many things we do in the course of the day. We study and work, but we also have time to enjoy ourselves.

7.1 Mini-scenes: Listening—J'étudie
Counter: 17:15–18:06

Watch these French young people describe what they're doing . . . and also what they're not doing.

CÉCILE: J'étudie.

PHILIPPE: Je n'étudie pas. Je travaille.

CÉCILE: Je ne travaille pas. Je regarde la télé.

ANTOINE: Je joue à un jeu vidéo.

CÉLINE: Il joue très bien!

CÉCILE: Je mange. Je mange un sandwich.

PHILIPPE: Je mange une pizza! Hmmm! C'est délicieux!

YANNICK: J'ecoute un CD de rock.

PHILIPPE: «Bonjour, madame. Est-ce que je peux parler à Dominique, s'il vous plaît?»
Je téléphone. Je téléphone à une copine. J'aime beaucoup téléphoner.
«Allô, Dominique? Comment vas-tu?»

7.2 Mini-scenes: Listening— Tu téléphones?
Counter: 18:07–18:41

Now watch as these people ask each other questions.

LÉA: Tu téléphones?

CÉLINE: Ben oui . . . je téléphone!

LÉA: Tu regardes la télé?

ANTOINE: Oui, je regarde le film de science-fiction.

MAMAN: Philippe! Phi . ˙. . li . . . ppe!!

PHILIPPE: Oui, Maman!

MAMAN: Est-ce que tu étudies?

PHILIPPE: Euh oui, Maman . . . Je travaille.

PAPA: Tu dînes à la maison ce soir?

NATHALIE: Non, je dîne avec une copine.
Au revoir, Papa.

PAPA: Au revoir.

7.3 Mini-scenes: Speaking—Est-ce qu'il travaille?
Counter: 18:42–19:45

Now it's your turn to speak. For each scene, you'll be asked a question. Answer the questions affirmatively or negatively.

—Est-ce qu'il travaille?   [screen card]
—Non, il ne travaille pas.

—Est-ce qu'ils travaillent?   [screen card]
—Non, ils ne travaillent pas.

—Est-ce qu'il voyage?   [screen card]
—Oui, il voyage.

—Est-ce qu'ils visitent Paris? [screen card]
—Oui, ils visitent Paris.

—Est-ce qu'ils jouent au tennis? [screen card]
—Non, ils ne jouent pas au tennis.

—Est-ce qu'elle chante bien?   [screen card]
—Non, elle ne chante pas bien.

—Est-ce qu'elle nage bien?   [screen card]
—Oui, elle nage bien.

7.4 Dialogue: Jean-Paul à la boum
Counter: 19:46–20:38

*This evening we are at a **boum**. Jean-Paul, who is not a very good dancer, is trying to find a partner. Watch.*

JEAN-PAUL: Tu aimes danser?

DOMINIQUE: Oui, j'aime danser.

JEAN-PAUL: Est-ce que tu danses bien?

DOMINIQUE: Oui, je danse très, très bien.
Et toi?

JEAN-PAUL: Euh non, pas très bien.

JEAN-PAUL: Tu aimes danser?

NATHALIE: Oui, j'aime danser . . . mais je ne danse pas très bien.

JEAN-PAUL: Est-ce que tu veux danser avec moi?

NATHALIE: Je te dis, je ne danse pas très bien.

JEAN-PAUL: Moi non plus, je ne danse pas très bien.

NATHALIE: Bon, d'accord.

7.5 Vignette culturelle: Une boum

Counter: 20:39–21:31

*On weekends, French teenagers like to go to parties which are organized at a friend's home. These parties are called a **boum**.*

*Usually there are about 15 to 25 guests. During the course of the year, everyone in the group will organize a **boum** and invite the others. What do they do at a party?*

*Well . . . first there's a buffet with lots of sandwiches and soft drinks. There's always music, of course, and dancing. French teenagers love to dance! Let's talk to some of the guests and ask them why they like to go to a **boum**.*

—Tu aimes les boums?

—J'adore les boums!

—Tu aimes danser?

—Non, je ne danse pas très bien . . . mais j'aime manger!

Discovering
FRENCH
Nouveau!

BLEU

Unité 3
Leçon 7

Audioscripts

LEÇON 7 Une boum

PE AUDIO

CD 2, Track 11

Compréhension orale, p. 92

Jean-Marc has been invited to a party. He is trying to decide whether to invite Béatrice or Valérie. First he talks to Béatrice.

JEAN-MARC: Dis, Béatrice, tu aimes danser?

BÉATRICE: Bien sûr, j'aime danser! Je danse très, très bien.

JEAN-MARC: Et toi Valérie, tu danses bien?

VALÉRIE: Non, je ne danse pas très bien.

JEAN-MARC: Est-ce que tu veux aller à une boum avec moi samedi?

VALÉRIE: Oui, d'accord, mais pourquoi est-ce que tu n'invites pas Béatrice? Elle adore danser...

JEAN-MARC: Oui, mais moi, je ne sais pas danser et je ne veux pas être ridicule...

BÉATRICE: Écoute. Entre copains, on n'est jamais ridicule.

JEAN-MARC: C'est vrai! Alors, je vous invite toutes les deux!

BÉATRICE: Super!

CD 2, Track 12

Écoutez et répétez., p. 92

You will now hear a paused version of the dialogue. Listen to the speaker and repeat right after he or she has completed the sentence.

CD 2, Track 13

Activité 10. Écoutez bien!, p. 99

You will hear French young people tell you what they do and do not do. Listen carefully to what they each say and determine if they do the following activities.

Modèle: Je ne joue pas au foot. Je joue au basket. #

Let's begin.

1. Je parle anglais. Je ne parle pas espagnol. #
2. Je n'habite pas à Tours. J'habite à Paris. #
3. Je dîne à la maison. Je ne dîne pas au restaurant. #
4. Je téléphone à un copain. Je ne téléphone pas à une copine. #
5. Je ne mange pas une pizza. Je mange un sandwich. #
6. J'étudie l'espagnol. Je n'étudie pas l'anglais. #
7. Je n'écoute pas la radio. J'écoute un CD. #

Prononciation, p. 101

CD 2, Track 14

Les voyelles /i/ et /u/

Écoutez: /u/ où /i/ ici

Be sure to pronounce the French "i" as in Mimi.

Répétez: /i/ # ici # Philippe # il # Mimi # Sylvie # visite #

Alice visite Paris avec Sylvie. #

/u/ # où # nous # vous # écoute # joue # toujours #

Vous jouez au foot avec nous? #

À votre tour!

CD 2, Track 15

1. Âllo!, p. 102

Sophie is phoning some friends. Match her questions on the left with her friends' answers on the right.

1. Est-ce que Marc est canadien?
   Oui, il habite à Montréal.

2. Est-ce que tu joues au tennis?
   Oui, mais pas très bien.

BLEU

3. Ton frère est à la maison?
   Non, il dîne au restaurant avec un copain.

4. Ta mère est en vacances?
   Non, elle travaille.

5. Tu invites Christine et Juliette à la boum?
   Bien sûr! Elles aiment beaucoup danser.

CD 2, Track 16

2. Créa-dialogue, p. 102

Listen to some sample *Créa-dialogues*.
Écoutez les conversations.

Modèle: —Robert, est-que tu joues au
            tennis?
         —Non, je ne joue pas au tennis.
         —Est-ce que tu écoutes la radio?
         —Oui, j'écoute souvent la radio.

Maintenant, écoutez le dialogue numéro 1.

—Louise, est-ce que tu nages?
—Non, je ne nage pas.
—Est-ce que tu chantes?
—Oui, je chante un peu.

WORKBOOK AUDIO

Section 1. Je parle français.

CD 7, Track 12

A. Questions et réponses, p. 69

You will hear a series of questions addressed to you. Answer them affirmatively. Listen to the model.

Modèle: Tu parles français. # Oui, je parle
          français.

Commençons. Let's begin.

1. Tu parles anglais? # Oui, je parle anglais.
2. Tu joues au basket? # Oui, je joue au basket.
3. Tu joues aux jeux vidéo? # Oui, je joue aux jeux vidéo.
4. Tu regardes la télé? # Oui, je regarde la télé.
5. Tu écoutes la radio? # Oui, j'écoute la radio.
6. Tu étudies? # Oui, j'étudie.
7. Tu organises une boum? # Oui, j'organise une boum.
8. Tu invites un copain? # Oui, j'invite un copain.

CD 7, Track 13

B. Regardez et parlez., p. 69

You will hear the names of different people. Say that each one is doing the activity shown in your Workbook. Use **il** or **elle**, as appropriate.

Listen to the model.

Modèle: Pauline # Elle joue au foot.

Commençons.
1. Thomas # Il joue au basket. #
2. Stéphanie # Elle nage. #
3. Marc # Il mange. #
4. Isabelle # Elle regarde la télé. #
5. Frédéric # Il téléphone. #
6. Mélanie # Elle chante. #
7. Monsieur Rémi # Il travaille. #
8. Madame Dupin # Elle voyage. #

Section 2. Nous parlons français.

CD 7, Track 14

C. Questions et réponses, p. 69

Now you will hear a series of questions about you and your friend. Answer them affirmatively, using **nous**.

Listen to the model.

Modèle: Vous parlez français? # Oui, nous
parlons français. #

Commençons.
1. Vous parlez anglais? # Oui, nous
parlons anglais.
2. Vous jouez au foot? # Oui, nous jouons
au foot.
3. Vous travaillez? # Oui, nous travaillons.
4. Vous étudiez? # Oui, nous étudions.
5. Vous invitez un copain # Oui, nous
invitons un copain.

Section 3. Oui ou non?

CD 7, Track 15

D. Compréhension orale, p. 70

You will hear what various people do or
don't do. Listen carefully to each sentence. If
the verb is in the affirmative, mark Row A. If
the verb is in the negative, mark Row B. You
will hear each sentence twice. Listen to the
model.

Modèle: Caroline ne parle pas espagnol.
Caroline does not speak Spanish.
Elle NE parle PAS espagnol.

The verb is negative so you would mark
Row B.

Commençons.
1. Éric et Sophie jouent au foot. #
2. Nous ne jouons pas au basket. #
3. Marc habite au Canada. #
4. Vous ne regardez pas la télé. #
5. Je n'écoute pas la radio. #
6. Vous parlez bien français. #
7. Ma cousine étudie à Paris. #
8. Monsieur Raymond ne travaille pas ici. #

Now check your answers. You should have
marked Row A for items 1, 3, 6 and 7. You
should have marked Row B for items 2, 4, 5
and 8.

CD 7, Track 16

E. Questions et réponses, p. 70

Look at the scenes in your Workbook. For
each scene you will be asked a question.
Answer affirmatively or negatively according
to the picture.

Listen to the model.

Modèle: Est-ce qu'il travaille? # Non, il ne
travaille pas.

Commençons.
1. Est-ce qu'ils travaillent? # Non, ils ne
travaillent pas.
2. Est-ce qu'il voyage? # Oui, il voyage.
3. Est-ce qu'ils visitent New York? # Non,
ils ne visitent pas New York.
4. Est-ce qu'ils jouent au tennis? # Non, ils
ne jouent pas au tennis.
5. Est-ce qu'elle chante bien? # Non, elle
ne chante pas bien.
6. Est-ce qu'elle nage bien? # Oui, elle
nage bien.

Section 4. Dictée

CD 7, Track 17

F. Écoutez et écrivez., p. 70

You will hear a short dialogue spoken twice.
First listen carefully to what the people are
saying. The second time you hear the
dialogue, fill in the missing words.

Écoutez.

—Est-ce que tu aimes jouer au basket?
—Oui, je joue souvent avec ma cousine.
—Est-ce qu'elle joue bien?
—Non, elle ne joue pas très bien, mais elle
aime jouer!

Listen again and fill in the missing words.

BLEU

LESSON 7 QUIZ

Part I: Listening

CD 14, Track 3

Conversations

You will hear a series of short conversations between Nathalie and Marc. Listen to each conversation carefully. Then answer the corresponding questions on your answer sheet by circling the appropriate letter (a, b, or c). You will hear each conversation twice.

Let's begin.

1. NATHALIE: Tu aimes chanter?
   MARC: Oui, j'aime beaucoup chanter.
   NATHALIE: Moi, je chante mal.

2. NATHALIE: Tu veux jouer au ping-pong avec moi?
   MARC: Oui, je veux bien.

NATHALIE: Est-ce que tu joues bien?
MARC: Non, je ne joue pas très bien.

3. MARC: Où est Thomas?
   NATHALIE: Il est à la maison.
   MARC: Il étudie?
   NATHALIE: Non, il joue aux jeux vidéo.

4. MARC: J'organise un pique-nique samedi.
   NATHALIE: Où?
   MARC: Chez moi!
   NATHALIE: Est-ce que tu invites Céline?
   MARC: Bien sûr! C'est une copine.

5. MARC: Ta cousine est canadienne, n'est-ce pas?
   NATHALIE: Oui, elle habite à Montréal.
   MARC: Tu parles anglais avec elle?
   NATHALIE: Non, nous parlons toujours français.

Nom _____

Classe _____ Date _____

Discovering
FRENCH
Nouveau!

B L E U

Unité 3
Leçon 7   Lesson Quiz

QUIZ 7

Part I: Listening

A. Conversations (30 points)

You will hear a series of short conversations between Nathalie and Marc. Listen to each conversation carefully. Then answer the corresponding questions on your answer sheet by circling the appropriate letter (a, b, or c). You will hear each conversation twice.

1. How does Nathalie sing?
   a. Well.
   b. Very well.
   c. Poorly.

2. What do we know about Marc's ping-pong game?
   a. He is a champion.
   b. He hates the game.
   c. He does not play very well.

3. What is Thomas doing?
   a. He is fixing dinner.
   b. He is watching TV.
   c. He is playing video games.

4. What is Marc doing on Saturday?
   a. He is having a party.
   b. He is going out with Céline.
   c. He is organizing a picnic.

5. What language does Nathalie speak with her cousin?
   a. English.
   b. French.
   c. Spanish.

Part II: Writing

B. Activités (30 points)

The following people are doing various things. Complete each sentence with the appropriate form of the verb in parentheses.

1. (parler)   Je _____ français.
2. (visiter)   Vous _____ Paris.
3. (travailler) Le docteur Laval _____ dans un hôpital.
4. (téléphoner) Nous _____ à un copain.
5. (étudier)   Tu _____ beaucoup.
6. (écouter)   Marie et Pierre _____ la radio.

Nom _____

Classe _____ Date _____

C. Non (20 points)

Say that the following people are NOT doing the things in parentheses.

1. (voyager)   Nous _____.

2. (inviter)   Céline et Pauline _____ Stéphanie.

3. (regarder)   Vous _____ la télé.

4. (habiter)   Tu _____ en France.

D. Expression personnelle (20 points)

Answer the following questions in French. Use complete sentences.

• In which city or town do you live?

   _____

• Do you study a lot?

   _____

Nom _____

Classe _____ Date _____

Discovering
FRENCH
Nouveau!

BLEU

Unité 3
Leçon 8

Workbook TE

LEÇON 8   Un concert de musique africaine

LISTENING ACTIVITIES

Section 1. Questions

A. Compréhension orale

	A	B	C	D	E	F
	où?	quand?	à quelle heure?	comment?	à qui?	avec qui?
▶	✔					
1			✔			
2						✔
3		✔				
4					✔	
5				✔		
6	✔					
7				✔		
8	✔					

B. Questions et réponses

Modèle: . . . à Québec.
   J'habite à Québec.

1. . . . à huit heures   Je regarde la télé à huit heures.
2. . . . bien   Je parle bien.
3. . . . en France   Je voyage en France.
4. . . . en été   Je voyage en été.
5. . . . à une copine   Je téléphone à une copine.
6. . . . avec mon oncle   Je dîne avec mon oncle.
7. . . . une pizza   Je mange une pizza.
8. . . . une promenade   Je fais une promenade.

Unité 3
Leçon 8

Workbook TE

Nom _____

Classe _____ Date _____

Discovering
FRENCH
Nouveau!

BLEU

Section 2. La réponse logique

C. Compréhension orale

1. a. À sept heures.
    b. Avec un copain.
    c. À la maison.

2. a. Dimanche.
    b. À huit heures.
    c. Avec ma cousine.

3. a. Oui, bien sûr!
    b. Très bien.
    c. Au club de sport.

4. a. À un copain.
    b. À la maison.
    c. Parce que je veux parler à ma mère.

5. a. Une omelette.
    b. À la cafétéria.
    c. À six heures et demie.

6. a. En France.
    b. Avec mon cousin.
    c. Parce que j'aime voyager.

Section 3. Dictée

D. Écoutez et écrivez.

—Dis, Patrick, qu'est-ce que tu _fais_ demain?

—Je joue au tennis avec ma cousine. Nous _faisons_ un match. _Pourquoi_?

—_Est-ce que_ je peux jouer avec vous?

—Oui, bien sûr!

Nom _____

Classe _____ Date _____ _____

Discovering
FRENCH
Nouveau!

BLEU

Unité 3
Leçon 8
Workbook TE

WRITING ACTIVITIES

A 1. Dialogue

Complete the following dialogues with the appropriate interrogative expressions.

1. —Où _____ est-ce que tu habites?
   —J'habite à Dakar.

2. —À quelle heure _____ est-ce que tu dînes?
   —En général, je dîne à huit heures.

3. —Comment _____ est-ce que tu chantes?
   —Je chante assez bien.

4. —Pourquoi _____ est-ce que tu étudies l'italien?
   —Parce que je veux visiter l'Italie.

5. —Quand _____ est-ce que tu voyages?
   —Je voyage en juillet.

6. —Où _____ est-ce que ta mère travaille?
   —Elle travaille dans *(in)* un hôpital.

B 2. Répétitions

Philippe did not quite hear what Annie told him and he asks her to repeat what she said.
Complete his questions.

ANNIE:	PHILIPPE:
▶ Je joue au tennis avec Vincent.	Avec qui est-ce que tu joues au tennis ?
1. Je téléphone souvent à Olivier.	À qui est-ce que tu téléphones souvent ?
2. Je parle rarement à Valérie.	À qui est-ce que tu parles rarement ?
3. J'étudie avec Jean-Claude.	Avec qui est-ce que tu étudies ?
4. Je travaille pour M. Bertrand.	Pour qui est-ce que tu travailles ?
5. Je parle anglais avec Vanessa.	Avec qui est-ce que tu parles anglais ?
6. Je parle de Pierre.	De qui est-ce que tu parles ?

Nom _____

Classe _____ Date _____

Discovering FRENCH *Nouveau*

BLEU

Unité 3
Leçon 8

Workbook TE

A/B/C 3. Curiosité

You want to know more about what the following people are doing. Write your questions using subject pronouns and the expressions in parentheses.

▶ Jérôme dîne. (avec qui?)

Avec qui est-ce qu'il dîne?

1. Madame Martin travaille. (où?)

Où est-ce qu'elle travaille?

2. Nathalie téléphone. (à qui?)

À qui est-ce qu'elle téléphone?

3. Antoine organise une boum. (quand?)

Quand est-ce qu'il organise une boum?

4. Thomas et Patrick étudient beaucoup. (pourquoi?)

Pourquoi est-ce qu'ils étudient beaucoup?

5. Hélène et Sylvie jouent au tennis. (à quelle heure?)

À quelle heure est-ce qu'elles jouent au tennis?

6. Béatrice étudie. (qu'est-ce que?)

Qu'est-ce qu'elle étudie?

D 4. Conversations

Complete the following mini-dialogues with the appropriate forms of **faire**.

1. —Qu'est-ce que tu <u>fais</u> à deux heures?

—Je <u>fais</u> un match de tennis.

2. —Qu'est-ce que vous <u>faites</u> maintenant?

—Nous <u>faisons</u> une salade de fruits.

3. —Où est ta cousine?

—Elle <u>fait</u> un voyage au Sénégal.

4. —Où sont Paul et Marc?

—Ils sont en ville. Ils <u>font</u> une promenade.

SÉNÉGAL

Nom _____

Classe _____ Date _____

Discovering FRENCH *Nouveau!*

B L E U

Unité 3
Leçon 8

Workbook TE

5. Communication

1. You want to invite your friend Nathalie to your home for dinner.

   Ask her . . .

   - *at what time she has dinner* À quelle heure est-ce que tu dînes?
   - *what she likes to eat* Qu'est-ce que tu aimes manger?

2. You are interviewing Madame Ricard, a French businesswoman, for your school newspaper. (Do not forget to address her as **vous!**)

   Ask her . . .

   - *where she lives* Où est-ce que vous habitez?
   - *where she works* Où est-ce que vous travaillez?
   - *when she travels* Quand est-ce que vous voyagez?

3. You meet your friend Marc.

   Ask him . . .

   - *what he is doing now* Qu'est-ce que tu fais maintenant?
   - *what he is doing tomorrow* Qu'est-ce que tu fais demain?
   - *if he wants to play video games* Est-ce que tu veux jouer aux jeux vidéo?

Nom _____

Classe _____ Date _____

Discovering
FRENCH *Nouveau!*

BLEU

Unité 3
Leçon 8
Activités pour tous TE

LEÇON 8   Un concert de musique africaine

A

Activité 1   Dialogues

Select the question word that would produce the given response.

1. —*À quelle heure /* (*Qu'*)est-ce que tu manges?
   —Un sandwich au fromage.
2. —*Quand /* (*Où*) est-ce que Martin habite?
   —Il habite à Minneapolis.
3. —(*À quelle heure*)*/ Comment* est-ce que les Dumont dînent, généralement?
   —Ils dînent à huit heures.
4. —*Quand /* (*Comment*) est-ce qu'Éric joue au foot?
   —Il joue bien.
5. —(*Quand*)*/ Comment* est-ce que tu étudies?
   —Le soir.

Activité 2   Répète, s'il te plaît.

You don't hear everything clearly on your cell phone. Ask for clarification, choosing one of the expressions below.

| Qui? | À qui? | De qui? | Pour qui? | Avec qui? |

1. Paul téléphone à Claire. À qui? _____
2. Ils parlent de Marie. De qui? _____
3. Elle aime étudier avec Robert. Avec qui? _____
4. Mais elle préfère Martin. Qui? _____
5. Et elle organise une boum pour Martin. Pour qui? _____

Activité 3   Qu'est-ce qu'ils font?

Your friend wants to find someone to go for a walk with her but everyone is busy doing something. Select the word that correctly completes each sentence.

—Qu'est-ce que tu (*fais*) */ font?* Tu veux faire une promenade avec moi?
—Moi, je (*fais*) */ fait* mes devoirs. Peut-être Suzanne et Hélène?
—Non, elles (*font*)*/ faisons* un match de foot. Et André, qu'est-ce qu'il *faire /* (*fait?*)
—Il *fais /* (*fait*) attention à la météo parce qu'il veut *fait /* (*faire*) un match de tennis à 4h.
—Bon. Nous (*faisons*)*/ faites* une pizza à 6h?
—D'accord!

Nom _____

Classe _____ Date _____

B

Activité 1 Questions

Select the question word or phrase that corresponds to each response.

| Où est-il? Quand? À quelle heure? Comment? Pourquoi? Qu'est-ce qu'il fait? |

À quelle heure? _____ 1. À six heures et demie.   Où est-il? _____ 4. Il est à la maison.

Pourquoi? _____ 2. Parce qu'il pleut.   Quand? _____ 5. Le matin.

Qu'est-ce qu'il fait? _____ 3. Il regarde la télé.   Comment? _____ 6. Bien!

Activité 2 Qu'est-ce qu'ils font?

Choose the best answer to each question.

1. À qui est-ce que tu téléphones?
   a. Je téléphone à ma copine.
   b. Je téléphone de chez moi.

2. Avec qui est-ce que Jean et Luc habitent?
   a. Ils habitent à Québec.
   b. Ils habitent avec leurs parents.

3. Pour qui est-ce que Claire travaille?
   a. Elle travaille pour TelNet.
   b. Elle travaille en ville.

4. De qui est-ce que vous parlez?
   a. Nous parlons de Thomas.
   b. Nous parlons à Véronique.

5. Qui est-ce que vous écoutez?
   a. Nous écoutons la radio.
   b. Nous écoutons le prof.

6. Qu'est-ce qu'il mange?
   a. Il mange avec une copine.
   b. Il mange un croissant.

Activité 3 Faire

Fill in the blanks with the correct form of **faire**.

1. Nous _faisons_ attention dans la rue.

2. Est-ce que vous _faites_ une promenade?

3. Est-ce que M. Lebeau _fait_ un voyage?

4. Tu ne _fais_ pas le dîner?

5. Éric et Yvette _font_ un match de tennis, non?

6. Moi, je peux peut-être _faire_ un voyage en été.

Nom

Classe _____ Date _____

Discovering FRENCH *Nouveau!*

BLEU

Unité 3
Leçon 8
Activités pour tous TE

C

Activité 1 Réponses (sample answers)

Answer the following questions.

1. À qui est-ce que tu téléphones souvent?

   Je téléphone souvent à ma copine Vanessa.

2. Avec qui est-ce que tu fais du sport?

   Je fais du sport avec mes copains.

3. À quelle heure est-ce que tu manges le soir?

   Je mange à 7h.

4. Comment est-ce que tu parles français?

   Je parle bien français.

Activité 2 Questions

Write a question to elicit the following answers.

1. *Comment est-ce qu'il chante?*

   —Il chante très mal.

2. *Pourquoi est-ce que tu travailles?*

   —Parce que je veux voyager en France.

3. *Qu'est-ce que tu n'aimes pas manger?*

   —Je n'aime pas le fromage.

4. *Où est-ce qu'elles habitent?*

   —Elles habitent à Chicago.

5. *Quand est-ce que vous jouez au foot?*

   —Nous jouons au foot au printemps.

6. *Est-ce que tu veux jouer au tennis?*

   —Non, je préfère étudier. Mais Simone aime le tennis.

Activité 3 Qu'est-ce qu'ils font?

Use the illustrations to write what people are doing. Use a form of **faire** in each sentence.

1. Mélanie *fait attention.*

2. David et Chantal *font un match.*

3. Tu *fais un voyage.*

4. Nous *faisons une pizza.*

5. Vous *faites une promenade.*

6. Je *fais une salade.*

LEÇON 8 Un concert de musique africaine, page 104

Objectives

Communicative Functions and Topics
To ask for information and to ask about people
To ask and to describe what people are doing
To express mild doubt or surprise

Linguistic Goals
To use the verb *faire*
To ask information questions with *est-ce que*
and to form questions with inversion
To pronounce the vowel /y/

Cultural Goals
To be aware of French heritage in Senegal

Motivation and Focus

❏ Ask students to preview the photos on pages 104–105. Ask where they think these pictures were taken. Then do SETTING THE SCENE, page 104 of the TE. You may then use the **Video** to present the lesson. Have students comment on the scenes and conversations.

Presentation and Explanation

❏ *Lesson Opener:* Read the introductory paragraph on page 104. Ask students to suggest interview questions. Play **Video** 8.4 or **Audio** CD 2, Tracks 17–18, or model the opening conversation. Have students read and summarize the dialogue.

❏ *Notes culturelles:* Read *En bref: Le Sénégal* and *Youssou N'Dour* on page 105. Show **Video** 8.5 or read the **Videoscript**. Do the CROSS-CULTURAL OBSERVATION, page 105 of the TE.

❏ *Grammar A* and *Vocabulaire:* Review times and activities with the WARM-UP AND REVIEW activity in the TE. Present information questions on page 106, pointing out intonation patterns. Introduce interrogative words in the *Vocabulaire* box, page 106.

❏ *Grammar B* and *C:* Present expressions with *qui*, page 108, and *qu'est-ce que?*, page 109. Use the question words to ask about students' activities.

❏ *Grammar D* and *Vocabulaire:* Present *faire* and expressions with *faire*, page 110. Practice by making sentences with *faire* using **Overhead Transparency** 18.

❏ *Grammar E:* Introduce inversion, page 111, as another way to ask questions in French. Point out word order in affirmative and interrogative forms.

❏ *Prononciation:* Model or use **Audio** CD 2, Tracks 20 to present and practice pronunciation of the vowel /y/. Students can read the information in the *Prononciation* box, page 111.

Guided Practice and Checking Understanding

❏ Use **Overhead Transparency** 18 and the activities described on page A66 to have students practice expressions with *faire*.

❏ To check understanding, use **Audio** CD 7, Tracks 18–21 or the **Audioscript** with **Workbook** Listening Activities A–D, pages 75–76.

❏ Play the **Video** or read the **Videoscript** and have students do **Video Activities** pages 114–116.

Independent Practice

❏ Model the Activities on pages 107–111. Students can do 4 and 9–11 alone or for homework and 1–3 and 5–8 for PAIR PRACTICE. Use **Audio** CD 2, Track 19 for Activity 1.

- The **Video Activities**, page 117, and **Communipak** *Interview* 4, page 129, *Conversations* 1–4, pages 132–133, *Échange* 2, page 135, and *Tête à tête* 3, pages 140–141, can be used for additional oral pair practice.
- Have students do the activities in **Activités pour tous,** pages 43–45.

Monitoring and Adjusting

- Assign Writing Activities 1–5 in the **Workbook**, pages 77–79.
- Monitor students as they work on the practice activities. Refer them to appropriate grammar and vocabulary boxes, pages 106–111. Use LANGUAGE and PRONUNCIATION notes and TEACHING STRATEGIES, pages 108–111 of the TE.

End-of-Lesson Activities

- *À votre tour!:* Do the Activities on pages 112–113. Students can check their own work on 1 and 3 with the **Audio** CD 2, Tracks 21–22 or **Audioscript**. Have pairs prepare and present the role plays in Activities 2 and 4. Students can practice writing questions in Activity 5.

Review

- Have students review the information they learned in this unit by completing the **Tests de contrôle** activities on pages 114–115. Encourage students to use the page references in the **Review . . .** tabs to verify/clarify grammar and vocabulary.

Reteaching

- Redo any appropriate activities from the **Workbook**.
- Assign the **Video** for students who need more review or make-up work.

Assessment

- After students have done all of the lesson's activities, administer Quiz 8 on pages 124–125. Use the **Test Generator** to adapt questions to your class. Administer Unit Test 3 (Form A or B) on pages 157–165 of **Unit Resources**. For additional assessment of specific language skills, use the **Performance Tests** for the unit. You may also administer Comprehensive Test 1 (Form A or B) on pages 185–204 of **Unit Resources**.

Extension and Enrichment

- Play the GAME: GETTING ACQUAINTED, page 108 of the TE.

Summary and Closure

- Have pairs of students prepare role play interviews modeled on the opening conversation on pages 104–105. As they present the interviews, have other students summarize the linguistic and communicative goals of the lesson.
- Do PORTFOLIO ASSESSMENT on page 113 of the TE.

End-of-Unit Activities

- *Entracte 3:* Follow the suggestions in the TE margins to read the selections on pages 118–123. Encourage reading for meaning using cognates and context clues.
- *Reading and Culture Activities:* Use **Workbook** pages 81–84 to review cultural information and activities.

LEÇON 8   Un concert de musique africaine, page 104

Block Schedule (5 days to complete – including unit test)

Objectives

Communicative Functions and Topics	To ask for information and to ask about people
	To ask and to describe what people are doing
	To express mild doubt or surprise
Linguistic Goals	To use the verb *faire*
	To ask information questions with *est-ce que* and to form questions with inversion
	To pronounce the vowel /y/
Cultural Goals	To be aware of French heritage in Senegal

Block Schedule

Variety On slips of paper, write questions in French using the interrogatives on page 106 of the TE. Write one answer to each question on separate slips of paper. Give each student a question or an answer. Have students move around the room asking and responding to the questions until they find the student whose question or answer matches their own. ■

Day 1

Motivation and Focus

❑ Ask students to preview the photos on pages 104–105. Ask where they think these pictures were taken. Then do SETTING THE SCENE, page 104 of the TE. You may then use the **Video** to present the lesson. Have students comment on the scenes and conversations.

Presentation and Explanation

❑ *Lesson Opener:* Read the introductory paragraph on page 104. Ask students to suggest interview questions. Play **Video** 8.4 or **Audio** CD 2, Tracks 17–18, or model the opening conversation. Have students read and summarize the dialogue.

❑ *Note culturelle:* Read *En bref: Le Sénégal* and *Youssou N'Dour* on page 105. Show **Video** 8.5 or read the **Videoscript**. Do the CROSS-CULTURAL OBSERVATION, page 104 of the TE.

❑ *Grammar A* and *Vocabulaire:* Review times and activities with the WARM-UP AND REVIEW activity in the TE. Present information questions on page 106, pointing out intonation patterns. Introduce interrogative words in the *Vocabulaire* box, page 106.

❑ *Grammar B* and *C:* Present expressions with *qui*, page 108, and *qu'est-ce que?*, page 109. Use the question words to ask about students' activities.

❑ *Grammar D* and *Vocabulaire:* Present *faire* and expressions with *faire*, page 110. Practice by making sentences with *faire* using **Overhead Transparency** 18.

❑ *Grammar E:* Introduce inversion, page 111, as another way to ask questions in French. Point out word order in affirmative and interrogative forms.

❑ *Prononciation:* Model or use **Audio** CD 2, Track 20 to present and practice pronunciation of the vowel /y/. Students can read the information in the *Prononciation* box, page 111.

Guided Practice and Checking Understanding

❑ Use **Overhead Transparency** 18 and the activities described on page A66 to have students practice expressions with *faire*.

❑ To check understanding, use the **Audio** CD 7, Tracks 18–21 or **Audioscript** with **Workbook** Listening Activities A–D, pages 75–76.

Day 2

Motivation and Focus

❑ Play the **Video** or read the **Videoscript** and have students do **Video Activities** pages 114–116.

❑ Have students do the **Block Schedule Activity** on the previous page.

❑ Use **Block Scheduling Copymasters** pages 57–64.

Independent Practice

❑ Model the Activities on pages 107–111. Students can do 4 and 9–11 alone or for homework and 1–3 and 5–8 for PAIR PRACTICE. Use **Audio** CD 2, Track 19 for activity 1.

❑ The **Video Activities**, page 117, and **Communipak** *Interview* 4, page 129, *Conversations* 1–4, pages 132–133, *Échange* 2, page 135, and *Tête à tête* 3, pages 140–141, can be used for additional oral pair practice.

❑ Have students do the activities in **Activités pour tous,** pages 43–45.

Monitoring and Adjusting

❑ Assign Writing Activities 1–5 in the **Workbook**, pages 77–79.

❑ Monitor students as they work on the practice activities. Refer them to appropriate grammar and vocabulary boxes, pages 106–111. Use LANGUAGE AND PRONUNCIATION NOTES and TEACHING STRATEGIES, page 108–111 of the TE.

Day 3

End-of-Lesson Activities

❑ *À votre tour!:* Do the Activities on pages 112–113. Students can check their own work on 1 and 3 with the **Audio** CD 2, Tracks 21–22 or **Audioscript**. Have pairs prepare and present the role plays in Activities 2 and 4. Students can practice writing questions in Activity 5.

Review

❑ Have students review the information they learned in this unit by completing the **Tests de contrôle** activities on pages 114–115. Encourage students to use the page references in the **Review . . .** tabs to verify/clarify grammar and vocabulary.

Reteaching (as needed)

❑ Redo any appropriate activities from the **Workbook**.

❑ Assign the **Video** for students who need more review or make-up work.

Extension and Enrichment (as desired)

❑ Play the GAME: GETTING ACQUAINTED, page 108 of the TE.

❑ For expansion activities, direct students to www.classzone.com.

Unité 3
Leçon 8

Block Scheduling
Lesson Plans

Discovering
FRENCH
Nouveau!

BLEU

Summary and Closure

❏ Have pairs of students prepare role play interviews modeled on the opening conversation on page 104. As they present the interviews, have other students summarize the linguistic and communicative goals of the lesson.
❏ Do PORTFOLIO ASSESSMENT on page 113 of the TE.

Assessment

❏ After students have completed all of the lesson's activities, administer Quiz 8 on pages 124–125. Use the **Test Generator** to adapt questions to your class's needs.

Day 4

End-of-Unit Activities

Note: These activities may be done at the end of the unit, or at any time that seems appropriate during the unit.

❏ *Entracte 3:* Follow the suggestions in the TE margins to read the selections on pages 118–123. Encourage reading for meaning using cognates and context clues.
❏ *Reading and Culture Activities:* Use **Workbook**, pages 81–84 to review cultural information and activities.

Day 5

Assessment

❏ Administer Unit Test 3 (Form A or B) on pages 157–165 of **Unit Resources**.
❏ For additional assessment of specific language skills, use the **Performance Tests** for the unit. You may also administer Comprehensive Test 1 (Form A or B) on pages 185–204 of **Unit Resources**.

Nom _____

Classe _____ Date _____

Discovering
FRENCH
Nouveau!

Unité 3
Leçon 8

Absent Student
Copymasters

B L E U

LEÇON 8   Un concert de musique africaine, pages 104–105

Materials Checklist

- **Student Text**
- **Audio CD** 2, Tracks 17–18
- **Video** 2 or **DVD** 1; Counter 25:36–27:59

Steps to Follow

- Read the dialogue *Un concert de musique africaine* (p. 104). Before you listen to the audio or watch the video or **DVD**, read the *Compréhension* questions (p. 104).
- Watch **Video** 2 or **DVD** 1; Counter 25:36–27:59, or listen to **Audio CD** 2, Tracks 17–18.
- Answer the *Compréhension* questions (p. 104) on a separate sheet of paper.
- Read the *Note Culturelle* and look at the photos on p. 105. Who is Youssou N'Dour? What kind of music does he play?

If You Don't Understand . . .

- Watch the **Video** or **DVD** in a quiet place. Try to stay focused. If you get lost, stop the **Video** or **DVD**. Replay it and find your place in the text.
- Listen to the **CD** in a quiet place. Try to stay focused. If you get lost, stop the **CD**. Replay it and find your place in the text.
- Repeat aloud with the audio. Try to sound like the people on the recording.
- On a separate sheet of paper, write down the words that are underlined in the text. Check for meaning.
- Write down questions so that you can ask your partner or your teacher later.

Self-Check

Answer the following questions on a separate sheet of paper. Use the appropriate pronoun, and write in complete sentences.

1. Est-ce que Fatou est sénégalaise?
2. Est-ce que Fatou habite maintenant à Dakar?
3. Est-ce que Fatou aime Paris?
4. Est-ce que Youssou N'Dour est français?

Answers

1. Oui, elle est sénégalaise.   2. Non, elle habite maintenant à Paris.   3. Oui, elle aime Paris.   4. Non, il est sénégalais.

Nom _____

Classe _____ Date _____

A. Les questions d'information, pages 106–107
Vocabulaire: Expressions interrogatives, Expressions pour la conversation, pages 106–107

Materials Checklist

- **Student Text**
- **Audio CD** 2, Track 19
- **Video** 2 or **DVD** 1; Counter 22:39–24:04
- **Workbook**

Steps to Follow

- Study *Les questions d'information* (p. 106).
- Study *Vocabulaire: Expressions interrogatives* (p. 106). Write the expressions on a separate sheet of paper.
- Watch **Video** 2 or **DVD** 1; Counter 22:39–24:04.
- Do Activity 1 in the text (p. 107). Use **Audio CD** 2, Track 19. Then listen to the audio a second time. Select the logical answer to each question from the list, and write it on a separate sheet of paper.
- Study *Vocabulaire: Expressions pour la conversation* (p. 107).
- Do Activities 2 and 3 in the text (p. 107). Write out the parts for both speakers on a separate sheet of paper.
- Do Activity 4 in the text (p. 107). Write the answers in complete sentences on a separate sheet of paper.
- Do **Writing Activities** A 1 in the **Workbook** (p. 77).

If You Don't Understand . . .

- Watch the **Video** or **DVD** in a quiet place. Try to stay focused. If you get lost, stop the **Video** or **DVD**. Replay it and find your place.
- Listen to the **CD** in a quiet place. Try to stay focused. If you get lost, stop the **CD**. Replay it and find your place.
- Repeat aloud with the audio. Try to sound like the people on the recording. Imitate their sounds and accents. Pause the **CD** if you need to.
- Reread the activity directions. Put the directions in your own words.
- Say aloud everything that you write. Be sure you understand what you are saying.
- Write down questions so that you can ask your partner or your teacher later.
- When writing a sentence, ask yourself, "What do I mean? What am I trying to say?"

Self-Check

Write the questions that correspond to the following answers.

1. Nous habitons en ville.
2. Je dîne à 8 heures.
3. Jean chante bien.
4. Nous organisons une boum ce (*this*) samedi.
5. Elles étudient le français parce qu'elles aiment les langues (*languages*).

Answers

1. Où est-ce que vous habitez? 2. À quelle heure est-ce que tu dînes/vous dînez? 3. Comment est-ce que Jean chante? 4. Quand est-ce que vous organisez une boum? 5. Pourquoi est-ce qu'elles étudient le français?

Nom _____

Classe _____ Date _____

Discovering
FRENCH *Nouveau!*

BLEU

Unité 3
Leçon 8

Absent Student
Copymasters

B. Les expressions interrogatives avec *qui,* pages 108–109
C. Qu'est-ce que?, page 109

Materials Checklist

- **Student Text**
- **Audio CD** 7, Tracks 18–20
- **Video** 2 or **DVD** 1; Counter 24:05–25:35
- **Workbook**

Steps to Follow

- Study *Les expressions interrogatives avec **qui*** (p. 108).
- On a separate sheet of paper, write the list of interrogative expressions and the model sentences. Underline the expressions in the model sentences.
- Watch **Video** 2 or **DVD** 1; Counter 24:05–25:35. Repeat what you hear.
- On a separate sheet of paper, do Activity 5 in the text (p. 108). Write the questions and answers in complete sentences for both speakers.
- Do Activity 6 in the text (p. 108). Write the survey questions in complete sentences.
- Study ***Qu'est-ce que?*** (p. 109).
- On a separate sheet of paper, write the model sentences and underline **qu'est-ce que/qu'**.
- Do Activity 8 in the text (p. 109). Write the parts for both speakers in complete sentences on a separate sheet of paper.
- Do **Writing Activities** B 2 and **Writing Activities** A/B/C 3 in the **Workbook** (pp. 77–78).
- Do **Listening Activities** A–C in the **Workbook** (pp. 75–76). Use **Audio CD** 7, Tracks 18–20.

If You Don't Understand . . .

- Watch the **Video** or **DVD** in a quiet place. Try to stay focused. If you get lost, stop the **Video** or **DVD**. Replay it and find your place.
- Reread the activity directions. Put the directions in your own words.
- Say aloud everything that you write. Be sure you understand what you are saying.
- Write down questions so that you can ask your partner or your teacher later.
- When writing a sentence, ask yourself, "What do I mean? What am I trying to say?"

Self-Check

Complete the following questions with **qui, à qui, de qui, avec qui, pour qui,** or **qu'est-ce que/qu'**.

1. . . . nage tous les jours (*every day*)?
2. . . . vous regardez?
3. . . . est-ce que vous parlez?
4. . . . est-ce qu'Anne travaille?
5. . . . est-ce que tu parles?
6. . . . est-ce que Jean organise la boum?

Answers

1. Qui nage tous les jours? 2. Qu'est-ce que vous regardez? 3. De qui est-ce que vous parlez? / Avec qui est-ce que vous parlez? 4. Avec qui est-ce qu'Anne travaille? / Pour qui est-ce qu'Anne travaille? 5. De qui est-ce que tu parles? / Avec qui est-ce que tu parles? 6. Pour qui est-ce que Jean organise la boum? / Avec qui est-ce que Jean organise la boum?

Nom _____

Classe _____ Date _____

Discovering
FRENCH
Nouveau!

B L E U

D. Le verbe *faire*, page 110
Vocabulaire: Expressions avec *faire*, page 110

Materials Checklist

- **Student Text**
- **Audio CD** 7, Track 21
- **Workbook**

Steps to Follow

- Study *Le verbe faire* (p. 110).
- On a separate sheet of paper, write the model sentences. Underline all the forms of **faire**.
- Study *Vocabulaire: Expressions avec faire* (p. 110). On a separate sheet of paper, write the model sentences. Underline all the expressions using **faire**.
- Do Activities 9 and 10 in the text (p. 110). Write the answers in complete sentences on a separate sheet of paper.
- Do **Writing Activities** D 4, 5 in the **Workbook** (pp. 78–79).
- Do **Listening Activity** D in the **Workbook** (p. 76). Use **Audio CD** 7, Track 21.

If You Don't Understand . . .

- Reread the activity directions. Put the directions in your own words.
- Say aloud everything that you write. Be sure you understand what you are saying.
- Write down questions so that you can ask your partner or your teacher later.
- When writing a sentence, ask yourself, "What do I mean? What am I trying to say?"

Self-Check

Complete the following sentences with the appropriate form of **faire**.

1. Jean et Alain / faire / un match de tennis
2. Hélène / faire / un voyage en France
3. Nous / faire / attention en classe
4. Vous / faire / une promenade en ville
5. Anne et Léa / faire / attention
6. Je / faire / un voyage à Montréal

Answers

1. Jean et Alain font un match de tennis. 2. Hélène fait un voyage en France. 3. Nous faisons attention en classe. 4. Vous faites une promenade en ville. 5. Anne et Léa font attention. 6. Je fais un voyage à Montréal.

Unité 3, Leçon 8
Absent Student Copymasters

Discovering French, Nouveau! Bleu

Nom _____

Classe _____ Date _____

Discovering
FRENCH *Nouveau!*

BLEU

Unité 3
Leçon 8

Absent Student
Copymasters

E. L'interrogation avec inversion, page 111

Materials Checklist

- **Student Text**
- **Audio CD** 2, Tracks 20–22

Steps to Follow

- Study *L'interrogation avec inversion* (p. 111).
- Do Activity 11 in the text (p. 111). On a separate sheet of paper, write the questions and underline the inversion.
- Read the expressions in *Prononciation: La voyelle /y/* (p. 111) before you listen to the audio.
- Listen to the audio for *Prononciation: La voyelle /y/*. Use **Audio CD** 2, Track 20. Repeat what you hear.
- Do Activities 1–5 of *À votre tour!* in the text (pp. 112–113). Use **Audio CD** 2, Tracks 21–22 with Activities 1 and 3.

If You Don't Understand . . .

- Reread the activity directions. Put the directions in your own words.
- Say aloud everything that you write. Be sure you understand what you are saying.
- Write down questions so that you can ask your partner or your teacher later.
- When writing a sentence, ask yourself, "What do I mean? What am I trying to say?"
- Listen to the **CD** in a quiet place. Try to stay focused. If you get lost, stop the **CD**. Replay it and find your place.
- Repeat aloud with the audio. Try to sound like the people on the recording.

Self-Check

Write questions using inversion and the following expressions. Write in complete sentences on a separate sheet of paper.

1. comment / chanter / elle
2. où / habiter / il
3. où / travailler / il
4. avec qui / parler français / vous
5. à quelle heure / dîner / nous
6. à quelle heure / écouter la radio / tu

Answers

1. Comment chante-t-elle? 2. Où habite-t-il? 3. Où travaille-t-il? 4. Avec qui parlez-vous français? 5. À quelle heure dînons-nous? 6. À quelle heure écoutes-tu la radio?

Discovering
FRENCH
Nouveau!

B L E U

Nom _____

Classe _____ Date _____

LEÇON 8   Un concert de musique africaine

À quelle heure . . . ?

Ask a family member at what time he or she eats dinner. Have that person choose the time closest to one of the pictures.

- First, explain your assignment.
- Help him or her pronounce the phrases correctly by modeling the pronunciation of the words below each image. Point to the picture as you model each answer.
- Then, ask the question: **À quelle heure est-ce que tu dînes?**
- After you get the answer, complete the sentence at the bottom of the page.

à cinq heures

à neuf heures

à huit heures

**à six heures
et demie**

_____ dîne à _____.

Nom _____

Classe _____ Date _____

Qu'est-ce que tu fais ce week-end?

Find out what a family member is doing this weekend. Have him or her pick the most likely activity.

- First, explain your assignment.
- Model the pronunciation of each phrase below the pictures. Point to the picture as you model each answer.
- Then, ask the question: **Qu'est-ce que tu fais ce week-end?**
- Write your answer in a sentence.

organiser une boum

travailler

faire une promenade

regarder la télé

Discovering
FRENCH
Nouveau

B L E U

MODULE 8   Un concert de musique africaine

Video 2, DVD 1

8.1 Activité 1. Des renseignements, s'il vous
plaît! *(Information please!)*

Counter 22:39–24:04

After you watch the video segment about asking
questions, draw a line from the question on the left to
the logical answer on the right.

1. **Où** est-ce que vous travaillez?

2. **Quand** est-ce que tu fais ta boum?

3. **À quelle heure** est-ce que tu dînes?

4. **Comment** est-ce que tu joues au tennis?

5. **Comment** est-ce que tu t'appelles?

6. **À qui** est-ce que tu téléphones?

7. **Avec qui** est-ce que tu joues au tennis?

a. Je m'appelle Delphine.

b. Samedi.

c. À ma copine Alice.

d. Pas très bien.

e. Je travaille dans une banque.

f. Avec Éric.

g. À sept heures et demie.

8.2 Activité 2. Qu'est-ce que tu fais?

Counter 24:05–24:53

As people in the video tell you what they are doing, put an **X** in front of the completion to
each sentence.

1. **Je fais . . .** _____ un sandwich   _____ une pizza

2. **Je fais . . .** _____ un sandwich   _____ une tarte

3. **Je fais . . .** _____ une glace   _____ une crêpe

4. **Je regarde . . .** _____ un film d'aventures   _____ un film de science-fiction

5. **J'écoute . . .** _____ un CD de jazz   _____ la radio

6. **Je mange . . .** _____ une crêpe   _____ une tarte

Nom _____

Classe _____ Date _____

Discovering
FRENCH
Nouveau!

B L E U

Unité 3
Leçon 8

Video Activities

8.3 Activité 3. Questions

After you watch the video segment, circle the letter of the correct completion to each sentence.

1. Il mange . . .
   a. un sandwich
   b. une pizza

2. Elle mange . . .
   a. un sandwich
   b. une pizza

3. Elle dîne avec . . .
   a. son père
   b. un copain

4. Ils dînent . . .
   a. au restaurant
   b. à la maison

5. Ils dînent . . .
   a. à huit heures
   b. à six heures

8.4 Activité 4. Un concert de musique africaine

Let's find out about Fatou. Listen and watch as Nicolas interviews her. Circle the letter of the correct completion to each sentence below.

1. Nicolas et Fatou sont . . .   a. au café   b. à la maison

2. Fatou est . . .   a. française   b. sénégalaise

3. Elle est de . . .   a. Dakar   b. Fort-de-France

4. Maintenant, elle habite à . . .   a. Paris   b. Lyon

5. Elle adore . . .   a. Nice   b. Paris

6. Le week-end, elle . . .   a. regarde la télé   b. joue au tennis

7. Fatou invite Nicolas à . . .   a. une boum   b. un concert

Nom _____

Classe _____ Date _____

8.5 Activité 5. Le Sénégal

Counter 26:27–27:59

As you watch the **Vignette culturelle,** fill in the index card below with the appropriate information about **le Sénégal.** You might choose another French-speaking country from the map and look it up in an encyclopedia or other reference book. Then fill in the information in the blank index card as you did for **le Sénégal.**

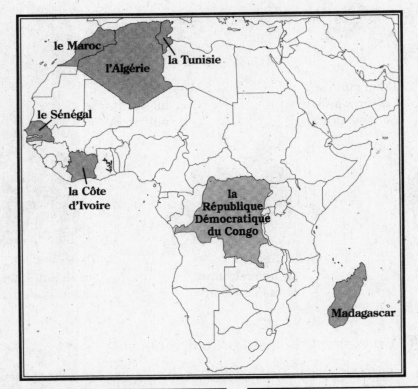

Country:	le Sénégal
Population:	
Capital:	
Languages:	
Continent:	

Country:	
Population:	
Capital:	
Languages:	
Continent:	

Nom _____

Classe _____ Date _____

Activité 6. Des interviews

Imagine you are one of the people pictured below. A classmate will interview you. Answer your classmate's questions according to the information given for each photo. When you have answered all the questions, interview your classmate. Continue until you and your classmate interview all four people. (NOTE: The question marks (**??**) indicate that you may mention other activities of your choice.)

Nom:	Philippe Martin
Âge:	15 ans
Ville/Pays:	Paris, France
Activités:	danser, écouter la radio, regarder la télé **??**

Nom:	Stéphanie Malle
Âge:	14 ans
Ville/Pays:	Paris, France
Activités:	travailler à la maison, inviter des copains à nager en été **??**

Nom:	Prak Maph
Âge:	15 ans
Ville/Pays:	Paris, France
Activités:	jouer au hockey en hiver, écouter la radio, jouer au tennis en été **??**

Nom:	Sophie Lafont
Âge:	14 ans
Ville/Pays:	Toulouse, France
Activités:	jouer au foot, skier en hiver, travailler dans un restaurant **??**

Phrases utiles	
Comment t'appelles-tu?	Quel âge as-tu?
Je m'appelle . . .	J'ai . . . ans.
Qu'est-ce que tu fais le week-end?	Où est-ce que tu habites?
Je . . .	J'habite à . . .

MODULE 8   Un concert de musique africaine

Video 2, DVD 1

We're all curious about other people. We want to know where they're going, what they're doing and why.

For instance, this gentleman . . . Where is he going? **Où est-ce qu'il va?** *It looks like he's going to a café. But why? Because he's meeting his date there!*

And where is this bus going?
It was going to Notre Dame.

And these people, what are they watching?
Why, they're watching a mime!

8.1 Mini-scenes: Listening—Où est-ce qu'il va?
Counter: 22:39–24:04

When we need information, it's important to know how to ask the right questions. We may want to ask WHERE *people do certain things: where do they work? where do they study? where do they live? In French, these questions begin with* **où.** [screen card]

—Où est-ce que tu habites?
—J'habite à Fort-de-France.

—Où est-ce que vous habitez?
—J'habite à Nantes.

—Où est-ce que vous travaillez?
—Je travaille dans une banque.

There are other types of information you may want to find out. For example, WHEN *something is happening.* **Quand?** [screen card]

PHILIPPE: Quand est-ce que tu fais ta boum?
FRANÇOIS: Samedi.

Or at WHAT TIME. **À quelle heure?** [screen card]

NICOLAS: À quelle heure est-ce que tu dînes?
NATHALIE: À sept heures et demie.

Perhaps you want to know HOW WELL *people do certain things.* **Comment?** [screen card]

—Comment est-ce que tu joues au tennis?
—Pas très bien.

Or what their name is, that is, how they call themselves. [screen card]

—Comment est-ce que tu t'appelles?
—Je m'appelle Delphine.

You may also want to know WHO *is involved in a certain activity.* **À qui?** [screen card]

—À qui est-ce que tu téléphones?
—À ma copine Alice.

Avec qui? [screen card]

—Avec qui est-ce que tu joues au tennis?
—Avec Éric.

8.2 Mini-scenes: Listening—Qu'est-ce que tu fais?
Counter: 24:05–24:53

When you want to know WHAT *people are doing, begin your question with* **qu'est-ce que.** [screen card]

CÉCILE: Qu'est-ce que tu fais?
PHILIPPE: Je fais un sandwich.

—Qu'est-ce que tu fais?
—Je fais une tarte.

—Qu'est-ce que vous faites?
—Je fais une crêpe.

LÉA: Qu'est-ce que tu regardes?
ANTOINE: Je regarde un film de science-fiction.

—Et toi, qu'est-ce que tu écoutes?
—J'écoute un CD de jazz.

—Qu'est-ce que tu manges?
—Je mange une tarte.
—Hmm, c'est délicieux!

8.3 Mini-scenes: Speaking— Questions

Counter: 24:54–25:35

Now it's your turn to speak. Watch the scenes and answer the questions.

—Qu'est-ce qu'il mange?   [screen card]
—Il mange un sandwich.

—Qu'est-ce qu'elle mange?   [screen card]
—Elle mange une pizza.

—Avec qui est-ce qu'elle dîne?   [screen card]
—Elle dîne avec un copain.

—Où est-ce qu'ils dînent?   [screen card]
—Ils dînent au restaurant.

—À quelle heure est-ce
  qu'ils dînent?   [screen card]
—Ils dînent à huit heures.

8.4 Dialogue: Un concert de musique africaine

Counter: 25:36–26:26

Nicolas is at a café with his new friend Fatou. He's interviewing her for an article in his school newspaper. Listen to their conversation.

NICOLAS: Bonjour, Fatou. Ça va?
FATOU: Oui, ça va.
NICOLAS: Tu es sénégalaise, n'est-ce pas?
FATOU: Oui, je suis sénégalaise.
NICOLAS: Où est-ce que tu habites?
FATOU: Je suis de Dakar, mais maintenant j'habite à Paris avec ma famille.
NICOLAS: Est-ce que tu aimes Paris?
FATOU: J'adore Paris.
NICOLAS: Qu'est-ce que tu fais le week-end?
FATOU: Ça dépend. En général, je regarde la télé ou je sors avec mes copains. Dis, Nicolas! Est-ce que je peux te poser une question?

NICOLAS: Oui, bien sûr!
FATOU: Qu'est-ce que tu fais samedi?
NICOLAS: Euh, . . . je ne sais pas.
FATOU: Est-ce que tu veux aller avec nous à un concert de musique africaine?
NICOLAS: Super! Où? Quand? Et à quelle heure?

8.5 Vignette culturelle: Le Sénégal

Counter: 26:27–27:59

Remember our map of the French-speaking world? Let's look again at Africa. The French-speaking world covers the greatest area here. In yellow are the countries where French is the official language. One of these countries is Senegal.

Although small in size, Senegal is one of the most dynamic and most attractive countries in Africa. It has a population of about ten and a half million. Its capital is Dakar, a city of one million people. Let's see more of Senegal.

—Bonjour, comment est-ce que vous vous appelez?
—Je m'appelle Monsieur Li.
—Vous parlez français?
—Oui, je parle français, et le wolof aussi.

There are many other countries in Africa that use French as their official language, from the Democratic Republic of the Congo, the largest one, to Mali, Niger, the Ivory Coast, and Burkina Faso. As you've seen, French is quite a useful language for people traveling in Africa.

Unité 3
Leçon 8

Audioscripts

Discovering
FRENCH
Nouveau

BLEU

LEÇON 8   Un concert de musique africaine

PE AUDIO

CD 2, Track 17
Compréhension orale, p. 104

Nicolas is at a café with his new friend Fatou. He's interviewing her for an article in his school newspaper.

NICOLAS: Bonjour Fatou. Ça va?
FATOU: Oui, ça va.
NICOLAS: Tu es sénégalaise, n'est-ce pas?
FATOU: Oui, je suis sénégalaise.
NICOLAS: Où est-ce que tu habites?
FATOU: Je suis de Dakar, mais maintenant j'habite à Paris avec ma famille.
NICOLAS: Est-ce que tu aimes Paris?
FATOU: J'adore Paris.
NICOLAS: Qu'est-ce que tu fais le week-end?
FATOU: Ça dépend. En général, je regarde la télé ou je sors avec mes copains. Dis, Nicolas! Est-ce que je peux te poser une question?
NICOLAS: Oui, bien sûr!
FATOU: Qu'est-ce que tu fais ce week-end?
NICOLAS: Euh, . . .je ne sais pas.
FATOU: Est-ce tu veux aller avec nous à un concert de Youssou N'Dour, le musicien sénégalais?
NICOLAS: Super! Où? Et à quelle heure?

CD 2, Track 18
Écoutez et répétez., p. 104

You will now hear a paused version of the dialog. Listen to the speaker and repeat right after he or she has completed the sentence.

CD 2, Track 19
Activité 1. Écoutez bien!, p. 107

The questions that you will hear can be logically answered by only one of the following options. Listen carefully to each question and select the logical answer. You will hear each question twice. Let's begin.

1. Où est-ce que tu habites? #
2. À quelle heure est-ce que vous dînez? #
3. Comment est-ce que vous parlez français?#
4. Quand est-ce que vous visitez Dakar?#
5. Où est-ce que ton oncle travaille?#
6. Quand est-ce que ton copain voyage en France?#
7. À quelle heure est-ce que vous regardez la télé?#
8. Comment est-ce que tu chantes? #

Prononciation, p. 111

CD 2, Track 20
La voyelle /y/

Écoutez: super!

The vowel sound /y/ — represented by the letter "u" — does not exist in English.

To say super, first say the French word si. Then round your lips as if to whistle and say si with rounded lips: /sy/. Now say si-per. Then round your lips as you say the first syllable: super!

Répétez: /y/ # super # tu # étudie # bien sûr # Lucie # Luc # Tu étudies avec Lucie. #

À votre tour!

CD 2, Track 21
1. Allô!, p. 112

Fatou is phoning some friends. Match her questions on the left with her friends' answers on the right.

1. Qu'est-ce que tu fais?
   J'étudie.

2. Qu'est-ce que vous faites samedi?
   Nous faisons un match de tennis.

3. Où est ton père?
   Il fait une promenade.

4. Quand est-ce que tu veux jouer au tennis avec moi?
   Dimanche. D'accord?

5. Qui est-ce que tu invites au cinéma?
   Ma cousin Alice.

6. Pourqoui est-ce que tu études l'anglais?
   Parce que je voudrais habiter à New York.

CD 2, Track 22

3. Créa-dialogue, p. 113

Listen to some sample *Créa-dialogues*.
Écoutez les conversations.

Modèle: —Qu'est-ce que tu fais lundi?
—Je joue au tennis.
—Ah bon? À quelle heure est-ce que tu joues?
—À deux heures.
—Et avec qui?
—Avec Anne-Marie.

Maintenant, écoutez le dialogue numéro 1.

—Qu'est-ce que tu fais mardi?
—J'étudie.
—Ah bon? À quelle heure est-ce que tu étudies?
—À six heures.
—Et avec qui?
—Avec un copain.

WORKBOOK AUDIO

Section 1. Questions

CD 7, Track 18

A. Compréhension orale, p. 75

In each of the following dialogues, someone is asking for information. Listen carefully and check the corresponding question words in your Workbook.

Modèle: —Où est-ce que tu habites?
—J'habite à Fort-de-France.

You would place a checkmark under column A: où.

1. NICOLAS: À quelle heure est-ce que tu dînes?
   NATHALIE: À sept heures et demie. #

2. —Avec qui est-ce que tu joues au tennis?
   —Avec Éric. #

3. PHILIPPE: Quand est-ce que tu fais ta boum?
   FRANÇOIS: Samedi. #

4. —À qui est-ce que tu téléphones?
   —À ma copine Alice. #

5. —Comment est-ce que tu t'appelles?
   —Je m'appelle Delphine. #

6. —Où est-ce que vous habitez?
   —J'habite à Nantes. #

7. —Comment est-ce que tu joues au tennis?
   —Hmm, pas très bien. #

8. —Où est-ce que vouz travaillez?
   —Je travaille dans une banque. #

Now check your answers. You should have marked the columns as follows: 1-C, 2-F, 3-B, 4-E, 5-D, 6-A, 7-D, and 8-A.

CD 7, Track 19

B. Questions et réponses, p. 75

You will hear a series of questions. Answer each one with the information suggested in your Workbook. You will hear each question twice. Listen to the model.

Modèle: Où est-ce que tu habites? # J'habite à Québec. #

Commençons.

1. À quelle heure est-ce que tu regardes la télé? #
   Je regarde la télé à huit heures.

2. Comment est-ce que tu parles français? #
   Je parle bien.

3. Où est-ce que tu voyages? #
   Je voyage en France.

4. Quand est-ce que tu voyages? #
   Je voyage en été.

5. À qui est-ce que tu téléphones? #
   Je téléphone à une copine.

6. Avec qui est-ce que tu dînes? #
   Je dîne avec mon oncle.

7. Qu'est-ce que tu manges? #
   Je mange une pizza.

8. Qu'est-ce que tu fais? #
   Je fais une promenade.

Section 2. La réponse logique

CD 7, Track 20

C. Compréhension orale, p. 76

You will hear Stéphanie asking her friend Christophe several questions. In your Workbook, select the most logical response and circle the corresponding letter, a, b or c. You will hear each question twice.

Commençons.

1. Où est-ce que tu dînes aujourd'hui? #
2. Quand est-ce que tu organises une boum? #
3. Comment est-ce que tu joues au tennis? #
4. Pourquoi est-ce que tu téléphones? #
5. Qu'est-ce que tu manges? #
6. Avec qui est-ce que tu aimes voyager? #

Now check your answers. You should have circled 1-c, 2-a, 3-b, 4-c, 5-a, and 6-b.

Section 3. Dictée

CD 7, Track 21

D. Écoutez et écrivez., p. 76

You will hear a short dialogue spoken twice. First listen carefully to what the people are saying. The second time you hear the dialogue, fill in the missing words.

Écoutez.

– Dis, Patrick, qu'est-ce que tu fais demain?
– Je joue au tennis avec ma cousine. Nous faisons un match. Pourquoi?
– Est-ce que je peux jouer avec vous?
– Oui, bien sûr!

Listen again and fill in the missing words.

Discovering
FRENCH
Nouveau!

BLEU

Unité 3
Leçon 8

Audioscripts

LESSON 8 QUIZ

Part I: Listening

CD 14, Track 4

A. Questions et réponses

You will hear your French friend Luc ask you eight questions. Select the MOST LOGICAL response and circle the corresponding letter (a, b, or c). You will hear each question twice.

Let's begin.

1. *Luc has spotted you at a café table. He comes up and asks:*
   Qu'est-ce que tu fais?

2. *Luc continues the conversation. He asks:*
   Qu'est-ce que tu manges?

3. *Luc has another question. He asks:*
   Où est-ce que tu dînes?

4. *Luc is asking you about your travel plans. He asks:*
   Avec qui est-ce que tu visites Montréal?

5. *You and Luc are talking about your families. He asks:*
   Où est-ce que ta mère travaille?

6. *You and Luc are discussing sports. He asks:*
   Comment est-ce que tu joues au foot?

7. *Luc is curious about your weekend plans. He asks:*
   Quand est-ce que tu organises une boum?

8. *You and Luc are in town. You take out your cell phone. He asks:*
   Pourquoi est-ce que tu téléphones?

Nom _____

Classe _____ Date _____

Discovering
FRENCH
Nouveau!

B L E U

QUIZ 8

Part I: Listening

A. Questions et réponses (40 points)

You will hear your French friend Luc ask you eight questions. Select the MOST LOGICAL response and circle the corresponding letter (a, b, or c). You will hear each question twice.

1. Luc has spotted you at a café table. He comes up. You reply:
   a. J'étudie.
   b. Très bien.
   c. Merci.

2. Luc continues the conversation. You reply:
   a. Au restaurant.
   b. Une glace.
   c. Non, je ne mange pas.

3. Luc has another question. You reply:
   a. À sept heures.
   b. Au restaurant.
   c. Un sandwich.

4. Luc is asking you about your travel plans. You reply:
   a. En juillet.
   b. Le 3 septembre.
   c. Avec mon cousin Martin.

5. You and Luc are talking about your families. You reply:
   a. Dans une pharmacie.
   b. À huit heures.
   c. Elle travaille beaucoup.

6. You and Luc are discussing sports. You reply:
   a. Mardi.
   b. Avec Paul.
   c. Bien. Et toi?

7. Luc is curious about your weekend plans. You reply:
   a. À la maison.
   b. Samedi.
   c. Oui, bien sûr.

8. You and Luc are in town. You take out your cell phone. You reply:
   a. À mon copain Éric.
   b. Oui, j'aime téléphoner.
   c. Parce que je veux inviter une copine au cinéma.

Part II: Writing

B. Questions (24 points)

Read each of the following conversations and complete the question with the logical interrogative expression.

1. —_____ est-ce que tu invites ta copine au restaurant?

   —Vendredi.

2. —_____ est-ce que tu dînes maintenant?

   —Parce que j'ai faim.

3. —_____ est-ce que tu danses?

   —Bien!

Nom _____

Classe _____ Date _____

Discovering
FRENCH
Nouveau!

B L E U

Unité 3
Leçon 8
Lesson Quiz

4. —_____ est-ce que ton copain habite?

—Il habite à Nice.

5. —_____ est-ce que tu téléphones?

—À Trinh.

6. —_____ tu écoutes?

—J'écoute un CD de rock.

C. Voyages (16 points)

The following people are traveling this summer. Complete each statement with the appropriate form of **faire.**

1. Nous _____ un voyage en Italie.

2. M. et Mme Caron _____ un voyage en Chine.

3. Je _____ un voyage en Égypte.

4. Vous _____ un voyage en Hollande.

D. Expression personnelle (20 points)
(8 points for the first answer; 12 points for the second answer)

It's Saturday. You meet your French friend Caroline downtown. Ask her in French . . .

• what she is doing

_____

• if she wants to go for a walk with you

_____

UNITÉ 3
Qu'est-ce qu'on fait?

CULTURAL CONTEXT: Daily activities at home, at school, on weekends

---

FUNCTIONS:

- describing daily activities: what people are doing and like to do
- finding out what is going on: asking questions
- talking about where people are
- Inviting friends to do things
- expressing agreement and disagreement

RELATED THEMES:

- daily activities
- affirmative and negative expressions

 **POUR COMMUNIQUER**   **Communicative Expressions and Thematic Vocabulary**

Nom _____

Classe _____ Date _____

UNITÉ 3 Interviews

In this section you will be interviewed by different people who want to get to know you better. If you wish, you may write the answers to the interview questions in the space provided.

Interview 1

I am preparing a mailing list for a French magazine: Please let me know in which cities your friends and relatives live. Invent an answer, if necessary.

- **Où habite ta cousine?**
- **Où habite ton copain?**
- **Où habitent ton oncle et ta tante?**
- **Où habite ta grand-mère?**

ADRESSES

- Cousine: _____
- Copain: _____
- Oncle et tante: _____
- Grand-mère: _____

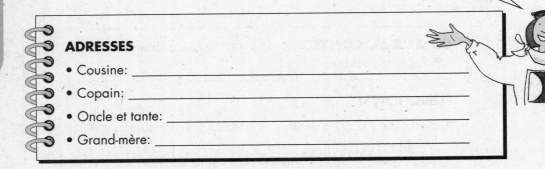

Interview 2

I would like to know more about you. For instance, how well you do certain things.

- **Comment est-ce que tu chantes?**
- **Comment est-ce que tu nages?**
- **Comment est-ce que tu joues au basket?**
- **Comment est-ce que tu joues aux jeux vidéo?**

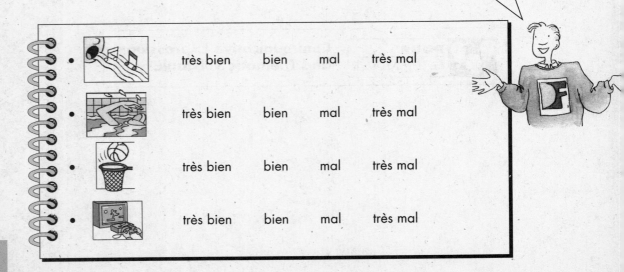

	très bien	bien	mal	très mal
	très bien	bien	mal	très mal
	très bien	bien	mal	très mal
	très bien	bien	mal	très mal

Nom _____

Classe _____ Date _____

Discovering
FRENCH
Nouveau!

BLEU

Unité 3
Resources

Communipak

Interview 3

I am taking a survey about what
American teenagers like to do.
Tell me about your preferences.

> • **Tu préfères jouer au foot ou au basket?**
> • **En classe, tu préfères parler français ou anglais?**
> • **À la maison, tu préfères regarder la télé ou écouter la radio?**
> • **En été, tu préfères voyager ou travailler?**

PRÉFÉRENCES

• Sports: _____

• En classe: _____

• À la maison: _____

• En été: _____

Interview 4

Tell me a little bit about
what you do in the course
of the day.

> • **À quelle heure est-ce que tu dînes?**
> • **Quels programmes de télé est-ce que tu regardes?**
> • **À qui est-ce que tu téléphones?**
> • **Quelle station de radio est-ce que tu écoutes?**

Nom _____

Classe _____ Date _____

Tu as la parole

Read the instructions on the cards below, and give your partner the corresponding information in French. Take turns reading your cards and listening to each other.

TU AS LA PAROLE 1 — UNITÉ 3

Describe one thing you like to do in each of the following situations.

- **En vacances, j'aime . . .**
- **Avec mes** *(my)* **copains, . . .**
- **Au restaurant, . . .**

TU AS LA PAROLE 2 — UNITÉ 3

Describe one thing you do NOT like to do in each of the following situations.

- **En classe, je n'aime pas . . .**
- **En vacances, . . .**
- **À la maison, . . .**

TU AS LA PAROLE 3 — UNITÉ 3

Describe three things you do when you are at home in the evening.

- **À la maison, je (j') . . .**
-
-

Nom _____

Classe _____ Date _____

Discovering
FRENCH
Nouveau!

B L E U

Unité 3
Resources

Communipak

TU AS LA PAROLE 4 — UNITÉ 3

Select three sports and say how well you play each of them.

▶ **Je joue au baseball. Je ne joue pas très bien.**

-
-
-

TU AS LA PAROLE 5 — UNITÉ 3

Select three people you know well—for example, friends or members of your family. Describe what each one likes to do.

-
-
-

TU AS LA PAROLE 6 — UNITÉ 3

Select a person whom you know well. Say . . .

- where this person lives
- what language(s) he/she speaks
- what he/she likes to do

Discovering
FRENCH
Nouveau

BLEU

Side A

Conversations

Act out the following situations with your partner. Take turns:

- In the odd-numbered situations, you will be asking the questions.
- In the even-numbered situations, you will be answering your partner's questions.

CONVERSATION 1	**UNITÉ 3**

It is vacation time. You are going to France for the first time. On the plane you meet another student.

◆————————————————————————————◆

Ask your partner . . .

- where he/she lives
- if he/she speaks French well
- if he/she travels often

CONVERSATION 2

It is Saturday afternoon and you are in town. You have just phoned your partner, who is at home. Your friend wants to know where you are and what you are doing.

Answer your partner's questions.

CONVERSATION 3	**UNITÉ 3**

At the sports club you meet a French classmate.

◆————————————————————————————◆

Ask your partner . . .

- if he/she likes to swim
- if he/she wants to play tennis with you
- if he/she wants to go for a walk afterwards **(après)**

CONVERSATION 4

A French friend has invited you to his/her home. Now your friend is asking you what you want to do.

Answer your partner's questions.

Nom _____

Classe _____ Date _____ _____

Discovering
FRENCH *Nouveau!*

B L E U

Side B

Unité 3
Resources
Communipak

Conversations

Act out the following situations with your partner. Take turns:

- In the odd-numbered situations, you will be answering your partner's questions.
- In the even-numbered situations, you will be asking the questions.

CONVERSATION 1

It is vacation time and you are on a plane going to France. The student seated across the aisle is going to France for the first time and is asking you some questions.

Answer your partner's questions

CONVERSATION 2   UNITÉ 3

You are at home on a Saturday afternoon. Your friend is phoning you from downtown.

◆━━━━━━━━━━━━━━━━━━━━━━━━━━◆

Ask your partner . . .

- where he/she is
- what he/she is doing
- what he/she wants to do

CONVERSATION 3

You are a French teenager and you are spending the day at the sports club. You meet a classmate and you strike up a conversation.

Answer your partner's questions

CONVERSATION 4   UNITÉ 3

You have invited your friend to your home. Since you are a good host/hostess, you are asking what your friend wants to do.

◆━━━━━━━━━━━━━━━━━━━━━━━━━━◆

Ask your partner . . .

- what he/she wants to watch on TV **(à la télé)**
- at what time he/she wants to have dinner
- what he/she wants to eat

Nom _____

Classe _____ Date _____

Échanges

1 You want to know who in your class is interested in the same activities as you.

- List four activities you enjoy doing.
- Then ask several classmates if they also like to do these things.

ACTIVITÉS	AMIS			
J'aime . . .	Pierre			
▶ nager				
1				
2				
3				
4				

- How many classmates are interested in at least <u>three</u> of the same activities as you?

Nom _____

Classe _____ Date _____

Discovering
FRENCH
Nouveau!

BLEU

2 You want to know more about your classmates' talents.

- Interview three friends and find out if they can do the following activities and how well they can do them.

- Write the names of your friends in the boxes that correspond to their answers.

ACTIVITÉS	oui, très bien	oui, bien	oui, comme ci, comme ça	oui, mais mal	non
	Claire				

Nom _____

Classe _____ Date _____

Tête à tête

1 Où sont-ils?

a

■ Find out from your partner where the following people are.

> Où est Isabelle?

Write your partner's answers in the spaces provided.

- **Isabelle?**

  Elle est _____

- **Jean-Paul?**

  Il est _____

- **Madame Lambert?**

  Elle est _____

- **Monsieur Thomas?**

  Il est _____

b

You know where the following people are, but your partner does not.

■ Answer your partner's questions.

• **Pauline**

• **Marc**

• **Mademoiselle Joli**

• **Madame Leblanc**

Nom _____

Classe _____ Date _____

Discovering
FRENCH *Nouveau!*

BLEU

Élève B

Unité 3
Resources Communipak

Tête à tête

1 | Où sont-ils?

a

You know where the following people are, but your partner does not.

■ Answer your partner's questions.

• Isabelle

• Jean-Paul

• Madame Lambert

• Monsieur Thomas

b

■ Now find out from your partner where the following people are.

> **Où est Pauline?**

✎ Write your partner's answers in the spaces provided.

• Pauline?

Elle est _____

• Marc?

Il est _____

• Mademoiselle Joli?

Elle est _____

• Madame Leblanc?

Elle est _____

Nom _____

Classe _____ Date _____

Tête à tête

2 **Qu'est-ce que tu aimes faire?**

a

First indicate whether or not you like to do each of the following activities by circling **oui** or **non**.

■ Then answer your partner's questions accordingly.

 oui non

 oui non

 oui non

 oui non

 oui non

b

■ Now find out what your partner likes to do.

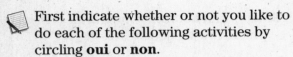
Est-ce que tu aimes voyager?

Mark your partner's answers by circling **oui** or **non**.

 oui non

 oui non

 oui non

 oui non

 oui non

Nom _____

Classe _____ Date _____

Discovering
FRENCH *Nouveau!*

BLEU

Unité 3
Resources Communipak

Tête à tête

2 Qu'est-ce que tu aimes faire?

a

 ■ First find out what your partner likes to do.

> **Est-ce que tu aimes chanter?**

 Mark your partner's answers by circling **oui** or **non**.

  oui   non

  oui   non

  oui   non

  oui   non

  oui   non

b

 Now indicate whether or not you like to do each of the following activities by circling **oui** or **non**.

■ Then answer your partner's questions accordingly.

  oui   non

  oui   non

  oui   non

  oui   non

  oui   non

Nom _____

Classe _____ Date _____

Tête à tête

3 Que font-ils?

a

Your friends are all busy today.

 Assign an activity to each one by drawing a line connecting the person's name to one of the illustrations.

■ Then answer your partner's questions.

Catherine	Florence	Jérôme	Philippe	Stéphanie

· ·

b

■ Ask your partner what the following people are doing.

Que fait Christine?

 Write down the information that your partner gives you.

- **Christine?** _____

- **Jean-Pierre?** _____

- **Éric?** _____

- **Delphine?** _____

- **Marc?** _____

Nom _____

Classe _____ Date _____

Discovering
FRENCH *Nouveau!*

B L E U

Unité 3
Resources
Communipak

Tête à tête

3 Que font-ils?

a

Your friends are all busy today.

■ Ask your partner what the following people are doing.

Que fait Catherine?

Write down the information that your partner gives you.

- **Catherine?** _____

- **Florence?** _____

- **Jérôme?** _____

- **Philippe?** _____

- **Stéphanie?** _____

b

Now, assign an activity to each of the following people by drawing a line connecting the person's name to one of the illustrations.

■ Then answer your partner's questions.

| Christine | Jean-Pierre | Éric | Delphine | Marc |

Nom _____

Classe _____ Date _____

Communicative Expressions and Thematic Vocabulary

Pour communiquer

Talking about likes and preferences

Est-ce que tu aimes	parler anglais?	*Do you like*	*to speak English?*
J'aime		*I like*	
Je n'aime pas		*I don't like*	
Je préfère	parler français.	*I prefer*	*to speak French.*
Je veux		*I want*	
Je voudrais		*I would like*	
Je ne veux pas		*I don't want*	

Inviting a friend

Est-ce que tu veux [jouer au tennis]?   *Do you want to [play tennis]?*
Est-ce que tu peux [jouer au foot] avec moi?   *Can you [play soccer] with me?*

Accepting or declining an invitation

Oui, bien sûr.	*Yes, of course.*	Je regrette, mais je ne peux pas.	*I'm sorry, but I can't.*
Oui, merci.	*Yes, thanks.*		
Oui, d'accord.	*Yes, all right, okay.*	Je dois [travailler].	*I have to, I must [work].*
Oui, je veux bien.	*Yes, I'd love to.*		

Expressing approval, regret, or surprise

Super!	*Terrific!*
Dommage!	*Too bad!*
Ah bon?	*Oh? Really?*

Answering a yes/no question

Oui!	*Yes!*	Non!	*No!*
Mais oui!	*Sure!*	Mais non!	*Of course not!*
Bien sûr!	*Of course!*	Peut-être . . .	*Maybe . . .*

Asking for information

où?	*where?*	qu'est-ce que . . .?	*what?*
quand?	*when?*	qui?	*who, whom?*
à quelle heure?	*at what time?*	à qui?	*to who(m)?*
comment?	*how?*	de qui?	*about who(m)?*
pourquoi?	*why?*	avec qui?	*with who(m)?*
parce que . . .	*because?*	pour qui?	*for who(m)?*

Saying where people are

Pierre est . . .

ici	*here*	à la maison	*at home*	en classe	*in class*
là	*here, there*	au café	*at the café*	en France	*in France*
là-bas	*over there*	au cinéma	*at the movies*	en vacances	*on vacation*
à [Paris]	*in [Paris]*	au restaurant	*at the restaurant*	en ville	*in town*

Nom _____

Classe _____ Date _____

Discovering FRENCH *Nouveau!*

B L E U

Unité 3
Resources

Communipak

Saying how well, how often, and when

bien	*well*	beaucoup	*a lot, much, very much*	maintenant	*now*
très bien	*very well*	un peu	*a little, a little bit*	souvent	*often*
mal	*badly, poorly*	rarement	*rarely, seldom*	toujours	*always*

Mots et expressions

Verbes réguliers en –er

aimer	*to like*	jouer aux jeux vidéo	*to play video games*
chanter	*to sing*	manger	*to eat*
danser	*to dance*	nager	*to swim*
dîner	*to have dinner*	organiser une boum	*to organize a party*
dîner au restaurant	*to eat out*	parler anglais	*to speak English*
écouter	*to listen, to listen to*	parler espagnol	*to speak Spanish*
écouter la radio	*to listen to the radio*	parler français	*to speak French*
étudier	*to study*	regarder	*to watch, to look at*
habiter (à Paris)	*to live (in Paris)*	regarder la télé	*to watch TV*
inviter	*to invite*	téléphoner (à Céline)	*to phone (Céline)*
jouer au basket	*to play basketball*	travailler	*to work*
jouer au foot	*to play soccer*	visiter Paris	*to visit Paris*
jouer au tennis	*to play tennis*	voyager	*to travel*

Verbes irréguliers

être	*to be*	faire	*to do, make*
être d'accord	*to agree*	faire un match	*to play a game (match)*
		faire une promenade	*to go for a walk*
		faire un voyage	*to take a trip*
		faire attention	*to pay attention*

Mots utiles

à	*at, in*	et	*and*
aussi	*also*	mais	*but*
avec	*with*	ou	*or*
de	*from, of*	pour	*for*

Nom _____

Classe _____ Date _____

Discovering
FRENCH
Nouveau!

B L E U

Unité 3
Resources

Activités pour tous TE
Reading

UNITÉ 3   Reading Comprehension

A

Muzzik

la chaîne

classique | jazz |

danse | musiques

du monde

MUZZIK

la chaîne
classique, jazz, danse
musiques du monde

www.muzzik.net

Muzzik est diffusé 7j/7, 24h/24
en qualité et son numériques

Muzzik est disponible sur:

CANALSATELLITE 0 803 804 804
LE MEILLEUR DU NUMÉRIQUE   (0.15 € /mn)

et le câble 08 91 67 60 60
                    (0.225 € /mn)

Compréhension

1. This ad would interest people who like:

    museums   movies   (music)

2. What do you think Muzzik is?

    (a channel available   a radio station
      via cable and
      satellite)

3. How many days a week does it broadcast?

    Monday   weekends   (every
    through   only   day)
    Friday

4. During what hours does it broadcast?

    mornings   evenings   (24 hours
                                        a day)

5. What does **musiques du monde** mean?

    foreign   (world   mountain
    music   music)   music

Qu'est-ce que vous en pensez?

1. How does one say "channel" in French? _chaîne_

2. What do you think **son numérique** means?

    (digital sound)   analog sound   high fidelity sound

3. How do the French say a show is "broadcast?"

    lancé   (diffusé)   joué

Unité 3
Resources

Activités pour tous TE
Reading

Discovering
FRENCH
Nouveau!

BLEU

Nom _____

Classe _____ Date _____

B

Musique et Patrimoine

MUSIQUE ET
PATRIMOINE

UN DIMANCHE PAR MOIS
À 16 HEURES *

LA MAIRIE DE PARIS
VOUS INVITE À DÉCOUVRIR
UN MONUMENT OU UN MUSÉE
AVEC UN CONCERT

MAIRIE DE PARIS

* sauf horaires particuliers

Informations

Direction des
Affaires culturelles
de la Ville de Paris
31, rue des Francs-
Bourgeois
Paris IVᵉ

01 42 76 84 00
01 42 76 84 01

Entrée libre

28 OCTOBRE 2001
Église Notre-Dame de Lorette
18 bis, rue de Chateaudun
Paris ixᵉ

25 NOVEMBRE 2001
Église Sainte-Marguerite
36, rue Saint-Bernard
Paris xiᵉ

20 JANVIER 2002
Couvent des Cordeliers
15, rue de l'École de médecine
Paris vⁱᵉ

24 FÉVRIER 2002
Musée Bourdelle
à 14 h 30 et 16 h
*Réservation obligatoire
au 01 42 76 56 18*
16, rue Antoine Bourdelle
Paris xvᵉ

17 MARS 2002
Église Saint-Pierre de Chaillot
31 bis, avenue Marceau
Paris viiᵉ

28 AVRIL 2002
Église Notre-Dame de la Croix
de Ménilmontant
3, place de Ménilmontant
Paris xxᵉ

26 MAI 2002
Église Saint-Germain des Prés
à 15 h
1, place Saint-Germain des Prés
Paris vⁱᵉ

23 JUIN 2002
Musée Carnavalet
à 14 h 30 et 16 h
*Réservation obligatoire
au 01 42 76 56 18*
23, rue de Sévigné
Paris iiiᵉ

Compréhension

1. What kind of event is this?

   rock concert   church and museum concert series

2. What day of the week do these events take place?

   Sunday   Wednesday   Saturday

3. How frequently do they happen?

   every day   once a week   once a month

4. What time do they take place? 2 P.M.   4 P.M.   6 P.M.

5. For which events are reservations required?

   church concerts   museum concerts

Qu'est-ce que vous en pensez?

1. What is the government trying to encourage?

   sightseeing   visits to museums and monuments   concert attendance

2. What do you think **patrimoine** means?

   exhibit   fatherhood   national heritage

3. The brochure is produced by Paris City Hall. How do you say "City Hall" in French?

   la mairie _____

Nom _____

Classe _____ Date _____

BLEU

Unité 3 Resources
Activités pour tous TE
Reading

Discovering
FRENCH
Nouveau!

C

Compréhension

1. Where is Sea Life located? Paris

2. What days and during what hours is it open? every day from 10 a.m.

3. What age do you have to be to get in free? 3 years old or younger.

4. How many aquariums are there? Over 30

5. Name two kinds of sea creatures you could see there. requins, pieuvres

Qu'est-ce que vous en pensez? (sample answers)

1. Who do you think this place would appeal to?

   Older adults   Young adults   Children   (All ages)

2. Which exhibits do you think would appeal the most to children? Why? L'aire de jeux,
   Au coeur du Titanic, because of the play pen and the slide.

3. What do you think **falaise** (#7) means? cliff

Nom _____

Classe _____ Date _____

Discovering
FRENCH
Nouveau!

BLEU

Unité 3
Resources

Workbook TE
Reading and Culture Activities

UNITÉ 3 Reading and Culture Activities

A. En France et en Louisiane

Nous avons besoin de nouvelles voix
pour renforcer notre groupe.

CHANTEZ AVEC NOUS...

... J.S. BACH, VIVALDI, MOZART,
CHANTS GREGORIENS,
REPERTOIRE CONTEMPORAIN.

——INSCRIPTIONS: Père A. Batselaere——
8, rue Massillon Paris 4ᵉ - Téléphone: **01 43 54 71 53**
ou 01 56 33 01 01

1. You would pay attention to this ad if you
   were interested in . . .
   ☑ singing
   ☐ traveling
   ☐ going to a concert
   ☐ visiting a church

ICI,
ON PARLE FRANÇAIS.

(FAITES VOTRE DEMANDE
EN FRANÇAIS).

NOUS SOMMES FIERS
DE PARLER
FRANÇAIS.

2. If you were traveling in Louisiana, you
   might see this sign in certain shops.
   What does it mean?
   ☐ We are French.
   ☑ French is spoken here.
   ☐ We sell French products.
   ☐ We like French people.

3. Here is another sign you might see in
   Louisiana. What does it mean?
   ☐ We do not speak French.
   ☑ We are proud to speak French.
   ☐ We sell French products.
   ☐ We love people who speak French.

Nom _____

Classe _____ Date _____

B. La Maison des Jeunes et de la Culture

Sandrine Moreau has dropped by Les Marquisats to get more information about their activities. She was asked to fill out the following form.

Je souhaite recevoir régulièrement des informations sur les activités culturelles de la Maison des Jeunes et de la Culture "Les Marquisats" d'Annecy.

Je suis plus particulièrement intéressé(e) par :

☐ CINÉMA   ☑ DANSES SPÉCIALES   ☐ CONFÉRENCES

☑ STAGES DANSE   ☐ JAZZ   ☐ ROCK   ☐ CHANSON

NOM _MOREAU, Sandrine_

INSTITUTION / PROFESSION _Étudiante_

ADRESSE _136, rue Descartes_

74000 Annecy

TÉL. _____ (facultatif).

LES MARQUISATS
M. J. C. 52, RUE DES MARQUISATS
74000 ANNECY TEL. 04.50.45.08.80

1. Sandrine is especially interested in . . .
   ☐ movies
   ☐ music
   ☑ dance
   ☐ lectures

2. Who is Sandrine?
   ☑ A student.
   ☐ A homemaker.
   ☐ A guitarist.
   ☐ A retired person.

Discovering
FRENCH
Nouveau!

B L E U

Unité 3
Resources

Workbook TE
Reading and Culture Activities

C. Conversation

Carefully read the following phone conversation between Carole and her friend Julien.

CAROLE: Allô, Julien?

JULIEN: Ah, c'est toi, Carole. Mais où es-tu?

CAROLE: Je suis à Tours.

JULIEN: À Tours? Mais pourquoi es-tu là-bas?

CAROLE: Je fais un voyage avec ma cousine.

JULIEN: Ah bon! Qu'est-ce que vous faites?

CAROLE: Oh là là, nous faisons beaucoup de choses. Nous visitons les châteaux. Nous dînons dans les restaurants. Nous . . .

JULIEN: Quand est-ce que vous rentrez à Paris?

CAROLE: Le quinze août.

JULIEN: Alors, bonnes vacances et bon retour!

- Where is Carole when she calls Julien? in Tours

  Where is Julien? in Paris

- With whom is Carole traveling? with her cousin

- What have the two of them been doing?

  They have been visiting castles and eating in restaurants.

  _____

- When is Carole returning home? on August 15

Unité 3
Resources

Workbook TE
Reading and Culture Activities

Discovering
FRENCH
Nouveau!

BLEU

Nom _____

Classe _____ Date _____

D. Invitations

1. You recently received two invitations. (Note: **venir** means *to come*.)

BOUM

Où? chez Daniel Lebrousse
32, rue Lecourbe

Quand? samedi
de 5 h 30 à 9 h 30

R.S.V.P. 01. 41. 12. 45 .30

Invitation

Est-ce que tu veux
venir dîner avec moi
samedi à 7 h 30?
Réponds-moi avant
jeudi.

Christophe

- What is Daniel's invitation for? a party
  What day and what time? Saturday from 5:30 to 9:30 P.M.

- What is Christophe's invitation for? dinner
  What day and what time? Saturday at 7:30 P.M.

- Which invitation are you going to accept, and why?
  Answers will vary.
  _____

2. Write a note to the person whose invitation you have to turn down.
   - Express your regret.
   - Explain that you have other plans.
   - Sign your note.

Sample answer:

Cher __Daniel (Christophe)__ ,

Je regrette, mais je ne peux pas

venir à la boum (dîner avec toi)

samedi. Je dois étudier.

_____

John (Katie)

Discovering FRENCH *Nouveau!* BLEU

IMAGES À l'école en France, page 124

Objectives

Cultural Goals
To learn about the French school system: grade levels and grading system
To compare typical French and American class days
To learn about French courses of study: subjects, schedule
To compare classrooms and buildings

Note: This **Images** presents information about the French school system and challenges students to compare their own school experiences in the U.S. to those of a typical student in France. You may want to refer back to this essay as students study more language for daily activities and communicating with friends.

Motivation and Focus

- As students preview the photos on pages 124–127, ask them to describe the scenes and suggest what a school day in France is like. Who are the people? Where are they? What are they doing? Together, read the photo captions on pages 125–127.
- Encourage students to describe their school and to talk about their favorite classes.
- As an overview of *À l'école en France*, play the **Video** or **DVD** sections B.1–B.4. Pause occasionally to allow students to comment on people and places.

Presentation and Explanation

- Together, read the letter and information about Nathalie on pages 124–125. Guide students to notice information about her family and home. Help students pronounce the names of Nathalie's school and town.
- Guide students as they look at the class schedule on page 131, noting days and times. Ask students to read *Le programme scolaire* and *L'emploi du temps de Nathalie*. Have students complete the *Comparaisons Culturelles* activities on pages 130–131.
- Present the information about French schools and grade levels on page 128. Have students read about the three teens on page 129. Ask them which student they would like to meet. Why? Point out the floor plan of the school building in the background on page 127. Encourage students to comment on classroom set-up. Ask students how they might feel in the French classroom pictured on page 127. Discuss the chart on page 128. Guide students to notice differences in identifying class levels in the French and American school systems. Point out French names for schools. Have students read pages 126–127, assisting with pronunciation as needed. Have students do the *Comparaisons Culturelles* activity on page 127.
- Use **Overhead Transparency** 50 to present classroom objects. Model the names of objects and have students repeat. Students can point to or find the objects in the rooms as you name them.

Guided Practice and Checking Understanding

- Have students try to identify the classes listed in the chart on page 130. Then guide students to talk about what subjects they take now.
- Use the COMPREHENSION CLASSROOM OBJECTS suggestions on page 133 of the TE to practice listening and following simple classroom directions with the objects on page 133. Students do not need to read and write the expressions on page 132; the focus is on comprehension. Help students use the *Tu dis . . .* expressions on page 133 to ask questions and talk about what they do and do not understand.

Unité 3
Resources

Lesson Plans for Images

Independent Practice

❑ Students can work in small groups to compare French and American schools with the CLASSROOM MANAGEMENT GROUPS activity on page 125 of the TE. Invite groups to share their lists.

Monitoring and Adjusting

❑ Monitor students' understanding of the French school system as they share their responses to the *Comparaisons Culturelles*. Clarify information as needed.

Assessment

❑ Use students' responses to *Comparaisons Culturelles* as an informal assessment of their awareness of cultural differences.
❑ To assess understanding of classroom objects, show **Overhead Transparency** S5. Invite students to point to objects as you say them.

Reteaching

❑ Use **Overhead Transparency** 50 to reteach names of classroom objects; then follow the instructions for the vocabulary game on page A121.

Extension and Enrichment

❑ Use **Overhead Transparency** S1 to introduce the SUPPLEMENTARY VOCABULARY on page 133 of the TE. Then have students find the objects in the classroom scene on Transparency S2.
❑ Have students note the way times are written on Nathalie's class schedule. Students may want to rewrite their class schedules using the 24-hour system. If students are interested, have them find examples of schedules or situations where times are written in similar fashion in the U.S. Some examples might be transportation schedules or military times.
❑ Encourage students to discuss or debate the pros and cons of the French school system. Students may want to consider Saturday classes, number of subjects studied, the grading system, and the ***baccalauréat*** test. Students should support their opinions.

Summary and Closure

❑ Show **Overhead Transparency** S5. Ask students to pretend they are one of the students in the picture and talk about their school life. Encourage them to share what they have learned about the French school system.

Discovering
FRENCH
Nouveau!

BLEU

Unité 3
Resources

Block Scheduling
Lesson Plans for Images

IMAGES À l'école en France, page 124

Block Schedule (1 day to complete – optional)

Objectives

Cultural Goals   To learn about the French school system: grade levels and grading system
To compare typical French and American class days
To learn about French courses of study: subjects, schedule
To compare classrooms and buildings

Note: This **Images** presents information about the French school system and challenges students to compare their own school experiences in the U.S. to those of a typical student in France. You may want to refer back to this essay as students study more language for daily activities and communicating with friends.

Block Schedule

Categorize Have students imagine that a group of French exchange students is arriving to attend classes for a semester. Tell them that you will read a list of the French students' names and their French school system grade levels. Students should write down the students' names and the grade in which the students should be placed under the American school system.

Day 1

Motivation and Focus

❑ As students preview the photos on pages 124–127, ask them to describe the scenes and suggest what a school day in France is like. Who are the people? Where are they? What are they doing? Together, read the photo captions on pages 125–127.

❑ Encourage students to describe their school and to talk about their favorite classes.

❑ As an overview of *À l'école en France*, play the **Video** or **DVD** sections B.1–B.4. Pause occasionally to allow students to comment on people and places.

Presentation and Explanation

❑ Together, read the letter and information about Nathalie on pages 124–125. Guide students to notice information about her family and home. Help students pronounce the names of Nathalie's school and town.

❑ Guide students as they look at the class schedule on page 131, noting days and times. Ask students to read *Le programme scolaire* and *L'emploi du temps de Nathalie*. Have students do the *Comparaisons Culturelles* activities on pages 130–131.

❑ Present the information about French schools and grade levels on page 128. Have students read about the three teens on page 129. Ask them which student they would like to meet. Why? Point out the floor plan of the school building in the background on page 127. Encourage students to comment on classroom set-up. Ask students how they might feel in the French classroom pictured on page 127. Discuss the chart on page 128. Guide students to notice differences in identifying class levels in the French and American school systems. Point out French names for schools. Have students read pages 126–127, assisting with pronunciation as needed. Have students do the *Comparaisons Culturelles* activity on page 127.

❑ Use **Overhead Transparency** 50 to present classroom objects. Model the names of objects and have students repeat. Students can point to or find the objects in the rooms as you name them.

Guided Practice and Checking Understanding

❏ Have students try to identify the classes listed in the chart on page 130. Then guide students to talk about what subjects they take now.

❏ Have students do the **Block Schedule Activity** on the previous page.

❏ Use the COMPREHENSION: CLASSROOM OBJECTS suggestions on page 133 of the TE to practice listening and following simple classroom directions with the objects on page 133. Students do not need to read and write the expressions on page 132; the focus is on comprehension. Help students use the *Tu dis. . .* expressions on page 133 to ask questions and talk about what they do and do not understand.

Independent Practice

❏ Students can work in small groups to compare French and American schools with the CLASSROOM MANAGEMENT GROUPS activity on page 125 of the TE. Invite groups to share their lists.

Monitoring and Adjusting

❏ Monitor students' understanding of the French school system as they share their responses to the *Comparaisons Culturelles*.

Reteaching (as needed)

❏ Use **Overhead Transparency** 50 to reteach names of classroom objects; then follow the instructions for the vocabulary game on page A125.

Extension and Enrichment (as desired)

❏ Use **Overhead Transparency** S1 to introduce the SUPPLEMENTARY VOCABULARY on page 133 of the TE. Then have students find the objects in the classroom scene on Transparency S2.

❏ Have students note the way times are written on Nathalie's class schedule. Students may want to rewrite their class schedules using the 24-hour system. If students are interested, have them find examples of schedules or situations where times are written in similar fashion in the U.S. Some examples might be transportation schedules or military times.

❏ Encourage students to discuss or debate the pros and cons of the French school system. Students may want to consider Saturday classes, number of subjects studied, the grading system, and the *baccalauréat* test. Students should support their opinions.

Summary and Closure

❏ Show **Overhead Transparency** S5. Ask students to pretend they are one of the students in the picture and talk about their school life. Encourage them to share what they have learned about the French school system.

Assessment

❏ Use students' responses to *Comparaisons Culturelles* as an informal assessment of their awareness of cultural differences.

❏ To assess understanding of classroom objects, show **Overhead Transparency** S5. Invite students to point to objects as you say them.

Nom _____

Classe _____ Date _____

Discovering
FRENCH
Nouveau!

B L E U

Unité 3
Resources

Unit Test Form A

UNIT TEST 3 (Lessons 5, 6, 7, 8)

FORM A

Part I. Listening Comprehension

1. The Logical Answer (20 points)

You will hear a series of ten questions. Listen carefully to each question and select the most logical answer on your test sheet. Circle the corresponding letter: a, b, or c. You will hear each question twice.

Modèle: [Quelle heure est-il?]
   a. Vendredi.
   b. Il fait beau.
   c. Deux heures et demie.

1. a. Là-bas.
   b. Bien, merci.
   c. Il est français.

2. a. Au restaurant.
   b. Peut-être.
   c. À huit heures.

3. a. Oui, il voyage.
   b. Oui, il regarde la télé.
   c. Oui, il fait une promenade.

4. a. Oui, bien sûr.
   b. Oui, je veux bien.
   c. Donne-moi un sandwich, s'il te plaît.

5. a. Oui, j'aime nager.
   b. Je regrette, mais je ne peux pas.
   c. Oui, je suis d'accord avec toi.

6. a. Français et anglais.
   b. À ma tante Isabelle.
   c. Je parle très bien.

7. a. Oui, elle est canadienne.
   b. Oui, elle aime voyager.
   c. Oui, elle visite le Canada.

8. a. D'accord, je veux bien.
   b. Oui, nous sommes d'accord.
   c. Oui, vous aimez danser.

9. a. Oui, je veux regarder la télé.
   b. Je ne suis pas d'accord avec toi.
   c. Je regrette, mais je dois étudier.

10. a. Oui, ils aiment chanter.
    b. Non, ils ne font pas attention.
    c. Non, ils ne parlent pas français.

Nom _____

Classe _____ Date _____

Part II. Language

2. The Right Choice (12 points)

Choose the word or expression which logically completes each of the following sentences.
Circle the corresponding letter: a, b, or c.

1. Ma cousine habite ____ Paris.
   a. à
   b. en
   c. au

2. Philippe est au restaurant ____ un copain.
   a. à
   b. aussi
   c. avec

3. Je parle français ____ je ne parle pas italien.
   a. ou
   b. mais
   c. souvent

4. Mon oncle travaille ____ une firme américaine.
   a. ici
   b. pour
   c. avec qui

5. Claire écoute ____ radio.
   a. à la
   b. la
   c. à

6. Martin joue ____ basket avec Marc et Robert.
   a. à
   b. au
   c. le

7. Je chante très mal. Je ne chante pas ____.
   a. bien
   b. bien sûr
   c. un peu

8. Léa fait une promenade ____.
   a. en classe
   b. en ville
   c. à la maison

9. Dis, Philippe, est-ce que tu ____ une limonade?
   a. veux
   b. peux
   c. manges

10. Je regrette, mais je ne ____ pas faire une promenade avec toi.
    a. suis
    b. peux
    c. voudrais

11. Isabelle étudie l'espagnol ____ elle veut visiter le Mexique.
    a. pourquoi
    b. parce qu'
    c. comment

12. Dis, Guillaume, ____ tu invites à la boum?
    a. est-ce que
    b. qu'est-ce que
    c. qui est-ce que

Nom _____

Classe _____ Date _____ _____

BLEU

Discovering
FRENCH
Nouveau!

Unité 3
Resources

Unit Test Form A

3. Être or Faire? (8 points)

Complete the following sentences with the appropriate forms of **être** or **faire**.

1. Madame Paquette, vous _____ canadienne, n'est-ce pas?

2. Nous _____ attention quand le professeur parle.

3. Pauline et Marc _____ au café.

4. Les touristes _____ une promenade en ville.

4. The Right Activity (16 points)

Complete each of the following sentences with the appropriate form of one of the verbs in the box. Be logical.

chanter	danser	dîner	écouter	habiter
jouer	manger	parler	regarder	travailler

Il est sept heures. Antoine et Sylvie *dînent* _____ au restaurant.

1. Patrick et Anne sont bilingues. Ils _____ français et anglais.

2. Jacques _____ une crêpe.

3. Est-ce que tu _____ bien au ping-pong?

4. Nous _____ un film à la télé.

5. Vous _____ un concert de rock.

6. Vous êtes français, n'est-ce pas? Est-ce que vous _____ à Paris?

7. Béatrice, est-ce que tu _____ dans une chorale *(choir)*?

8. Le samedi, mon copain et moi, nous _____ dans un supermarché.

5. Non! (12 points)

Complete the answers to the following questions with a NEGATIVE verb.

1. Est-ce que tu voyages souvent?

   Non, je _____ souvent.

2. Est-ce que Paul nage bien?

   Non, il _____ bien.

3. Est-ce que vous invitez Vincent?

   Non, nous _____ Vincent.

4. Est-ce que les touristes visitent la cathédrale?

   Non, ils _____ la cathédrale.

6. The Right Question (12 points)

Write the questions that correspond to the following answers and ask for the underlined information. Use **tu** in your questions.

1. _____?

   Je parle <u>à ma tante.</u>

2. _____?

   Je travaille <u>dans *(in)* un restaurant.</u>

3. _____?

   J'écoute <u>un CD de rock.</u>

4. _____?

   J'organise une boum <u>le samedi 15 mars.</u>

Part III. Written Expression

7. Composition (20 points)

On this part of the test, you can express yourself freely. However, use only the vocabulary and the expressions that you know in French.

Le week-end

Write a paragraph of five or six sentences describing what you and your friends do on weekends.

Le week-end, _____

_____

_____

_____

_____

_____

_____

_____

_____

_____

Nom _____

Classe _____ Date _____

Discovering
FRENCH
Nouveau!

Unité 3
Resources

Unit Test Form B

B L E U

UNIT TEST 3 (Lessons 5, 6, 7, 8)

FORM B

Part I. Listening Comprehension

1. The Logical Answer (20 points)

You will hear a series of ten questions. Listen carefully to each question and select the most logical answer on your test sheet. Circle the corresponding letter: a, b, or c. You will hear each question twice.

Modèle: [Quelle heure est-il?]
  a. Vendredi.
  b. Il fait beau.
  c. Deux heures et demie.

1. a. En ville.
   b. Très bien.
   c. Elle est canadienne.

2. a. Oui, elle est là-bas.
   b. Oui, elle est en classe.
   c. Non, elle travaille.

3. a. Oui, ils aiment nager.
   b. Oui, ils jouent aux jeux vidéo.
   c. Oui, ils font une promenade.

4. a. À six heures.
   b. Au restaurant.
   c. Dans *(in)* dix minutes.

5. a. Samedi, le 3 novembre.
   b. Avec mon copain.
   c. Oui, j'aime danser.

6. a. Je téléphone.
   b. Je suis au cinéma.
   c. Je ne fais pas attention.

7. a. Souvent.
   b. Rarement.
   c. Très bien.

8. a. Oui, bien sûr.
   b. Oui, Valérie est d'accord.
   c. Oui, il est avec moi.

9. a. Je n'écoute pas la radio.
   b. Je dois étudier.
   c. Je suis à la maison.

10. a. Oui, je joue au foot.
    b. Non, je n'aime pas chanter.
    c. D'accord, mais je ne joue pas bien.

Nom _____

Classe _____ Date _____ _____

Part II. Language

2. The Right Choice (12 points)

Choose the word or expression which logically completes each of the following sentences. Circle the corresponding letter: a, b, or c.

1. Catherine, est-ce que tu es française ___ canadienne?
   a. et
   b. ou
   c. souvent

2. Luis parle anglais. Il parle espagnol ___.
   a. aussi
   b. avec
   c. mais

3. Pierre n'est pas à la maison. Il est ___ cinéma avec une copine.
   a. à
   b. au
   c. en

4. J'habite ___.
   a. ou
   b. où
   c. ici

5. Nicolas regarde ___ télévision.
   a. —
   b. la
   c. à la

6. Sylvie joue ___ tennis avec Michelle.
   a. à
   b. au
   c. le

7. Marc ne danse pas bien. Il danse ___.
   a. mal
   b. aussi
   c. maintenant

8. Je regrette, mais je ne suis pas ___ avec toi!
   a. rarement
   b. en ville
   c. d'accord

9. Un jour, ___ visiter Montréal.
   a. j'aime
   b. je préfère
   c. je voudrais

10. Je ne regarde pas la télé. Je ___ étudier!
    a. dois
    b. peux
    c. n'aime pas

11. Vous parlez français, ___?
    a. pas
    b. mais non
    c. n'est-ce pas

12. Dis, Émilie, ___ est-ce que tu téléphones?
    a. qui
    b. à qui
    c. de qui

Nom _____

Classe _____ Date _____

Discovering
FRENCH
Nouveau!

B L E U

Unité 3
Resources

Unit Test Form B

3. Être or Faire? (8 points)

Complete the following sentences with the appropriate forms of **être** or **faire**.

1. Nous _____ au cinéma.

2. Qu'est-ce que vous _____ samedi?

3. Les élèves _____ en classe.

4. Tu _____ un match de tennis avec un copain.

4. The Right Activity (16 points)

Complete each of the following sentences with the appropriate form of one of the verbs in the box. Be logical.

chanter	danser	dîner	écouter	habiter
jouer	manger	parler	regarder	travailler

▶ Il est sept heures. Antoine et Sylvie *dînent* _____ au restaurant.

1. Madame Renaud, est-ce que vous _____ français à la maison?

2. Jean-Louis _____ une pizza.

3. Marc et moi, nous _____ souvent aux jeux vidéo.

4. Thomas et Claire _____ une comédie à la télé.

5. Tu _____ un concert à la radio.

6. Tu es américain et tu _____ à Boston, n'est-ce pas?

7. Alice et François _____ le tango.

8. Monsieur Rimbaud est ingénieur *(engineer)*. Il _____ pour Renault.

5. Non! (12 points)

Complete the answers to the following questions with a NEGATIVE verb.

1. Est-ce que tu téléphones à Catherine?

   Non, je _____ à Catherine.

2. Est-ce que Monsieur Renaud dîne en ville?

   Non, il _____ en ville.

3. Est-ce que vous étudiez l'anglais?

   Non, nous _____ l'anglais.

4. Est-ce que Sylvie et Claire voyagent beaucoup?

   Non, elles _____ beaucoup.

Discovering
FRENCH *Nouveau!*

BLEU

6. The Right Question (12 points)

Write the questions that correspond to the following answers and ask for the underlined information. Use **tu** in your questions.

1. _____?
   Je téléphone <u>à ma copine Léa</u>.

2. _____?
   Je mange <u>une glace</u>.

3. _____?
   J'étudie le japonais <u>parce que je voudrais visiter le Japon</u>.

4. _____?
   Je chante <u>très bien</u>.

Part III. Written Expression

7. Composition (20 points)

On this part of the test, you can express yourself freely. However, use only the vocabulary and the expressions that you know in French.

Activités

Describe what you and your friends do or do not do at certain times and in certain places. Complete the following sentences with expressions of your choice.

À la maison, je _____

    Je ne (n') _____

Le week-end, mes copains et moi, nous _____

    Nous ne (n') _____

En classe, les élèves _____

    Ils ne (n') _____

Nom _____

Classe _____ Date _____ _____

Discovering
FRENCH
Nouveau!

B L E U

Unité 3
Resources

Unit Test Part III (Alternate)
Cultural Awareness

Part III. Cultural Awareness (Alternate) FORMS A and B

7. Culture (20 points)

Choose the completion which best reflects the cultural information that you read about in this unit. Circle the corresponding letter: a, b, or c.

1. A French **collège** is the equivalent of an American . . .
   a. middle school.
   b. junior college.
   c. state university.

2. In general, French middle school students do not have classes on . . .
   a. Monday mornings.
   b. Wednesday afternoons.
   c. Friday afternoons.

3. A **lycée** is . . .
   a. a sports complex.
   b. a high school.
   c. a large auditorium.

4. The sport that French people call **foot** is known in the United States as . . .
   a. hiking.
   b. soccer.
   c. football.

5. When the French talk about their **portable,** they are referring to their . . .
   a. cell phone.
   b. computer.
   c. radio.

6. When French teenagers go to **une boum,** they are going to . . .
   a. an outdoor concert.
   b. a music store.
   c. a party at a friend's house.

7. The French **Minitel** was a precursor of . . .
   a. satellite TV.
   b. the cell phone.
   c. the Internet.

8. In recent years, France has welcomed many Southeast Asian immigrants from . . .
   a. Burma.
   b. Thailand.
   c. Vietnam.

9. Senegal is a country which has French as its official language. Senegal is located in . . .
   a. the Middle East.
   b. Southern Asia.
   c. Western Africa.

10. Youssou N'Dour is an internationally known . . .
    a. movie star.
    b. musician.
    c. writer.

Nom _____

Classe _____ Date _____

UNITÉ 3   Listening Comprehension Performance Test

Partie A. Conversations

This part of the Listening Comprehension Performance Test will let you see how well you understand spoken French. You will hear five short conversations. Look at your Listening Comprehension Performance Test Answer Sheet and read the corresponding questions. After you have heard each conversation the second time, select the correct answer and mark the corresponding letter (a, b, c, or d) on your answer sheet.

1. Listen to the following conversation between two friends.
   What do we know about the boy who is speaking?
   a. He is French.
   b. He lives in Paris.
   c. He does not like to speak French.
   d. He is from Montreal.

2. Listen to the following conversation between Thomas and his sister Cécile.
   What does Cécile want to do?
   a. To go for a walk.
   b. To stay home.
   c. To watch TV.
   d. To do her homework.

3. Listen to the following conversation between two friends.
   Where does the conversation take place?
   a. At school.
   b. In the street.
   c. At a party.
   d. At a movie theater.

4. Listen to the following phone conversation between Marc and Caroline.
   Whom does Marc want to talk to?
   a. To Caroline.
   b. To Caroline's brother.
   c. To a friend of Caroline's.
   d. To a friend of Caroline's brother.

5. Listen to the following conversation between Jérôme and Alice.
   Why does Alice turn down Jérôme's invitation to play tennis?
   a. She is tired.
   b. She is upset at Jérôme.
   c. She does not know how to play.
   d. She has other plans.

Nom _____

Classe _____ Date _____

Discovering
FRENCH *Nouveau!*

BLEU

Unité 3
Resources

Listening Comprehension
Performance Test

Partie B. Questions et réponses

This part of the Listening Comprehension Performance Test will let you see how well you can handle French questions. You will hear your French friend François ask you five questions. Listen carefully. Then look at your Listening Comprehension Performance Test Answer Sheet and select the MOST LOGICAL answer to each question. Mark the corresponding letter (a, b, c, or d) on your answer sheet. You will hear each question twice.

6. You and François are walking past the tennis court.
   You reply:
   a. Oui, très souvent.
   b. Pas très bien. Et toi?
   c. Avec mon ami Jérôme.
   d. Non, je n'aime pas jouer.

7. You and François are walking down the street.
   You reply:
   a. Je fais attention.
   b. J'organise une boum.
   c. Non, il n'est pas là.
   d. Oui, il fait une promenade.

8. You and François are at a café.
   You reply:
   a. Oui, d'accord.
   b. Moi aussi, je parle avec elle.
   c. Oui, elle parle français.
   d. Elle est à la maison.

9. Soccer practice is over and you are talking with your teammates.
   You reply:
   a. Oui, nous dînons au restaurant.
   b. Non, je ne suis pas avec vous.
   c. Je regrette, mais je dois étudier.
   d. Oui, j'aime jouer au foot.

10. You and your best friend are talking before class begins.
    You reply:
    a. Nous nageons et nous jouons au tennis.
    b. Oui, nous aimons être en vacances.
    c. Non, nous sommes en classe.
    d. Non, je n'aime pas voyager.

Discovering
FRENCH
Nouveau!

B L E U

UNITÉ 3 Speaking Performance Test

1. Conversations

In this part of the Speaking Performance Test, I will describe a situation and then ask you some related questions. In your answers, use the vocabulary and structures you have learned. Use your imagination.

CONVERSATION A   UNITÉ 3

I would like to help you find a French pen pal, but first I would like to ask you a few questions.

- Comment t'appelles-tu?
- Où est-ce que tu habites?
- Est-ce que tu aimes parler français?
- Pourquoi est-ce que tu étudies le français?

CONVERSATION B   UNITÉ 3

You and I are working on a skit for school. You have phoned me to see if we can get together tonight to practice. I am asking you some questions.

- Es-tu à la maison maintenant?
- Qu'est-ce que tu fais?
- À quelle heure est-ce que tu dînes?
- À quelle heure est-ce que tu veux travailler?

CONVERSATION C   UNITÉ 3

I would like to invite you to my home in Quebec this summer. I have a few questions about what kinds of things you like to do.

- Est-ce que tu joues au tennis?
- Est-ce que tu nages bien ou mal?
- Est-ce que tu aimes voyager?
- Est-ce que tu veux visiter Québec avec moi?

Nom _____

Classe _____ Date _____ _____

Discovering
FRENCH
Nouveau!

B L E U

Unité 3
Resources

Speaking Performance Test

CONVERSATION D   UNITÉ 3

I am looking for your sister Caroline, but cannot find her.
Please answer my questions.

- Est-ce qu'elle étudie?
- Est-ce qu'elle est au cinéma?
- Où est-ce qu'elle est?
- Qu'est-ce qu'elle fait?

CONVERSATION E   UNITÉ 3

I am trying to find people for the French talent show, and
would like to know if you are interested.

- Est-ce que tu danses bien?
- Est-ce que tu veux danser dans le show?
- Est-ce que tu aimes chanter?
- Comment est-ce que tu chantes?

CONVERSATION F   UNITÉ 3

I am a journalist writing an article on what young
Americans do in their free time. I would like to ask you
some questions about what you and your friends do on
weekends.

- Est-ce que vous travaillez?
- Est-ce que vous regardez la télé?
- Est-ce que vous écoutez la radio?
- Est-ce que vous jouez aux jeux vidéo?

Nom _____

Classe _____ Date _____

2. Tu as la parole

In this part of the Speaking Performance Test, you have the opportunity to make three comments about a familiar topic. Use only the structures and vocabulary you know. Use your imagination.

TU AS LA PAROLE (A)   UNITÉ 3

You are at a party and have met a French student, Sophie. Ask her . . .

- where she lives
- if she speaks English
- if she likes to travel

TU AS LA PAROLE (B)   UNITÉ 3

You have invited Nicolas, a French friend, to spend Saturday afternoon at your house. Ask him . . .

- if he likes to watch TV
- if he wants to play video games
- what he wants to eat

TU AS LA PAROLE (C)   UNITÉ 3

Your friend Valérie has invited you to have dinner with her tonight, but unfortunately you have other plans. Tell Valérie . . .

- that you are sorry
- that you cannot have dinner with her
- that you have to do something else (for example, study, work, . . .)

Nom _____

Classe _____ Date _____

Discovering FRENCH *Nouveau!*

B L E U

Unité 3
Resources

Speaking Performance Test

TU AS LA PAROLE (D) UNITÉ 3

Think about THREE people and tell me where they are right now (or where they are not). You may consider the following people:

- mon copain (ma copine)
- mon frère (ma soeur)
- mon (ma) prof de français

TU AS LA PAROLE (E) UNITÉ 3

You are already thinking about the next vacation. Tell me TWO things you like to do and ONE thing you do not like to do. For example, you might say . . .

- on vacation you like to swim
- you like to travel
- you don't like to study

TU AS LA PAROLE (F) UNITÉ 3

Tell me TWO things you want to do tonight and ONE thing you do not want to do. For example, you might say . . .

- you want to watch TV
- you want to listen to the radio
- you don't want to work

UNITÉ 3   Reading Comprehension Performance Test

Look at the following ad from a French newspaper. Then read the question. On your Answer Sheet, mark the correct answer by placing a check next to the corresponding letter.

1. What does the ad want us to do?
   a. Be kind to animals.
   b. Listen to rock music.
   c. Buy a certain type of TV set.

Look at the following brochure cover. Then read the question. On your Answer Sheet, mark the correct answer by placing a check next to the corresponding letter.

2. To whom is this brochure
   primarily addressed?
   a. To businesspeople.
   b. To tourists.
   c. To construction workers.

Nom _____

Classe _____ Date _____

Discovering
FRENCH
Nouveau!

B L E U

Unité 3 Reading Comprehension Resources Performance Test

Read carefully the following ad from a French newspaper. Then read the questions. On your Answer Sheet, mark the correct answers by placing a check next to the corresponding letter.

3. What is being promoted in this ad?
   a. A TV set.
   b. An ocean trip.
   c. A computer.

4. What are people invited to do?
   a. Watch a sports event.
   b. Watch game shows.
   c. Play electronic games.

Read the following note that Olivier wrote to his cousin Patrick. Then read the questions. On your Answer Sheet, mark the correct answers by placing a check next to the corresponding letter.

5. Why did Olivier write Patrick?
   a. To accept his invitation.
   b. To decline his invitation.
   c. To invite him to a new restaurant.

6. Where is Olivier going to go on Saturday?
   a. To a party.
   b. To the movies.
   c. To a concert.

7. With whom is Olivier going out on Saturday?
   a. With his cousin.
   b. With a girlfriend.
   c. With a classmate.

> Mardi
>
> Cher Patrick,
>   Merci de ton invitation. Je voudrais bien
> dîner au restaurant samedi soir avec toi, mais je
> ne peux pas. J'ai un rendez-vous avec une copine.
> Nous sommes invités à une boum. Excuse-moi!
>
>   Olivier

Nom _____

Classe _____ Date _____

Read carefully the following request for pen pals that appeared in a French teen magazine. Then read the questions. On your Answer Sheet, mark the correct answers by placing a check next to the corresponding letter.

Je m'appelle Valérie Legrand et j'habite à Toulouse. J'aime nager, jouer au tennis et danser. Je parle un peu anglais et je voudrais correspondre avec filles ou garçons de nationalité américaine pour échanger posters et CD. Joindre une photo, s'il vous plaît.

> Valérie Legrand
> 35, rue d'Austerlitz
> 31000 Toulouse

Je m'appelle Nicolas Fournier et j'habite à Strasbourg. J'aime écouter la radio et regarder

8. According to her letter, which of the following does Valérie prefer?
   a. Reading and television.
   b. Sports and dancing.
   c. Traveling abroad.

9. Does Valérie speak English?
   a. Yes, a little.
   b. Yes, very well.
   c. No, not at all.

10. Why does Valérie want to have pen pals?
   a. So she can practice her English.
   b. So she can visit the United States one day.
   c. So she can trade posters and CDs.

Nom _____

Classe _____ Date _____

Discovering FRENCH *Nouveau!*

BLEU

Unité 3
Resources

Writing Performance Test

UNITÉ 3 Writing Performance Test

A. Lettre à Stéphanie (10 points)

Write a short note to your French pen pal Stéphanie introducing yourself. Give her the following information:

- your name
- the city or town where you live
- what sport(s) you play

Sign your name

> Chère Stéphanie,
>
> _____
> _____
> _____
> _____
> _____
> _____
> _____
>   _____

B. Préférences (20 points)

Make a list of three things you like to do and two things you do not like to do.

▶ LIKES: **J'aime téléphoner.**

   DISLIKES: **Je n'aime pas danser.**

LIKES: • _____
     • _____
     • _____

DISLIKES: • _____
       • _____

Unité 3 Resources

Writing Performance Test

Nom _____

Classe _____ Date _____

Discovering
FRENCH
Nouveau!

B L E U

C. Activités (30 points)

List one thing you and your friends do and one thing that you do not do in the following circumstances. Name eight different activities.

À la maison, nous _____.

Nous ne/n' _____.

En classe, nous _____.

Nous ne/n' _____.

Le week-end, nous _____.

Nous ne/n' _____.

En vacances, nous _____.

Nous ne/n' _____.

D. Questions (20 points)

An exchange student from Canada is arriving at your school next week. You would like to know more about her. Prepare a list of four questions using the following suggestions as a guide. (If you prefer, you may make up your own questions.)

? ? ? ?

- Where do you live?
- Do you speak English?
- Do you like to travel?
- Do you want to visit *[name of your city]* with me?

- _____
- _____
- _____
- _____

E. Note à Christophe (20 points)

Your friend Christophe has invited you to play tennis today, but unfortunately you have to work. Write him a short note explaining the situation. Ask him for a rain check for next Saturday.

Tell Christophe that . . .
- you are sorry
- you cannot play tennis with him today
- you have to work

Ask Christophe . . .
- what he is doing on Saturday
- if he wants to play with you at two o'clock

Sign your note.

Christophe,

_____

_____

_____

_____

_____

_____

_____

Nom _____

Classe _____ Date _____

Discovering FRENCH Nouveau!

BLEU

UNITÉ 3 Multiple Choice Test Items

Leçon 5

1. —Tu aimes parler anglais?
   —Oui, mais je préfère _____.
   a. parler français
   b. au volley
   c. parler anglais

2. Tu aimes _____ la radio?
   a. regarder
   b. travailler
   c. écouter

3. J'aime _____ au café.
   a. voyager
   b. manger
   c. nager

4. Est-ce que tu aimes _____ au foot?
   a. travailler
   b. jouer
   c. téléphoner

5. Avec mon copain le week-end, je n'aime pas _____.
   a. voyager
   b. regarder la télé
   c. travailler

6. —Est-ce que tu aimes parler espagnol?
   —Non, je n'aime pas _____.
   a. parler espagnol
   b. parler français
   c. parler anglais

7. —Est-ce que tu aimes écouter le professeur?
   —Non, je préfère _____.
   a. écouter un CD
   b. travailler
   c. étudier

8. —Est-ce que tu veux jouer au tennis avec moi?
   —Oui, _____.
   a. je veux bien
   b. je ne peux pas
   c. je dois étudier

9. —Tu veux jouer au basket?
   —Non, _____.
   a. je veux bien
   b. je regrette
   c. d'accord

Nom _____

Classe _____ Date _____

Discovering
FRENCH
Nouveau!

BLEU

10. —Tu veux dîner avec moi?
    —Oui, _____.
    a. je veux bien
    b. je regrette
    c. je ne veux pas

11. —Tu as faim?
    —Oui, je veux _____.
    a. jouer aux jeux vidéo
    b. parler espagnol
    c. dîner au restaurant

12. Tu voudrais _____ au tennis avec ta copine?
    a. parler
    b. jouer
    c. voyager

13. Je ne veux pas _____ le CD.
    a. regarder
    b. manger
    c. écouter

14. —Je voudrais _____ à six heures.
    —Tu as faim?
    a. dîner au restaurant
    b. jouer aux jeux vidéo
    c. téléphoner

15. —Est-ce que tu veux dîner au restaurant?
    — Non merci, je dois _____.
    a. chanter
    b. danser
    c. travailler

16. Je voudrais _____ un croissant.
    a. jouer
    b. voyager
    c. manger

17. —Est-ce que tu veux _____ une glace?
    a. chanter
    b. manger
    c. écouter

18. —Est-ce que tu peux étudier avec moi?
    —Oui, _____.
    a. je dois étudier avec ma copine
    b. je regrette
    c. d'accord

19. —Est-ce que tu veux jouer aux jeux vidéo?
    —Non, _____.
    a. bien sûr
    b. je ne peux pas
    c. je veux bien

Nom _____

Classe _____ Date _____

Discovering
FRENCH
Nouveau!

B L E U

Unité 3
Resources

Multiple Choice Test Items

20. —Est-ce que tu voudrais travailler avec mon père samedi?
    —Non, _____.
    a. je dois étudier
    b. bien sûr
    c. je veux bien

Leçon 6

1. Je _____ de Montréal.
   a. sommes
   b. suis
   c. est

2. —Luc est de Boston?
   —Oui, il _____ de Boston.
   a. es
   b. est
   c. êtes

3. —Tu _____ française?
   —Oui, je suis de Paris.
   a. es
   b. êtes
   c. sont

4. Non, nous ne _____ pas français.
   a. sommes
   b. sont
   c. êtes

5. Toi et Vincent, vous _____ de Tours?
   a. sont
   b. es
   c. êtes

6. Madame Dumont, est-ce que _____ anglaise?
   a. vous êtes
   b. tu es
   c. il est

7. Pierre et Jean-Marie
   a. elles
   b. vous
   c. ils

8. Madame Moreau et Annie
   a. tu
   b. elles
   c. ils

9. Est-ce que Marc _____ en France?
   a. êtes
   b. es
   c. est

10. —Nous sommes d'accord?
    —Oui, _____.
    a. ils sont d'accord
    b. nous ne sommes pas d'accord
    c. nous sommes d'accord

11. Où est mon prof de français? Il est _____.
    a. huit heures
    b. en classe
    c. mon prof

12. Tu es au restaurant, _____?
    a. mais oui
    b. n'est-ce pas
    c. à la maison

13. Ton copain n'est pas en classe?
    a. Non, il est à la maison.
    b. Oui, il est en ville.
    c. Mais oui, il est en vacances.

14. Où _____ ta maison?
    a. suis
    b. êtes
    c. est

15. Luc et Claire _____ de Nice?
    a. est
    b. sommes
    c. sont

16. —Est-ce que vous êtes d'accord?
    —Oui, _____.
    a. nous sommes d'accord
    b. je veux bien
    c. n'est-ce pas

17. —Tu es curieux, n'est-ce pas?
    —Non, _____.
    a. tu n'es pas curieux
    b. je suis curieux
    c. je ne suis pas curieux

18. Ils sont en vacances en France.
    a. Ils sont ici.
    b. Ils sont en classe.
    c. Ils sont là-bas.

19. Marie-France est au café, _____?
    a. est-ce que
    b. n'est-ce pas
    c. mais non

Nom _____

Classe _____ Date _____ _____

Discovering
FRENCH
Nouveau!

BLEU

Unité 3
Resources

Multiple Choice Test Items

20. —Vous êtes là-bas?
—Non, _____.
   a. nous sommes ici
   b. je suis là-bas
   c. vous êtes là-bas

Leçon 7

1. Je _____ anglais.
   a. parle
   b. parles
   c. parlez

2. Tu _____ à Paris?
   a. habite
   b. habites
   c. habitez

3. Est-ce que ton copain _____ une boum?
   a. organisent
   b. organise
   c. organiser

4. Isabelle et Caroline _____ Marc et Paul.
   a. inviter
   b. invitent
   c. invitez

5. —Tu étudies au café?
—Oui, _____
   a. je n'étudie pas
   b. j'étudie
   c. tu étudies

6. Marc _____ au restaurant.
   a. visite
   b. dîne
   c. nage

7. Alain et Suzanne _____ à Strasbourg.
   a. habites
   b. habitez
   c. habitent

8. —José parle espagnol?
—Oui, _____.
   a. il parle espagnol
   b. elle ne parle pas espagnol
   c. il ne parle pas espagnol

9. —Vous chantez bien?
—Oui, _____
   a. vous chantez bien
   b. tu chantes bien
   c. nous chantons bien

Nom _____

Classe _____ Date _____

10. Est-ce que Jean-Paul et Claire _____ le professeur?
    a. travaillent
    b. écoutent
    c. parlent

11. Nous ne _____ pas en France.
    a. voyagez
    b. voyageons
    c. voyagent

12. Je dois _____
    a. étudie
    b. étudier
    c. étudiez

13. —Tu aimes danser?
    —Non, _____.
    a. tu n'aimes pas danser
    b. j'aime danser
    c. je n'aime pas danser

14. —Tu aimes le foot?
    —Non, _____ le foot.
    a. j'aime
    b. tu n'aimes pas
    c. je n'aime pas

15. Je _____ à Sophie.
    a. regarde
    b. téléphone
    c. danse

16. Non, il n'aime pas _____.
    a. étudier
    b. étudie
    c. étudies

17. Est-ce qu'elle chante souvent?
    —Non, elle chante _____.
    a. rarement
    b. beaucoup
    c. toujours

18. —Les Yankees jouent au football?
    —Non, _____.
    a. ils ne jouent pas aux jeux vidéo
    b. ils ne jouent pas au baseball
    c. ils ne jouent pas au football

19. Je voudrais _____ en France.
    a. voyage
    b. voyagez
    c. voyager

Nom _____

Classe _____ Date _____

Discovering
FRENCH *Nouveau!*

B L E U

Unité 3
Resources

Multiple Choice Test Items

20. Philippe aime chanter mais il préfère _____.
    a. danse
    b. danser
    c. inviter

Leçon 8

1. —_____ est Michelle?
    —Au cinéma.
    a. Qui
    b. Alors
    c. Où

2. _____ est-ce que tu nages? Bien ou mal?
    a. Comment
    b. Pourquoi
    c. Qui

3. —_____ est-ce que tu n'aimes pas chanter?
    —Parce que je chante mal.
    a. Pourquoi
    b. Comment
    c. Qu'est-ce que

4. _____ est-ce que tu travailles? À trois heures?
    a. Comment
    b. Où
    c. À quelle heure

5. _____ est-ce que ton copain organise une fête?
    a. Quand
    b. Qu'est-ce que
    c. Parce que

6. —Pourquoi est-ce que vous étudiez le français?
    —_____ je veux voyager en France.
    a. Quand
    b. Parce que
    c. Où

7. _____ est à la maison?
    a. Qui
    b. Où
    c. À qui

8. —Marie dîne avec un copain.
    —Ah bon? _____?
    a. À qui
    b. Avec qui
    c. Pour qui

9. _____ est-ce que Paul téléphone?
    a. Qui
    b. De qui
    c. À qui

Nom _____

Classe _____ Date _____ _____

Discovering
FRENCH
Nouveau!

B L E U

10. _____ est-ce que tu étudies?
    a. De qui
    b. Avec qui
    c. À qui

11. Qu'est-ce que tu _____?
    a. téléphones
    b. fais
    c. habites

12. Avec _____ est-ce que Paul dîne?
    a. où
    b. qui
    c. quelle heure

13. _____ vous regardez?
    a. De qui
    b. Qu'est-ce qu'
    c. Qu'est-ce que

14. _____ elle mange?
    —Elle mange une pizza.
    a. Qui
    b. Qu'est-ce qu'
    c. Comment

15. Où _____?
    a. est-ce que
    b. est-il
    c. au café

16. —Quand _____ en France?
    —En octobre.
    a. voyagez-vous
    b. vous voyagez
    c. voyagez

17. Mes amies _____ un voyage en été.
    a. faire
    b. faites
    c. font

18. Qu'est-ce que vous _____ maintenant?
    a. faites
    b. font
    c. faisons

19. Nous _____ une promenade.
    a. faire
    b. faisons
    c. faites

20. Est-ce que tu _____ attention quand le prof parle?
    a. fais
    b. faisons
    c. faites

Discovering
FRENCH *Nouveau!*

B L E U

UNITÉ 3   Comprehensive Test 1 (Units 1, 2, 3)   **FORM A**

Part I. Listening Comprehension (25 points)

1. Loto! (5 points)

You and your friends are playing French **Loto.** You will hear five numbers called out. Listen carefully to each item and select the appropriate number of your test paper. Then, blacken the corresponding letter—a, b, or c—on your answer sheet. You will hear each item twice.

Modèle: [Dix]

      a. 2 (b.) 10   c. 6

1. a. 45	b. 25	c. 35	4. a. 3	b. 13	c. 30
2. a. 15	b. 51	c. 59	5. a. 71	b. 61	c. 91
3. a. 98	b. 18	c. 88			

2. Quelle heure est-il? (5 points)

You will hear five short conversations in which a time is mentioned. Listen carefully to each item to determine if the clock on your test paper matches the time you hear. Then, blacken the corresponding letter—a. **oui** or b. **non**—on your answer sheet. You will hear each item twice.

Modèle: [—Quelle heure est-il?
       —Il est une heure.]

    (a.) oui   b. non

8.

    a. oui   b. non

6.

    a. oui   b. non

9.

    a. oui   b. non

7.

    a. oui   b. non

10.

    a. oui   b. non

Nom _____

Classe _____ Date _____

3. Invitations (5 points)

You will hear five short conversations. In each one, a student is asking a friend to do something. Listen carefully to the invitation to determine if the friend a. **accepts,** b. **declines,** or c. **does neither.** Then, blacken the corresponding letter—a, b, or c—on your answer sheet. You will hear each item twice.

Modèle: [—Est-ce que tu veux jouer au tennis?
—Oui, merci.]
(a.) accepts   b. declines   c. does neither

11. a. accepts
     b. declines
     c. does neither

12. a. accepts
     b. declines
     c. does neither

13. a. accepts
     b. declines
     c. does neither

14. a. accepts
     b. declines
     c. does neither

15. a. accepts
     b. declines
     c. does neither

4. La réponse logique (10 points)

You will hear a series of ten questions. Listen carefully to each question and select the most logical response on your test paper. Then, blacken the corresponding letter—a, b, or c—on your answer sheet. You will hear each question twice.

Modèle: [Quel temps fait-il?]
a. C'est le printemps.   (b.) Il pleut.   c. Il est trois heures.

16. a. C'est Roger.
     b. C'est une copine.
     c. C'est mon prof.

17. a. Ça va, merci.
     b. Lundi.
     c. À demain!

18. a. Oui, elle habite à Paris.
     b. Non, elle est anglaise.
     c. Non, il est français.

19. a. Bien sûr, je voudrais un steak.
     b. Oui, donne-moi une salade.
     c. Mais oui, j'ai soif!

20. a. Il a dix ans.
     b. Ça fait dix euros.
     c. A dix heures.

21. a. Mais oui, il fait un voyage.
     b. Oui, c'est l'été.
     c. Oui, il fait très mauvais.

22. a. À huit heures.
     b. Au café.
     c. Parce que j'aime manger.

23. a. Bien sûr, je veux bien.
     b. J'écoute mon baladeur.
     c. Je suis de Tours.

24. a. Je téléphone souvent.
     b. À oncle Bernard.
     c. Zut! Je dois téléphoner.

25. a. Super! Je danse au concert.
     b. Je chante rarement.
     c. Comme ci, comme ça. Et toi?

Nom _____

Classe _____ Date _____ _____

Discovering
FRENCH
Nouveau!

BLEU

Unité 3
Resources

Comprehensive Test 1
Form A

Part II. Language and Communication (40 points)

5. Au café (5 points)

François and Isabelle are watching people at **Le Sélect** café. Read portions of their conversation and decide which word from the box correctly completes each sentence. Then, mark the corresponding letter—a, b, or c—on your answer sheet.

> a. **le**   b. **la**   c. **l'**

26. —Tu connais ___ dame?
    a. ❏   b. ❏   c. ❏

27. —Comment s'appelle ___ monsieur?
    a. ❏   b. ❏   c. ❏

28. —Voilà ___ amie de Juliette!
    a. ❏   b. ❏   c. ❏

29. —Qui est ___ fille là-bas?
    a. ❏   b. ❏   c. ❏

30. —Et ça, c'est ___ prof de français!
    a. ❏   b. ❏   c. ❏

6. L'été (5 points)

People are busy in the summertime! Read the following sentences and choose the *one* word that correctly completes each item. Then, mark the corresponding letter—a, b, c, or d—on your answer sheet.

31. Aujourd'hui, nous ___ au tennis.
    a. jouer
    b. jouez
    c. jouons
    d. joue

32. Oui, j'adore ___ des promenades.
    a. fais
    b. fait
    c. faire
    d. font

33. Tu ___ nager, n'est-ce pas?
    a. veux
    b. fais
    c. es
    d. joues

34. Cet été, Éric et Vincent ___ en France.
    a. es
    b. être
    c. êtes
    d. sont

35. Super! Qui ___ la boum?
    a. organises
    b. organise
    c. organiser
    d. organisent

Nom _____

Classe _____ Date _____

7. Ma copine Sylvie (5 points)

Sylvie is an active person. Read the following sentences about her and decide which word from the box correctly completes each item. Then, mark the corresponding letter—a, b, or c—on your answer sheet.

a. **est** b. **a** c. **fait**

36. Oui, elle ____ 16 ans.
    a. ❑   b. ❑   c. ❑

37. Aujourd'hui, Sylvie ____ une promenade en ville.
    a. ❑   b. ❑   c. ❑

38. Elle mange au café parce qu'elle ____ très faim.
    a. ❑   b. ❑   c. ❑

39. Mais oui, Sylvie ____ une fille active!
    a. ❑   b. ❑   c. ❑

40. Elle ____ un match de tennis avec Éric et Isabelle.
    a. ❑   b. ❑   c. ❑

8. Une interview (5 points)

Marc is interviewing Stéphanie, an exchange student, for his school newspaper. Read parts of their conversation and select the correct question word to complete Stéphanie's answer. Then, mark the corresponding letter—a, b, c, d, or e—on your answer sheet. (Note: Some words may be used more than once and others not at all.)

a. **qui** b. **qu'** c. **comment** d. **où** e. **quand**

41. —____ est-ce que tu habites? —À Fort-de-France.
    a. ❑   b. ❑   c. ❑   d. ❑   e. ❑

42. —Avec ____ est-ce que tu joues au volley? —Avec ma copine Doris.
    a. ❑   b. ❑   c. ❑   d. ❑   e. ❑

43. —____ est-ce que tu nages? —Le week-end, d'habitude (usually).
    a. ❑   b. ❑   c. ❑   d. ❑   e. ❑

44. —À ____ est-ce que tu téléphones? —À mes copains.
    a. ❑   b. ❑   c. ❑   d. ❑   e. ❑

45. —____ est-ce que tu fais à l'école? —J'étudie, bien sûr!
    a. ❑   b. ❑   c. ❑   d. ❑   e. ❑

Nom _____

Classe _____ Date _____

Discovering
FRENCH
Nouveau!

B L E U

Unité 3
Resources

Comprehensive Test 1
Form A

9. L'intrus (7 points)

Which word is the intruder? Read each list carefully to determine the word that does *not* belong with the other three. Then, mark the corresponding letter—a, b, c, or d—on your answer sheet.

46. a. soda   b. glace   c. chocolat chaud   d. limonade
47. a. hiver   b. temps   c. automne   d. printemps
48. a. lundi   b. décembre   c. samedi   d. dimanche
49. a. dame   b. prof   c. chat   d. copain
50. a. rarement   b. souvent   c. toujours   d. demain
51. a. quarante   b. quand   c. quinze   d. quatre
52. a. chat   b. soir   c. chien   d. tigre

10. Allô! (8 points)

Awa is phoning her friends this weekend. Read her questions on the left and her friends' answers on the right. Then, select the most logical response and mark the corresponding letter—a, b, c, d, or e—on your answer sheet.

samedi

53. Est-ce que tu joues au volley?
54. Comment est-ce que tu chantes?
55. Est-ce que vous invitez Luc à la boum?
56. Ta soeur est à la maison?

a. Très mal. Et toi?
b. Bien sûr! Il adore danser.
c. Je suis à la maison.
d. Oui, mais pas très bien.
e. Elle est en classe.

dimanche

57. Ta soeur est là?
58. Tu connais M. Bernard?
59. Pourquoi est-ce que Luc est à Boston?
60. À quelle heure est-ce que tu joues?

a. Il étudie l'anglais.
b. À midi.
c. Mais non. Qui est-ce?
d. Non, elle est en ville.
e. À bientôt.

11. Situations (5 points)

What would you say in the following situations? Read each item carefully and select the *best* expression. Then, mark the appropriate letter—a, b, or c—on your answer sheet.

61. *You want to know who that student talking to Claude is. You ask:*
    a. Comment t'appelles-tu?
    b. Il s'appelle Claude?
    c. Comment s'appelle la fille?

62. *You would like to know what Pierre wants to do. You ask:*
    a. Qu'est-ce que tu veux faire?
    b. Avec qui est-ce que tu fais un match?
    c. Qu'est-ce que tu veux manger?

63. *Éric asks where you are from. You answer:*
    a. Moi, j'habite à Québec.
    b. Je suis à New York.
    c. Je suis de Boston. Et toi?

64. *You need to borrow five euros from a friend. You ask:*
    a. Prête-moi cinq euros, s'il te plaît.
    b. C'est tout? Ça fait cinq euros.
    c. Il coûte cinq euros.

65. *Isabelle asks you to go to the movies. You answer:*
    a. Oui, je suis au cinéma.
    b. D'accord, je veux bien.
    c. Je regarde un film maintenant.

Nom _____

Classe _____ Date _____

Discovering
FRENCH
Nouveau!

B L E U

Unité 3
Resources

Comprehensive Test 1
Form A

Part III. Reading Comprehension (20 points)

12. Quatre annonces (9 points)

Four young people are looking for pen pals. Read their messages and the conversations that follow, selecting the ad which *best* matches each exchange. Then, mark the corresponding letter—a, b, c, or d—on your answer sheet.

66. —Qu'est-ce que tu aimes faire?
    —J'aime beaucoup jouer au tennis.
    a. ❑   b. ❑   c. ❑   d. ❑

67. —Tu es canadienne?
    —Mais non, je suis française. Et toi?
    a. ❑   b. ❑   c. ❑   d. ❑

68. —Tu es français?
    —Oui, bien sûr!
    —Quel âge as-tu?
    —Moi, j'ai 15 ans.
    a. ❑   b. ❑   c. ❑   d. ❑

69. —Tu veux aller *(to go)* au match ou
    au concert?
    —Je préfère regarder le match.
    a. ❑   b. ❑   c. ❑   d. ❑

70. —Tu veux faire une promenade en
    ville?
    —Mais oui! Je voudrais voir un bon
    film.
    a. ❑   b. ❑   c. ❑   d. ❑

71. —Est-ce que tu veux correspondre avec les
    étudiants canadiens?
    —Euh . . . je préfère correspondre avec les
    étudiants anglais. D'accord?
    a. ❑   b. ❑   c. ❑   d. ❑

72. —Qui est-ce?
    —C'est Nathalie.
    —Quel âge a-t-elle?
    —Elle a 16 ans.
    a. ❑   b. ❑   c. ❑   d. ❑

73. —Allô, Éric? Qu'est-ce que tu fais
    maintenant?
    —J'écoute mes CD.
    a. ❑   b. ❑   c. ❑   d. ❑

74. —Je voudrais correspondre avec les
    étudiants de beaucoup de nationalités.
    a. ❑   b. ❑   c. ❑   d. ❑

a. Jeune° fille, 15 ans et demi, grande sportive, cherche° partenaires pour jouer au tennis.

young

is looking for

b. étudiant, 15 ans, aimant° le cinéma et la musique classique désire correspondre avec étudiants ou étudiantes du même° âge.

who likes

same

c. jeune Français, 16 ans, désire correspondre avec étudiant(e)s de toutes° nationalités pour échanger° cartes postales° et CD

all

to exchange

postcards

d. étudiante française, 16 ans, désire correspondre avec étudiants américains ou anglais.

Nom _____

Classe _____ Date _____

13. Une lettre de Christine (5 points)

You have just received a letter from Christine. Read her message carefully and decide whether the statements which follow are true (**vrai**) or false (**faux**). Then, mark the corresponding letter—a or b—on your answer sheet.

CT

Salut!

Je m'appelle Christine Tremblay et j'ai 15 ans. J'habite à Québec avec ma famille. À la maison, j'étudie beaucoup mais pas tout le temps *(all the time)*. Voici ce que j'aime faire:

J'aime les boums parce que j'adore danser (et manger)! J'aime aussi la musique, surtout le rock. Je préfère écouter la musique américaine.

J'aime les sports. En hiver je skie dans les Laurentides et en été je nage et je joue au tennis. Je joue assez *(rather)* bien mais je ne suis pas encore une championne! La fin de semaine *(weekend)*, j'aime faire des promenades à scooter. Ça, c'est l'fun!

J'aime assez bien mon école, surtout la classe d'anglais. Le prof est très sympa *(nice)*. Je n'aime pas trop les maths parce que le prof est très sévère.

À la maison, j'aime regarder les séries américaines à la télé. J'aime aussi écouter mes CD.

J'aime téléphoner à ma copine Mireille mais je téléphone rarement parce que ma mère proteste et je dois étudier. C'est dommage, n'est-ce pas?

Et toi, qu'est-ce que tu aimes faire? S'il te plaît, réponds-moi vite!

Amicalement,

Christine

---

75. Christine n'étudie pas souvent.	a. vrai	b. faux
76. Elle aime jouer au tennis en été.	a. vrai	b. faux
77. À l'école, elle préfère l'anglais.	a. vrai	b. faux
78. Elle aime regarder les séries françaises à la télé.	a. vrai	b. faux
79. Elle téléphone souvent à sa copine.	a. vrai	b. faux

Nom _____

Classe _____ Date _____

Discovering FRENCH *Nouveau!*

B L E U

Unité 3 Resources
Comprehensive Test 1
Form A

14. À la télé (6 points)

You are in France and want to watch TV. Read the television listing and the items which follow. Then, choose the correct answer and mark the corresponding letter—a, b, or c—on your answer sheet.

• In France, TV viewers have a choice of six main channels: **TF1, France 2, France 3, Cinquième Arte, M6,** and **Canal Plus.** (People who want to watch **Canal Plus** need to have a special decoding machine for which they pay a monthly fee.)
• Note that in TV listings, times are expressed using a 24-hour clock. In this system, 8 P.M. is **20.00 (vingt heures)**; 10 P.M. is **22.00 (vingt-deux heures).**

SÉLECTION DE LA SEMAINE　　VENDREDI

TF1

20.30 VARIÉTÉS
SALUT L'ARTISTE
émission présentée par
Yves Noël et Ophélie Winter

22.05 DOCUMENT
HISTOIRES NATURELLES

2 France

20.35 SÉRIE
HÔTEL DE POLICE
Le Gentil Monsieur
de Claude Barrois
avec Cécile Magnet

23.20 FILM
ALICE DANS LES VILLES
de Wim Wenders

france 3

21.30 SÉRIE
LE MASQUE
MADEMOISELLE EVELYNE
de Jean-Louis Fournier

23.45 CONCERT
MUSIQUES, MUSIQUE

france 5 arte

20.15 DOCUMENTAIRE
CENT ANS DE CINÉMA JAPONAIS

23.20 MAGAZINE
une vidéo inédite
DE BOB DYLAN

M6

20.30 FILM TV
LE MARIAGE DE MON MEILLEUR AMI
avec Julia Roberts

22.05 THÉÂTRE
RHINOCÉROS

CANAL+

20.30 FOOTBALL
CAEN - TOULOUSE
Championnat de France
28e journée

22.40 FILM
MALCOLM X
de Spike Lee

---

80. This TV listing is for ___.
   a. Monday
   b. Friday
   c. Saturday

81. At 8:30 viewers can watch ___.
   a. «Le Mariage de Mon Meilleur Ami»
   b. «Le Masque»
   c. «Hôtel de police»

82. There is a soccer match on ___.
   a. TF1
   b. Cinquième Arte
   c. Canal +

83. «Histoires naturelles» is a ___.
   a. comedy
   b. detective film
   c. documentary

84. There is *not* a weekly series on ___.
   a. France 3
   b. France 2
   c. M6

85. Overall, the *least* common type of programming is ___.
   a. featured movies
   b. weekly series
   c. sports events

Nom _____

Classe _____ Date _____

Discovering
FRENCH
Nouveau

B L E U

Part IV. Cultural Awareness (15 points)

15. Méli-mélo culturel (cultural jumble) (15 points)

How much do you know about French-speaking people and their everyday life? Read each sentence below and decide whether the item is true (**vrai**) or false (**faux**). Then, mark the corresponding letter—a or b—on your answer sheet.

86. a. vrai   b. faux   A **croissant** is a French candy bar.
87. a. vrai   b. faux   In France, **la famille** refers to all relatives, including aunts, uncles, grandparents and cousins.
88. a. vrai   b. faux   Martinique is a French island located in the South Pacific.
89. a. vrai   b. faux   French high school students generally do *not* have classes on Wednesday afternoons.
90. a. vrai   b. faux   To greet a woman teacher at school, French students usually say **Bonjour, ça va?**
91. a. vrai   b. faux   Youssou N'Dour is a famous musician from Senegal.
92. a. vrai   b. faux   In France, the most popular pets are birds.
93. a. vrai   b. faux   In a French **café,** the tip is usually included in the check.
94. a. vrai   b. faux   **Astérix** is the name of a French cartoon character.
95. a. vrai   b. faux   A French **collège** is the equivalent of an American junior college.
96. a. vrai   b. faux   In the province of Quebec, the majority of the population is French-speaking.
97. a. vrai   b. faux   A **portable** is a laptop computer.
98. a. vrai   b. faux   The **euro** is divided into 10 **cents** (or **centimes**).
99. a. vrai   b. faux   The second-largest French-speaking city in the world is Montreal.
100. a. vrai   b. faux   For French students, **la rentrée** is the first day of vacation.

Nom _____

Classe _____ Date _____

Discovering
FRENCH
Nouveau!

BLEU

UNITÉ 3 Comprehensive Test 1 (Units 1, 2, 3)   FORM B

Part I. Listening Comprehension (25 points)

1. Loto! (5 points)

You and your friends are playing French **Loto.** You will hear five numbers called out. Listen carefully to each item and select the appropriate number on your test paper. Then, blacken the corresponding letter—a, b, or c—on your answer sheet. You will hear each item twice.

Modèle: [Dix]
        a. 2. (b.) 10   c. 6

1. a. 2   b. 22   c. 12
2. a. 58   b. 15   c. 56
3. a. 72   b. 82   c. 92

4. a. 91   b. 61   c. 71
5. a. 76   b. 60   c. 16

2. Quelle heure est-il? (5 points)

You will hear five short conversations in which a time is mentioned. Listen carefully to each item to determine if the clock on your test paper matches the time you hear. Then, blacken the corresponding letter—a. **oui** or b. **non**—on your answer sheet. You will hear each item twice.

Modèle: [—Quelle heure est-il?
        —Il est une heure.]

(a.) oui   b. non

8.

a. oui   b. non

6.

a. oui   b. non

9.

a. oui   b. non

7.

a. oui   b. non

10.

a. oui   b. non

Nom _____

Classe _____ Date _____ _____

Unité 3 Resources

Comprehensive Test 1 Form B

Discovering
FRENCH
Nouveau!

B L E U

3. Invitations (5 points)

You will hear five short conversations. In each one, a student is asking a friend to do something. Listen carefully to the invitation to determine if the friend a. **accepts,** b. **declines,** or c. **does neither.** Then, blacken the corresponding letter—a, b, or c—on your answer sheet. You will hear each item twice.

Modèle: [—Est-ce que tu veux jouer au tennis?
        —Oui, merci.]
        (a.) accepts   b. declines   c. does neither

11. a. accepts
     b. declines
     c. does neither

12. a. accepts
     b. declines
     c. does neither

13. a. accepts
     b. declines
     c. does neither

14. a. accepts
     b. declines
     c. does neither

15. a. accepts
     b. declines
     c. does neither

4. La réponse logique (10 points)

You will hear a series of ten questions. Listen carefully to each question and select the most logical response on your test paper. Then, blacken the corresponding letter—a, b, or c—on your answer sheet. You will hear each question twice.

Modèle: [Quel temps fait-il?]
        a. C'est le printemps.   (b.) Il pleut.   c. Il est trois heures.

16. a. C'est Thomas.
     b. C'est mon cousin.
     c. C'est une copine.

17. a. Le deux août.
     b. À deux heures.
     c. Deux ans et demi.

18. a. Non, il est américain.
     b. Oui, il est français.
     c. Oui, il habite à New York.

19. a. Dommage! J'ai faim.
     b. Oui, merci, je veux bien.
     c. Mais oui, je suis végétarien.

20. a. Prête-moi deux euros.
     b. Elle coûte trois euros.
     c. Il coûte deux euros cinquante.

21. a. C'est le 14 juillet.
     b. Il fait très beau.
     c. Il fait un match maintenant.

22. a. Au restaurant.
     b. Parce que j'ai faim.
     c. Peut-être, merci.

23. a. Oui, je préfère faire un voyage.
     b. Je regrette, mais je ne peux pas.
     c. Moi, je ne fais pas attention.

24. a. Je voudrais manger au restaurant.
     b. Merci, je préfère manger.
     c. Je voudrais un steak, s'il te plaît.

25. a. Je fais un voyage ici.
     b. En France, bien sûr!
     c. Parce que je suis américaine.

Nom _____

Classe _____ Date _____ _____

Discovering
FRENCH
Nouveau!

B L E U

Unité 3
Resources

Comprehensive Test 1
Form B

Part II. Language and Communication (40 points)

5. Au café (5 points)

François and Isabelle are watching people at **Le Sélect** café. Read portions of their conversation and decide which word from the box correctly completes each sentence. Then, mark the corresponding letter—a, b, or c—on your answer sheet.

> a. **le**   b. **la**   c. **l'**

26. —Dis, voilà ____ ami de Marc.
   a. ❑   b. ❑   c. ❑

27. —Qui est ____ femme au cinéma là-bas?
   a. ❑   b. ❑   c. ❑

28. —Tiens, voilà ____ copine de Monique!
   a. ❑   b. ❑   c. ❑

29. —Oui, c'est ____ cousin de Christine.
   a. ❑   b. ❑   c. ❑

30. —Est-ce que tu connais ____ oncle de Stéphanie?
   a. ❑   b. ❑   c. ❑

6. L'été (5 points)

People are busy in the summertime! Read the following sentences and choose the *one* word that correctly completes each item. Then, mark the corresponding letter—a, b, c, or d—on your answer sheet.

31. Nous aimons ____ un match de tennis.
   a. faisons
   b. fais
   c. faire
   d. font

32. Est-ce que vous ____ au volley demain?
   a. jouez
   b. jouons
   c. jouent
   d. jouer

33. Nathalie ____ à Québec avec Isabelle.
   a. es
   b. est
   c. être
   d. sont

34. Qui ____ au Select?
   a. travailler
   b. travaillent
   c. travailles
   d. travaille

35. Je (J') ____ visiter New York.
   a. suis
   b. veux
   c. ai
   d. fais

Unité 3
Resources

Comprehensive Test 1
Form B

Discovering
FRENCH
Nouveau!

B L E U

Nom _____

Classe _____ Date _____

7. Ma copine Sylvie (5 points)

Sylvie is an active person. Read the following sentences about her and decide which word from the box correctly completes each item. Then, mark the corresponding letter—a, b, or c—on your answer sheet.

a. **est** b. **a** c. **fait**

36. Sylvie veut une limonade parce qu'elle ___ soif.
   a. ❑   b. ❑   c. ❑

37. Bien sûr, elle ___ attention en classe!
   a. ❑   b. ❑   c. ❑

38. Sylvie ___ au cinéma maintenant.
   a. ❑   b. ❑   c. ❑

39. Samedi, elle ___ un match de foot avec Philippe et Anne.
   a. ❑   b. ❑   c. ❑

40. Le copain de Sylvie ___ 17 ans. Toi aussi?
   a. ❑   b. ❑   c. ❑

8. Une interview (5 points)

Marc is interviewing Stéphanie, an exchange student, for his school newspaper. Read parts of their conversation and select the correct question word to complete Stéphanie's answer. Then, mark the corresponding letter—a, b, c, d, or e—on your answer sheet. (Note: Some words may be used more than once and others not at all.)

a. **qui**   b. **qu'**   c. **comment**   d. **où**   e. **quand**

41. —___ est-ce que tu regardes à la télé? —Un film de science-fiction.
   a. ❑   b. ❑   c. ❑   d. ❑   e. ❑

42. —___ est-ce que tu dînes? —À la maison.
   a. ❑   b. ❑   c. ❑   d. ❑   e. ❑

43. —Et ___ est-ce que tu fais le week-end? —Je nage avec mes (my) copains.
   a. ❑   b. ❑   c. ❑   d. ❑   e. ❑

44. —Avec ___ est-ce que tu étudies? —Avec mon frère Danou.
   a. ❑   b. ❑   c. ❑   d. ❑   e. ❑

45. —___ est-ce que tu parles anglais? —Comme ci, comme ça!
   a. ❑   b. ❑   c. ❑   d. ❑   e. ❑

Nom _____

Classe _____ Date _____

Discovering
FRENCH Nouveau!

B L E U

Unité 3
Resources

Comprehensive Test 1
Form B

9. L'intrus (7 points)

Which word is the intruder? Read each list carefully to determine the word that does *not* belong with the other three. Then, mark the corresponding letter—a, b, c, or d—on your answer sheet.

46. a. avril   b. automne   c. août   d. octobre
47. a. croissant   b. steak   c. thé   d. crêpe
48. a. euro   b. fille   c. tante   d. frère
49. a. maison   b. cinéma   c. copain   d. café
50. a. bien   b. super   c. mal   d. beaucoup
51. a. zéro   b. dix   c. zut   d. onze
52. a. bientôt   b. jour   c. mois   d. an

10. Allô! (8 points)

Awa is phoning her friends this weekend. Read her questions on the left and her friends' answers on the right. Then, select the most logical response and mark the corresponding letter—a, b, c, d, or e—on your answer sheet.

samedi

53. Pourquoi est-ce que tu invites Sylvie?   a. Luc.
54. Qu'est-ce que tu fais?   b. Demain, à quatre heures.
55. Quand est-ce que vous jouez au tennis?   c. Il fait un match.
56. Où est ton frère?   d. Je regarde la télé.
                                                  e. Parce qu'elle danse bien!

dimanche

57. Tu invites Catherine à la boum?   a. Très, très bien!
58. Comment est-ce que Monique parle   b. Je voudrais jouer au basket.
    anglais?   c. De M. Dubois, le prof d'anglais.
59. De qui est-ce que tu parles?   d. Mais non, elle travaille.
60. Qu'est-ce que tu veux faire demain?   e. Bien sûr, elle parle anglais.

Unité 3
Resources

Comprehensive Test 1
Form B

Nom _____

Classe _____ Date _____

Discovering
FRENCH
Nouveau!

B L E U

11. Situations (5 points)

What would you say in the following situations? Read each item carefully and select the *best* expression. Then, mark the corresponding letter—a, b, or c—on your answer sheet.

61. *You want to know if Philippe likes to dance. You ask:*
    a. Tu danses bien?
    b. Est-ce que tu aimes danser?
    c. Tu veux danser avec moi?

62. *You would like to know what Isabelle is doing. You ask:*
    a. Avec qui est-ce que tu fais un match?
    b. Qu'est-ce que tu veux faire demain?
    c. Qu'est-ce que tu fais maintenant?

63. *You're working in a café and the bill comes to five euros. You say:*
    a. Ça fait cinq euros, madame.
    b. S'il te plaît, prête-moi cinq euros.
    c. Il coûte cinq euros, monsieur.

64. *You want to know if Monique knows Jérôme. You ask:*
    a. Tu aimes Jérôme, n'est-ce pas?
    b. Est-ce que tu connais Jérôme?
    c. Tu es Jérôme?

65. *Catherine invites you to take a walk. You answer:*
    a. Oui, je fais une promenade.
    b. Peut-être, à quelle heure?
    c. Je préfère faire une promenade.

Nom _____

Classe _____ Date _____

Discovering
FRENCH
Nouveau!

B L E U

Unité 3
Resources

Comprehensive Test 1
Form B

Part III. Reading Comprehension (20 points)

12. Quatre annonces (9 points)

Four young people are looking for pen pals. Read their messages and the conversations that follow, selecting the ad which *best* matches each exchange. Then, mark the corresponding letter—a, b, c, or d—on your answer sheet.

66. —Je voudrais correspondre aussi
    avec les étudiants anglais.
    a. ☐   b. ☐   c. ☐   d. ☐

67. —Et qu'est-ce que tu veux
    regarder?
    —Je préfère regarder les films
    d'aventures.
    a. ☐   b. ☐   c. ☐   d. ☐

68. —Quel âge as-tu?
    —J'ai 16 ans.
    —Est-ce que tu es canadien?
    —Mais non, je suis français.
    a. ☐   b. ☐   c. ☐   d. ☐

69. —Moi, je préfère correspondre
    avec les étudiants de 15 ans.
    a. ☐   b. ☐   c. ☐   d. ☐

70. —Pardon, madame. Combien
    coûte la carte?
    —Elle coûte 2 euros.
    —Voilà.
    —Merci, monsieur.
    a. ☐   b. ☐   c. ☐   d. ☐

71. —Bien sûr, je voudrais correspondre avec les
    étudiants espagnols.
    a. ☐   b. ☐   c. ☐   d. ☐

72. —Comment s'appelle le garçon?
    —Il s'appelle Luc.
    —Quel âge a-t-il?
    —Il a 15 ans.
    a. ☐   b. ☐   c. ☐   d. ☐

73. —Je préfère faire du sport. Je n'aime pas
    beaucoup écouter la musique.
    a. ☐   b. ☐   c. ☐   d. ☐

a. Jeune fille, 15 ans et demi, grande, sportive, cherche partenaires pour jouer au tennis.

young

is looking for

b. étudiant, 15 ans, aimant le cinéma et la musique classique désire correspondre avec étudiants ou étudiantes du même âge

who likes

same

c. jeune Français, 16 ans, désire correspondre avec étudiant(e)s de toutes nationalités pour échanger cartes postales et CD

all

to exchange

postcards

d. étudiante française, 16 ans, désire correspondre avec étudiants américains ou anglais.

74. —Tu veux aller *(to go)* au match avec
    moi?
    —D'accord, je veux bien. À quelle
    heure?
    a. ☐   b. ☐   c. ☐   d. ☐

Unité 3
Resources

Comprehensive Test 1
Form B

BLEU

Discovering
FRENCH
Nouveau

Nom _____

Classe _____ Date _____

13. Une lettre de Christine (5 points)

You have just received a letter from Christine. Read her message carefully and decide whether the statements which follow are true (**vrai**) or false (**faux**). Then, mark the corresponding letter—a or b—on your answer sheet.

CT

Salut!
    Je m'appelle Christine Tremblay et j'ai 15 ans. J'habite à Québec avec ma famille. À la maison, j'étudie beaucoup mais pas tout le temps *(all the time)*. Voici ce que j'aime faire:
    J'aime les boums parce que j'adore danser (et manger)! J'aime aussi la musique, surtout le rock. Je préfère écouter la musique américaine.
    J'aime les sports. En hiver je skie dans les Laurentides et en été je nage et je joue au tennis. Je joue assez *(rather)* bien mais je ne suis pas encore une championne! La fin de semaine *(weekend)*, j'aime faire des promenades à scooter. Ça, c'est l'fun!
    J'aime assez bien mon école, surtout la classe d'anglais. Le prof est très sympa *(nice)*. Je n'aime pas trop les maths parce que le prof est très sévère.
    À la maison, j'aime regarder les séries américaines à la télé. J'aime aussi écouter mes CD.
    J'aime téléphoner à ma copine Mireille mais je téléphone rarement parce que ma mère proteste et je dois étudier. C'est dommage, n'est-ce pas?
    Et toi, qu'est-ce que tu aimes faire? S'il te plaît, réponds-moi vite!

                                    Amicalement,
                                    Christine

75. Christine étudie souvent.   a. vrai   b. faux

76. Elle habite au Canada.   a. vrai   b. faux

77. En été, elle aime jouer au basket.   a. vrai   b. faux

78. Le prof d'anglais est agréable.   a. vrai   b. faux

79. Christine ne téléphone pas souvent.   a. vrai   b. faux

Nom _____

Classe _____ Date _____ _____

Discovering FRENCH *Nouveau!*

B L E U

Unité 3 Resources

Comprehensive Test 1

Form B

14. À la télé (6 points)

You are in France and want to watch TV. Read the television listing and the items which follow. Then, choose the correct answer and mark the corresponding letter—a, b, or c—on your answer sheet.

• In France, TV viewers have a choice of six main channels: **TF1, France 2, France 3, Cinquième Arte, M6,** and **Canal Plus.** *(People who want to watch **Canal Plus** need to have a special decoding machine for which they pay a monthly fee.)*
• Note that in TV listings, times are expressed using a 24-hour clock. In this system, 8 P.M. is **20.00 (vingt heures)**; 10 P.M. is **22.00 (vingt-deux heures)**.

SÉLECTION DE LA SEMAINE   VENDREDI

20.30 VARIÉTÉS
SALUT L'ARTISTE
émission présentée par
Yves Noël et Ophélie Winter

22.05 DOCUMENT
HISTOIRES NATURELLES

20.15 DOCUMENTAIRE
CENT ANS DE CINÉMA JAPONAIS

23.20 MAGAZINE
une vidéo inédite
DE BOB DYLAN

20.35 SÉRIE
HÔTEL DE POLICE
Le Gentil Monsieur
de Claude Barrois
avec Cécile Magnet

23.20 FILM
ALICE DANS LES VILLES
de Wim Wenders

20.30 FILM TV
LE MARIAGE DE MON MEILLEUR AMI
avec Julia Roberts

22.05 THÉÂTRE
RHINOCÉROS

france 3

21.30 SÉRIE
LE MASQUE
MADEMOISELLE EVELYNE
de Jean-Louis Fournier

23.45 CONCERT
MUSIQUES, MUSIQUE

20.30 FOOTBALL
CAEN - TOULOUSE
Championnat de France
28e journée

22.40 FILM
MALCOLM X
de Spike Lee

---

80. At 9:30 you can watch ___.
   a. «Le Masque»
   b. «Salut l'artiste»
   c. «Alice dans les villes»

81. They are broadcasting a documentary on ___.
   a. Cinquième Arte
   b. M6
   c. France 3

82. The featured dramatic play is entitled ___.
   a. «Deux flics à Miami»
   b. «Rhinocéros»
   c. «Mon prof est un extra-terrestre»

83. The only musical presentation is on ___.
   a. France 3
   b. Cinquième Arte
   c. France 2

84. In general, the *most* common type of programming is ___.
   a. variety shows
   b. movies
   c. weekly series

85. The foreign programming is primarily ___.
   a. American
   b. English
   c. Italian

Nom _____

Classe _____ Date _____

Part IV. Cultural Awareness (15 points)

15. Méli-mélo culturel *(cultural jumble)* (15 points)

How much do you know about French-speaking people and their everyday life? Read each sentence below and decide whether the item is true **(vrai)** or false **(faux)**. Then, mark the corresponding letter—a or b—on your answer sheet.

86. a. vrai   b. faux   French teenagers often order milk as a beverage.
87. a. vrai   b. faux   The **tama** is a traditional Senegalese drum.
88. a. vrai   b. faux   **Jean** is a typical French name for a girl.
89. a. vrai   b. faux   In France, it is illegal to make a cell phone call while driving.
90. a. vrai   b. faux   The inhabitants of Martinique are mainly of European origin.
91. a. vrai   b. faux   When French teenagers go to **une boum,** they are going to an outdoor concert.
92. a. vrai   b. faux   There are 10 different euro bills.
93. a. vrai   b. faux   On the island of Martinique, most people speak French and Spanish.
94. a. vrai   b. faux   In a French **café,** you can usually order a variety of sandwiches.
95. a. vrai   b. faux   A famous monument given to the United States by the French people is the Statue of Liberty.
96. a. vrai   b. faux   Senegal, a French-speaking country, is located in the Middle East.
97. a. vrai   b. faux   100 **centimes** are worth five **euros.**
98. a. vrai   b. faux   When a French teenager talks about **ma copine,** he is talking about his girlfriend.
99. a. vrai   b. faux   **Minou,** a popular pet name in France, is usually given to dogs.
100. a. vrai   b. faux   For French students, **la rentrée** usually takes place in early September.

Nom _____

Classe _____ Date _____

Discovering
FRENCH *Nouveau!*

B L E U

Unité 3
Resources

Test Scoring Tools

UNITÉ 3   Listening Comprehension
Performance Test Answer Sheet

A. Conversations

1. a. ___   2. a. ___   3. a. ___   4. a. ___   5. a. ___
   b. ___   b. ___   b. ___   b. ___   b. ___
   c. ___   c. ___   c. ___   c. ___   c. ___
   d. ___   d. ___   d. ___   d. ___   d. ___

B. Questions et réponses

6. a. ___   7. a. ___   8. a. ___   9. a. ___   10. a. ___
   b. ___   b. ___   b. ___   b. ___   b. ___
   c. ___   c. ___   c. ___   c. ___   c. ___
   d. ___   d. ___   d. ___   d. ___   d. ___

UNITÉ 3   Reading Comprehension
Performance Test Answer Sheet

1. a. ___   2. a. ___   3. a. ___   4. a. ___   5. a. ___
   b. ___   b. ___   b. ___   b. ___   b. ___
   c. ___   c. ___   c. ___   c. ___   c. ___

6. a. ___   7. a. ___   8. a. ___   9. a. ___   10. a. ___
   b. ___   b. ___   b. ___   b. ___   b. ___
   c. ___   c. ___   c. ___   c. ___   c. ___

Nom _____

Classe _____ Date _____

Comprehensive Test 1 (Units 1, 2, 3)

Instructions

Please use a No. 2 pencil only. Make heavy black marks that fill the circle completely. Do not make any stray marks on this answer sheet. Make all erasures cleanly.

	A B C D E		A B C D E		A B C D E		A B C D E		A B C D E
1	① ② ③ ④ ⑤	11	① ② ③ ④ ⑤	21	① ② ③ ④ ⑤	31	① ② ③ ④ ⑤	41	① ② ③ ④ ⑤
2	① ② ③ ④ ⑤	12	① ② ③ ④ ⑤	22	① ② ③ ④ ⑤	32	① ② ③ ④ ⑤	42	① ② ③ ④ ⑤
3	① ② ③ ④ ⑤	13	① ② ③ ④ ⑤	23	① ② ③ ④ ⑤	33	① ② ③ ④ ⑤	43	① ② ③ ④ ⑤
4	① ② ③ ④ ⑤	14	① ② ③ ④ ⑤	24	① ② ③ ④ ⑤	34	① ② ③ ④ ⑤	44	① ② ③ ④ ⑤
5	① ② ③ ④ ⑤	15	① ② ③ ④ ⑤	25	① ② ③ ④ ⑤	35	① ② ③ ④ ⑤	45	① ② ③ ④ ⑤
6	① ② ③ ④ ⑤	16	① ② ③ ④ ⑤	26	① ② ③ ④ ⑤	36	① ② ③ ④ ⑤	46	① ② ③ ④ ⑤
7	① ② ③ ④ ⑤	17	① ② ③ ④ ⑤	27	① ② ③ ④ ⑤	37	① ② ③ ④ ⑤	47	① ② ③ ④ ⑤
8	① ② ③ ④ ⑤	18	① ② ③ ④ ⑤	28	① ② ③ ④ ⑤	38	① ② ③ ④ ⑤	48	① ② ③ ④ ⑤
9	① ② ③ ④ ⑤	19	① ② ③ ④ ⑤	29	① ② ③ ④ ⑤	39	① ② ③ ④ ⑤	49	① ② ③ ④ ⑤
10	① ② ③ ④ ⑤	20	① ② ③ ④ ⑤	30	① ② ③ ④ ⑤	40	① ② ③ ④ ⑤	50	① ② ③ ④ ⑤
51	① ② ③ ④ ⑤	61	① ② ③ ④ ⑤	71	① ② ③ ④ ⑤	81	① ② ③ ④ ⑤	91	① ② ③ ④ ⑤
52	① ② ③ ④ ⑤	62	① ② ③ ④ ⑤	72	① ② ③ ④ ⑤	82	① ② ③ ④ ⑤	92	① ② ③ ④ ⑤
53	① ② ③ ④ ⑤	63	① ② ③ ④ ⑤	73	① ② ③ ④ ⑤	83	① ② ③ ④ ⑤	93	① ② ③ ④ ⑤
54	① ② ③ ④ ⑤	64	① ② ③ ④ ⑤	74	① ② ③ ④ ⑤	84	① ② ③ ④ ⑤	94	① ② ③ ④ ⑤
55	① ② ③ ④ ⑤	65	① ② ③ ④ ⑤	75	① ② ③ ④ ⑤	85	① ② ③ ④ ⑤	95	① ② ③ ④ ⑤
56	① ② ③ ④ ⑤	66	① ② ③ ④ ⑤	76	① ② ③ ④ ⑤	86	① ② ③ ④ ⑤	96	① ② ③ ④ ⑤
57	① ② ③ ④ ⑤	67	① ② ③ ④ ⑤	77	① ② ③ ④ ⑤	87	① ② ③ ④ ⑤	97	① ② ③ ④ ⑤
58	① ② ③ ④ ⑤	68	① ② ③ ④ ⑤	78	① ② ③ ④ ⑤	88	① ② ③ ④ ⑤	98	① ② ③ ④ ⑤
59	① ② ③ ④ ⑤	69	① ② ③ ④ ⑤	79	① ② ③ ④ ⑤	89	① ② ③ ④ ⑤	99	① ② ③ ④ ⑤
60	① ② ③ ④ ⑤	70	① ② ③ ④ ⑤	80	① ② ③ ④ ⑤	90	① ② ③ ④ ⑤	100	① ② ③ ④ ⑤

Nom _____

Classe _____ Date _____

Discovering FRENCH *Nouveau!*

BLEU

Comprehensive Test 1 (Units 1, 2, 3)

FORM B

Instructions

Please use a No. 2 pencil only. Make heavy black marks that fill the circle completely. Do not make any stray marks on this answer sheet. Make all erasures cleanly.

1 A B C D E ① ② ③ ④ ⑤	11 A B C D E ① ② ③ ④ ⑤	21 A B C D E ① ② ③ ④ ⑤	31 A B C D E ① ② ③ ④ ⑤	41 A B C D E ① ② ③ ④ ⑤
2 A B C D E ① ② ③ ④ ⑤	12 A B C D E ① ② ③ ④ ⑤	22 A B C D E ① ② ③ ④ ⑤	32 A B C D E ① ② ③ ④ ⑤	42 A B C D E ① ② ③ ④ ⑤
3 A B C D E ① ② ③ ④ ⑤	13 A B C D E ① ② ③ ④ ⑤	23 A B C D E ① ② ③ ④ ⑤	33 A B C D E ① ② ③ ④ ⑤	43 A B C D E ① ② ③ ④ ⑤
4 A B C D E ① ② ③ ④ ⑤	14 A B C D E ① ② ③ ④ ⑤	24 A B C D E ① ② ③ ④ ⑤	34 A B C D E ① ② ③ ④ ⑤	44 A B C D E ① ② ③ ④ ⑤
5 A B C D E ① ② ③ ④ ⑤	15 A B C D E ① ② ③ ④ ⑤	25 A B C D E ① ② ③ ④ ⑤	35 A B C D E ① ② ③ ④ ⑤	45 A B C D E ① ② ③ ④ ⑤
6 A B C D E ① ② ③ ④ ⑤	16 A B C D E ① ② ③ ④ ⑤	26 A B C D E ① ② ③ ④ ⑤	36 A B C D E ① ② ③ ④ ⑤	46 A B C D E ① ② ③ ④ ⑤
7 A B C D E ① ② ③ ④ ⑤	17 A B C D E ① ② ③ ④ ⑤	27 A B C D E ① ② ③ ④ ⑤	37 A B C D E ① ② ③ ④ ⑤	47 A B C D E ① ② ③ ④ ⑤
8 A B C D E ① ② ③ ④ ⑤	18 A B C D E ① ② ③ ④ ⑤	28 A B C D E ① ② ③ ④ ⑤	38 A B C D E ① ② ③ ④ ⑤	48 A B C D E ① ② ③ ④ ⑤
9 A B C D E ① ② ③ ④ ⑤	19 A B C D E ① ② ③ ④ ⑤	29 A B C D E ① ② ③ ④ ⑤	39 A B C D E ① ② ③ ④ ⑤	49 A B C D E ① ② ③ ④ ⑤
10 A B C D E ① ② ③ ④ ⑤	20 A B C D E ① ② ③ ④ ⑤	30 A B C D E ① ② ③ ④ ⑤	40 A B C D E ① ② ③ ④ ⑤	50 A B C D E ① ② ③ ④ ⑤
51 A B C D E ① ② ③ ④ ⑤	61 A B C D E ① ② ③ ④ ⑤	71 A B C D E ① ② ③ ④ ⑤	81 A B C D E ① ② ③ ④ ⑤	91 A B C D E ① ② ③ ④ ⑤
52 A B C D E ① ② ③ ④ ⑤	62 A B C D E ① ② ③ ④ ⑤	72 A B C D E ① ② ③ ④ ⑤	82 A B C D E ① ② ③ ④ ⑤	92 A B C D E ① ② ③ ④ ⑤
53 A B C D E ① ② ③ ④ ⑤	63 A B C D E ① ② ③ ④ ⑤	73 A B C D E ① ② ③ ④ ⑤	83 A B C D E ① ② ③ ④ ⑤	93 A B C D E ① ② ③ ④ ⑤
54 A B C D E ① ② ③ ④ ⑤	64 A B C D E ① ② ③ ④ ⑤	74 A B C D E ① ② ③ ④ ⑤	84 A B C D E ① ② ③ ④ ⑤	94 A B C D E ① ② ③ ④ ⑤
55 A B C D E ① ② ③ ④ ⑤	65 A B C D E ① ② ③ ④ ⑤	75 A B C D E ① ② ③ ④ ⑤	85 A B C D E ① ② ③ ④ ⑤	95 A B C D E ① ② ③ ④ ⑤
56 A B C D E ① ② ③ ④ ⑤	66 A B C D E ① ② ③ ④ ⑤	76 A B C D E ① ② ③ ④ ⑤	86 A B C D E ① ② ③ ④ ⑤	96 A B C D E ① ② ③ ④ ⑤
57 A B C D E ① ② ③ ④ ⑤	67 A B C D E ① ② ③ ④ ⑤	77 A B C D E ① ② ③ ④ ⑤	87 A B C D E ① ② ③ ④ ⑤	97 A B C D E ① ② ③ ④ ⑤
58 A B C D E ① ② ③ ④ ⑤	68 A B C D E ① ② ③ ④ ⑤	78 A B C D E ① ② ③ ④ ⑤	88 A B C D E ① ② ③ ④ ⑤	98 A B C D E ① ② ③ ④ ⑤
59 A B C D E ① ② ③ ④ ⑤	69 A B C D E ① ② ③ ④ ⑤	79 A B C D E ① ② ③ ④ ⑤	89 A B C D E ① ② ③ ④ ⑤	99 A B C D E ① ② ③ ④ ⑤
60 A B C D E ① ② ③ ④ ⑤	70 A B C D E ① ② ③ ④ ⑤	80 A B C D E ① ② ③ ④ ⑤	90 A B C D E ① ② ③ ④ ⑤	100 A B C D E ① ② ③ ④ ⑤

Discovering French, Nouveau! Bleu

Unité 3 Resources
Test Scoring Tools

Unité 3 Resources

Audioscripts

Discovering
FRENCH
Nouveau!

BLEU

UNIT TEST 3 (Lessons 5, 6, 7, 8)   FORM A

Part I. Listening Comprehension

CD 14, Track 5

1. The Logical Answer (20 points)

You will hear a series of ten questions. Listen carefully to each question and select the most logical answer on your test sheet. Circle the corresponding letter: a, b, or c. You will hear each question twice. First listen to the model.

Modèle: Quelle heure est-il?
You should have circled the letter **"c"**: **Deux heures et demie.**

Let's begin. Écoutez.

Un.	Où est ton copain?
Deux.	Quand est-ce que vous dînez?
Trois.	Ton père est à la maison?
Quatre.	Dis, Caroline, qu'est-ce que tu veux manger?
Cinq.	Thomas, est-ce que tu veux dîner au restaurant avec moi?
Six.	À qui est-ce que tu parles, Charlotte?
Sept.	Ta copine habite à Montréal?
Huit.	Est-ce que nous sommes d'accord?
Neuf.	Dis, Thomas, tu veux jouer aux jeux vidéo avec moi?
Dix.	Est-ce que les élèves écoutent le prof?

UNIT TEST 3 (Lessons 5, 6, 7, 8)   FORM B

Part I. Listening Comprehension

CD 14, Track 6

1. The Logical Answer (20 points)

You will hear a series of ten questions. Listen carefully to each question and select the most logical answer on your test sheet. Circle the corresponding letter: a, b, or c. You will hear each question twice. First listen to the model.

Modèle: Quelle heure est-il?
You should have circled the letter **"c"**: **Deux heures et demie.**

Let's begin. Écoutez.

Un.	Où est Marie-Claire?
Deux.	Est-ce que ta cousine est en vacances?
Trois.	Est-ce que Philippe et Caroline sont à la maison?
Quatre.	Où dînez-vous aujourd'hui?
Cinq.	Dis, Jean-Claude, quand est-ce que tu organises une boum?
Six.	Dis, Philippe, qu'est-ce que tu fais?
Sept.	Comment est-ce que vous parlez espagnol?
Huit.	Est-ce que vous êtes d'accord avec moi?
Neuf.	Pourquoi est-ce que tu ne regardes pas la télé?
Dix.	Tu veux jouer au basket avec moi?

Listening Comprehension Performance Test

CD 14, Track 7

Partie A. Conversations

This part of the Listening Comprehension Test will let you see how well you understand spoken French. You will hear five short conversations. Look at your Listening Comprehension Test Sheet and read the corresponding questions. After you have heard each conversation the second time, select the correct answer and mark the corresponding letter (a, b, c, or d) on your answer sheet.

Let's begin.

1. *Listen to the following conversation between two friends.*
   FILLE: Tu parles français?
   GARÇON: Bien sûr! Je suis canadien.
   FILLE: Où est-ce que tu habites?
   GARÇON: Je suis de Montréal.

2. *Listen to the following conversation between Thomas and his sister Cécile.*
   THOMAS: Tu veux jouer aux jeux vidéo avec moi?
   CÉCILE: Non, merci.
   THOMAS: Pourquoi?
   CÉCILE: Je préfère faire une promenade.

3. *Listen to the following conversation between two friends.*
   FILLE: Tu veux danser?
   GARÇON: Hmm, je ne danse pas très bien.
   FILLE: Bon … alors … qu'est-ce que tu veux faire?
   GARÇON: Manger un sandwich et écouter la musique.

4. *Listen to the following phone conversation between Marc and Caroline.*
   MARC: Allô, Caroline!?
   CAROLINE: Salut, Marc. Ça va?
   MARC: Oui, ça va. Dis, est-ce que je peux parler à ton frère?
   CAROLINE: Il n'est pas à la maison.
   MARC: Ah bon? Où est-il?
   CAROLINE: Il est au cinéma avec une copine.

5. *Listen to the following conversation between Jérôme and Alice.*
   JÉRÔME: Dis, Alice, tu joues au tennis?
   ALICE: Oui, bien sûr. Pourquoi?
   JÉRÔME: Est-ce que tu veux jouer avec moi?
   ALICE: À quelle heure?
   JÉRÔME: À deux heures.
   ALICE: Je regrette, mais j'ai rendez-vous avec un copain.

CD 14, Track 8

Partie B. Questions et réponses

This part of the Listening Comprehension Test will let you see how well you can handle French questions. You will hear your French friend François ask you five questions. Listen carefully. Then look at your Listening Comprehension Test Sheet and select the MOST LOGICAL answer to each question. Mark the corresponding letter (a, b, c, or d) on your answer sheet. You will hear each question twice.

Let's begin.

6. *You and François are walking past the tennis court. He asks:*
   Comment joues-tu au tennis?

7. *You and François are walking down the street. He asks:*
   Dis, qu'est-ce que tu fais samedi?

8. *You and François are at a café. He says:*
   Je voudrais parler à Caroline. Où est-elle?

9. *Soccer practice is over and you are talking with your teammates. François asks:*
   Est-ce que tu veux dîner avec nous?

10. *You and your best friend are talking before class begins. François asks:*
    Qu'est-ce que vous faites quand vous êtes en vacances?

Comprehensive Test 1 (Units 1, 2, 3)

Part I. Listening Comprehension (25 points)

CD 14, Track 9

1. Loto! (5 points)

You and your friends are playing French **Loto.** You will hear five numbers called out. Listen carefully to each item and select the appropriate number on your test paper. Then, blacken the corresponding letter—a, b, or c—on your answer sheet. You will hear each item twice. First, listen to the model.

Modèle: Dix. # Dix.
You should have blackened the letter **"b": 10.**

Let's begin. Écoutez.

One.	Trente-cinq.
Two.	Cinquante et un.
Three.	Quatre-vingt-dix-huit.
Four.	Treize.
Five.	Soixante et onze.

CD 14, Track 10

2. Quelle heure est-il? (5 points)

You will hear five short conversations in which a time is mentioned. Listen carefully to each item to determine if the clock on your test paper matches the time you hear. Then, blacken the corresponding letter—a. **oui** or b. **non**—on your answer sheet. You will hear each item twice. First, listen to the model.

Modèle: —Quelle heure est-il?
—Il est une heure.
You should have blackened the letter **"a": oui.**

Let's begin. Écoutez.

Six.   —Bonjour, monsieur! Quelle heure est-il?
—Il est huit heures.
—Merci, monsieur.

Seven.   —À quelle heure est le concert?
—À deux heures et demie.

Eight.   —J'ai un rendez-vous avec Marc.
—À quelle heure?
—À quatre heures moins le quart.

Nine.   —Dis, Stéphanie, quelle heure est-il?
—Il est huit heures vingt-cinq.
—J'ai un rendez-vous dans cinq minutes. Au revoir, Stéphanie!

Ten.   —À quelle heure est le train de Marseille?
—À dix heures cinquante.
—Ça va. Nous avons le temps.

Discovering
FRENCH
Nouveau!

BLEU

Unité 3
Resources

Audioscripts

CD 14, Track 11

3. Invitations (5 points)

You will hear five short conversations. In each one, a student is asking a friend to do something. Listen carefully to the invitation to determine if the friend a. **accepts,** b. **declines,** or c. **does neither.** Then, blacken the corresponding letter—a, b, or c—on your answer sheet. You will hear each item twice. First, listen to the model.

Modèle: —Est-ce que tu veux jouer au tennis?
—Oui, merci.
You should have blackened the letter **"a"**: **accepts.**

Let's begin. Écoutez.

Eleven.   —Céline, est-ce que tu veux dîner avec moi?
—Oui, d'accord. Je veux bien.

Twelve.   —Est-ce que tu veux nager?
—Non, je ne peux pas nager avec toi.

Thirteen.   —Salut, Vincent! Est-ce que tu veux étudier avec moi?
—Euh, peut-être.

Fourteen.   —Caroline, est-ce que tu veux jouer au tennis?
—Je ne peux pas. Je dois travailler.

Fifteen.   —Tu veux chanter avec la chorale?
—Peut-être, mais je ne sais pas. Je ne chante pas très bien!

CD 14, Track 12

4. La réponse logique (10 points)

You will hear a series of ten questions. Listen carefully to each question and select the most logical response on your test paper. Then, blacken the corresponding letter—a, b, or c—on your answer sheet. You will hear each question twice. First, listen to the model.

Modèle: Quel temps fait-il?
You should have blackened the letter **"b"**: **Il pleut.**

Let's begin. Écoutez.

Sixteen.   Qui est le garçon?

Seventeen.   Quel jour est-ce?

Eighteen.   Ta cousine est américaine?

Nineteen.   Tu veux une limonade?

Twenty.   Ça fait combien?

Twenty-one.   Il fait froid à Montréal?

Twenty-two.   Quand est-ce que vous dînez?

Twenty-three. Dis, Anne, qu'est-ce que tu fais?

Twenty-four.   À qui est-ce que tu téléphones, Jacques?

Twenty-five.   Comment est-ce que tu chantes, Monique?

Discovering
FRENCH
Nouveau!

BLEU
FORM B

Comprehensive Test 1 (Units 1, 2, 3)

Part I. Listening Comprehension (25 points)

CD 14, Track 13

1. Loto! (5 points)

You and your friends are playing French **Loto.** You will hear five numbers called out. Listen carefully to each item and select the appropriate number on your test paper. Then, blacken the corresponding letter—a, b, or c—on your answer sheet. You will hear each item twice. First, listen to the model.

Modèle: Dix. # Dix.
    You should have blackened the letter **"b": 10.**

Let's begin. Écoutez.

One.	Douze.
Two.	Cinquante-six.
Three.	Quatre-vingt-deux.
Four.	Soixante et un.
Five.	Seize.

CD 14, Track 14

2. Quelle heure est-il? (5 points)

You will hear five short conversations in which a time is mentioned. Listen carefully to each item to determine if the clock on your test paper matches the time you hear. Then, blacken the corresponding letter—a. **oui** or b. **non**—on your answer sheet. You will hear each item twice. First, listen to the model.

Modèle: —Quelle heure est-il?
    —Il est une heure.
    You should have blackened the letter **"a": oui.**

Let's begin. Écoutez.

Six.	—Salut, Vincent! Quelle heure est-il?
	—Il est sept heures.
Seven.	—Dis, à quelle heure est le film?
	—À huit heures et demie.
Eight.	—J'ai un rendez-vous avec une copine.
	—À quelle heure?
	—À trois heures et quart.
Nine.	—David, quelle heure est-il maintenant?
	—Il est six heures dix.
	—Oh là là, j'ai un rendez-vous avec Isabelle. Au revoir, David. À bientôt!
Ten.	—Pardon, madame. À quelle heure est le train de Toulon?
	—À neuf heures trente-cinq.
	—Merci, madame.
	—Au revoir, monsieur.

Discovering
FRENCH
Nouveau!

BLEU

Unité 3
Resources

Audioscripts

CD 14, Track 15

3. Invitations (5 points)

You will hear five short conversations. In each one, a student is asking a friend to do something. Listen carefully to the invitation to determine if the friend a. **accepts,** b. **declines,** or c. **does neither.** Then, blacken the corresponding letter—a, b, or c—on your answer sheet. You will hear each item twice. First, listen to the model.

Modèle: —Est-ce que tu veux jouer au tennis?
　　　　—Oui, merci.
　　　　You should have blackened the letter "**a**": **accepts.**

Let's begin. Écoutez.

Eleven. 　　—David, est-ce que tu veux jouer au basket?
　　　　　　—Non, je ne peux pas.

Twelve. 　　—Dis, est-ce que tu veux manger une pizza?
　　　　　　—Oui, merci, j'ai faim!

Thirteen. 　—Stéphanie, est-ce que tu veux regarder la télé?
　　　　　　—Euh, je ne sais pas. Peut-être… mais j'ai un rendez-vous à huit heures.

Fourteen. 　—Est-ce que tu veux dîner au restaurant?
　　　　　　—Je regrette, mais je dois étudier.

Fifteen. 　　—Dis, Caroline, tu veux parler espagnol avec moi?
　　　　　　—Peut-être, mais je ne parle pas très bien!
　　　　　　—Dommage!

CD 14, Track 16

4. La réponse logique (10 points)

You will hear a series of ten questions. Listen carefully to each question and select the most logical response on your test paper. Then, blacken the corresponding letter—a, b, or c—on your answer sheeet. You will hear each question twice. First, listen to the model.

Modèle: Quel temps fait-il?
　　　　You should have blackened the letter "**b**": **Il pleut.**

Let's begin. Écoutez.

Sixteen. 　　　　Qui est la fille?
Seventeen. 　　Quelle est la date?
Eighteen. 　　Ton cousin est anglais?
Nineteen. 　　Tu veux un hamburger?
Twenty. 　　　Combien coûte le chocolat?
Twenty-one. 　Quel temps fait-il en été?
Twenty-two. 　Où dînez-vous demain?
Twenty-three. Tiens, Philippe, tu veux faire un match avec moi?
Twenty-four. 　Qu'est-ce que tu veux manger, Alice?
Twenty-five. 　Pourquoi est-ce que tu es à Paris?

IMAGES   À l'école en France

CD 2, Track 23

Écoutez bien!

Imagine you are in a school in France. Listen carefully to what different French teachers will ask you to do and carry out their instructions. If you have trouble understanding the commands, your teacher will mime the actions for you.

1. Prends ton crayon.
2. Prends ton livre.
3. Ouvre ton livre.
4. Ouvre ton cahier.
5. Montre-mon ton cahier.
6. Montre-moi ton stylo.
7. Montre-moi ton sac.
8. Lève-toi.
9. Va au tableau.
10. Montre-moi un morceau de craie.
11. Va à la porte.
12. Va à la fenêtre.
13. Assieds-toi.
14. Prends une feuille de papier.
15. Écris avec ton crayon.

Très bien.

Discovering
FRENCH *Nouveau!*

BLEU

Unité 3
Resources

Videoscripts

IMAGES À l'école en France

Bonjour! Today we are going to visit a French high school. But first we will meet our guide: Nathalie Aubin. We will ask her where she lives, and where she goes to school. And we will also ask her when her classes begin and end on a typical school day.

SÉBASTIEN: Bonjour!
NATHALIE: Bonjour!
SÉBASTIEN: Comment t'appelles-tu?
NATHALIE: Je m'appelle Nathalie Aubin.
SÉBASTIEN: Et où est-ce que tu habites?
NATHALIE: J'habite à Savigny-sur-Orge.
SÉBASTIEN: Et à quelle école est-ce que tu vas?
NATHALIE: Je vais au lycée Jean-Baptiste Corot.
SÉBASTIEN: En quelle classe es-tu?
NATHALIE: Je suis en seconde.
SÉBASTIEN: En général, à quelle heure est-ce que les classes commencent le matin?
NATHALIE: Les classes commencent à huit heures et demie.
SÉBASTIEN: Et à quelle heure est-ce qu'elles finissent l'après-midi?
NATHALIE: Elles finissent à quatre heures ou à cinq heures.
SÉBASTIEN: Merci.
NATHALIE: Au revoir.

Savigny-sur-Orge, the city where Nathalie lives, is a residential community located about 20 miles south of Paris. The high school is called le lycée Jean-Baptiste Corot. Like most schools in France, it is named after a famous French person. Jean-Baptiste Corot is a nineteenth century painter known for his landscapes. Let's accompany Nathalie as she goes to school.

As you can see, this is a very interesting lycée. Its main building is an old castle. Here is the moat, formed by a branch of the Orge River. The other buildings are more modern. What classes does Nathalie have this morning? Let's see. Today is Monday. Her

first class is history. At 9:30, Nathalie has an English class.

After her English class, Nathalie has sports. And now that the morning classes are over, Nathalie is going to show us around the lycée.

NATHALIE: Voici le château. C'est le bâtiment administratif.

Voici les bâtiments scolaires.
Voici le gymnase.
Voici le terrain de foot.
Voici la cantine. J'ai faim!

Before her afternoon classes begin, Nathalie meets her friends. She'll ask them what their favorite subjects are. Listen carefully and see how many responses you can understand.

—Quel est ton sujet favori?
—J'aime l'histoire.
—Quel est ton sujet favori?
—J'aime le français.
—Je préfère l'anglais.
—J'aime l'espagnol.
—J'aime les sports.
—J'aime les maths.
—J'aime la musique.
—J'aime l'anglais.
—J'aime les sports.
—J'aime les sciences naturelles.
—Je préfère la biologie.
—J'aime les maths.

After lunch, Nathalie has about an hour of free time before classes begin again. Depending on which day it is, she leaves school at four or five o'clock. It takes her about a half an hour to get home. Usually Nathalie begins her homework before dinner. She has about two or three hours of homework every day. At eight o'clock, the family has dinner. After dinner, Nathalie finishes her homework. Then she watches TV or reads in her room. French kids have a busy day, don't they? Au revoir, Nathalie!

NATHALIE: Au revoir!

UNITÉ 3 ANSWER KEY

Video Activities

Module 5: Le français pratique: Mes activités (Pages 21–24)

Activité 1. J'aime . . .

a. 12	b. 1
c. 9	d. 4
e. 13	f. 7
g. 3	h. 8
i. 6	j. 2
k. 11	l. 5
m. 10	

Activité 2. Tu aimes écouter la radio?
1. écouter la radio
2. jouer au tennis
3. jouer au foot
4. regarder la télé
5. manger
6. téléphoner
7. nager
8. voyager

Activité 3. Invitations
1. Oui, je veux bien.
2. Oui, je veux bien.
3. Oui, je veux bien.
4. Non, merci, je n'ai pas faim.

Activité 4. Tennis?
1. non
2. non
3. oui

Activité 5. Le téléphone
1. cell phone
2. when driving, at school, in a café or a restaurant

Activité 6. Pour téléphoner . . .
A.

1. b	2. d
3. a	4. b
5. e	6. c
7. f	

Activité 7. Une conversation téléphonique
Conversations will vary.

Module 6: Une invitation? (Pages 49–52)

Activité 1. Où sont les copains?

1. a	2. b
3. b	4. a

Activité 2. Où est tout le monde?
Students should have marked **à la maison, à Paris, en France,** and **en ville** once; **au café, en classe,** and **en vacances** twice.

Activité 3. Où sont-ils?

1. h	2. f
3. e	4. a
5. b	6. c
7. g	8. d

Activité 4. Au café
1. to meet their friends and talk
2. outside
3. They enjoy the sun and watch people passing by.
4. the indoor section
5. a table-top soccer game

Question personnelle sample answer:
I would go to a fast-food place because I like fast food!

Activité 5. Un jeu: Où es-tu?
Games will vary.

Module 7: Une boum (Pages 81–84)

Activité 1. Tout le monde

1. Cécile	2. Philippe
3. Cécile	4. Antoine
5. Cécile	6. Philippe
7. Yannick	8. Philippe

Activité 2. D'autre copains

1. téléphone	2. regarde
3. travaille	4. dîne

Activité 3. Est-ce qu'il travaille?

1. non	2. non
3. oui	4. oui
5. non	6. non
7. oui	

Activité 4. Comment dansent les copains?

1. oui	2. non
3. non	

Activité 5. Une boum

A.	B.
weekends	1. les boums
a friend's home	2. manger
15–25	
food, music, dancing	

Activité 6. Le week-end
Activities will vary

Module 8: Un concert de musique africain Une interview (Pages 114–117)

Activité 1. Des renseignements, s'il vous plaît!

1. e	2. b
3. g	4. d
5. a	6. c
7. f	

Activité 2. Qu'est-ce que tu fais?
1. un sandwich
2. une tarte
3. une crêpe
4. un film de science-fiction
5. un CD de jazz
6. une tarte

Activité 3. Questions

1. a	2. b
3. b	4. a
5. a	

Activité 4. Une interview

1. a	2. b
3. a	4. a
5. b	6. a
7. b	

Activité 5. Le Sénégal
about 10,500,000
Dakar
French and Wolof
Africa
Information on a second country will vary.

Activité 6. Des interviews
Interviews will vary.

Lesson Quizzes

Quiz 5

Part I: Listening

A. Conversations (40 points)

1. b	2. a
3. a	4. b
5. c	

Part II: Writing

B. Activités (30 points)

1. écouter	2. regarder
3. jouer	4. manger
5. parler	

C. Expression personnelle (30 points) Note: Answers will vary.
- J'aime voyager.
- J'aime jouer au tennis.
- Je n'aime pas travailler.

Quiz 6

Part I: Listening

A. Conversations (25 points)

1. c	2. b
3. a	4. a
5. c	

Part II: Writing

B. Oui et non (40 points)
1. est / sont
2. êtes / sommes
3. est / n'est pas
4. es / ne suis pas

C. Le mot juste (15 points)

1. ou	2. à
3. et	4. pour
5. mais	

D. Expression personnelle (20 points) <u>Note</u>: Answers will vary.
- Je suis en classe.
- Mon père est en ville.

Quiz 7

Part I: Listening

A. Conversations (30 points)

1. c	2. c
3. c	4. c
5. b	

Part II: Writing

B. Activités (30 points)

1. parle	2. visitez
3. travaille	4. téléphonons
5. études	6. écoutent

C. Non (20 points)
1. ne voyageons pas
2. n'invitent pas
3. ne regardez pas
4. n'habites pas

D. Expression personnelle (20 points) <u>Note</u>: Answers will vary.
- J'habite à Dallas.
- Ou, j'étudie beaucoup. (Non, je n'étudie pas beaucoup.)

Quiz 8

Part I: Listening

A. Questions et réponses (40 points)

1. a	2. b
3. b	4. c
5. a	6. c
7. b	8. c

Part II: Writing

B. Questions (24 points)

1. Quand	2. Pourquoi
3. Comment	4. Où
5. À qui	6. Qu' est-ce que

C. Voyages (16 points)

1. faisons	2. font
3. fais	4. faites

D. Expression personnelle (20 points) *(8 points for the first answer; 12 points for the second answer)*
- Qu'est-ce que tu fais?
- Est-ce que tu veux faire une promenade avec moi?

Communipak

Interviews

URB p. 216

Unité 3 Resources
Answer Key

Discovering French, Nouveau! Bleu

Unité 3 Resources

Answer Key

Discovering
FRENCH
Nouveau!

B L E U

Unité 3
Resources
Answer Key

Interview 1 (sample answers)

Elle habite à San Diego.
Il habite à Cleveland.
Ils habitent à Providence.
Elle habite à Jacksonville.

Interview 2

Answers will vary.

Interview 3 (sample answers)

Je préfère jouer au basket.
Je préfère parler en français.
Je préfère écouter la radio.
Je préfère voyager.

Interview 4 (sample answers)

Je dîne à sept heures.
Je regarde «The Practice», «Will and Grace»
et «Dharma and Greg».
Je téléphone à ma soeur.
J'écoute WGBH.

Tu as la parole

Tu as la parole 1 (sample answers)

voyager.
j'aime jouer au foot.
j'aime manger un steak-frites.

Tu as la parole 2 (sample answers)

parler français.
je n'aime pas nager.
je n'aime pas travailler.

Tu as la parole 3 (sample answers)

regarde la télé.
Je téléphone à une copine.
J'écoute la radio.

Tu as la parole 4 (sample answers)

Je joue au tennis. Je joue bien.
Je joue au foot. Je joue mal.
Je joue au basket. Je ne joue pas très bien.

Tu as la parole 5 (sample answers)

Ma mère aime chanter.
Mon cousin aime jouer au basket.
Ma copine Sarah aime nager.

Tu as la parole 6 (sample answers)

Nicole habite à Cambridge.
Elle parle français et anglais.
Elle aime dîner au restaurant.

Conversations Side A

Conversation 1

Où est-ce que tu habites?
Est-ce que tu parles bien français?
Est-ce que tu voyages souvent?

Conversation 2 (sample answers)

Je suis en ville.
Je fais du shopping.
Je voudrais aller au café et au cinéma.

Conversation 3

Est-ce que tu aimes nager?
Est-ce que tu veux jouer au tennis avec moi?
Est-ce que tu veux faire une promenade
après?

Conversation 4 (sample answers)

Je voudrais voir un film.
Je voudrais manger à six heures.
Je voudrais manger un hamburger.

Conversations Side B

Conversation 1 (sample answers)

J'habite à Bangor, Maine.
Non, je ne parle pas très bien français.
Oui, je voyage souvent.

Conversation 2

Où es-tu?
Qu'est-ce que tu fais?
Qu'est-ce que tu veux faire?

Conversation 3 (sample answers)

Oui, j'aime beaucoup nager.
Non merci, je n'aime pas jouer au tennis.
Oui, je voudrais bien faire un promenade avec
toi.

Conversation 4

Qu'est-ce que tu veux regarder à la télé?
À quelle heure est-ce que tu veux dîner?
Qu'est-ce que tu veux manger?

Échanges

Échange 1

Answers will vary.

Échange 2 (sample answers)

John, est-ce que tu chantes? Comment est-ce
que tu chantes?
Lisa, est-ce que tu joues au tennis? Comment
est-ce que tu joues?
Bill, est-ce que tu danses? Comment est-ce
que tu danses?
Amy, est-ce que tu joues au basket? Comment
est-ce que tu joues?

Tête à tête

Activité 1 Où sont-ils?

Élève A (sample answers)
a. au cinéma.
    Où est Jean-Paul?
    au café.
    Où est Madame Lambert?
    au restaurant.
    Où est Monsieur Thomas?
    à Paris.
b. Elle est en classe.
    Il est en vacances.
    Elle est à la maison.
    Elle est en ville.

Élève B (sample answers)
a. Elle est au cinéma.
    Il est au café.
    Elle est au restaurant.
    Il est à Paris.
b. en classe.
    Où est Marc?
    en vacances.
    Où est Mademoiselle Joli?
    à la maison.
    Où est Madame Leblanc?
    en ville.

Activité 2 Qu'est-ce que tu aimes faire?

Élève A (sample answers)
a. Oui, j'aime chanter. (Non, je n'aime pas
    chanter.)
    Oui, j'aime danser. (Non, je n'aime pas
    danser.)
    Oui, j'aime travailler. (Non, je n'aime pas
    travailler.)
    Oui, j'aime jouer aux jeux vidéo. (Non, je
    n'aime pas jouer aux jeux vidéo.)
    Oui, j'aime parler espagnol. (Non, je n'aime
    pas parler espagnol.)
b. Est-ce que tu aimes jouer au foot?
    Est-ce que tu aimes parler français?

Est-ce que tu aimes étudier?
Est-ce que tu aimes manger?

Élève B (sample answers)
a. Est-ce que tu aimes danser?
    Est-ce que tu aimes travailler?
    Est-ce que tu aimes jouer aux jeux vidéo?
    Est-ce que tu aimes parler espagnol?
b. Oui, j'aime voyager. (Non, je n'aime pas
    voyager.)
    Oui, j'aime jouer au foot. (Non, je n'aime
    pas jouer au foot.)
    Oui, j'aime parler français. (Non, je n'aime
    pas parler français.)
    Oui, j'aime étudier. (Non, je n'aime pas
    étudier.)
    Oui, j'aime manger. (Non, je n'aime pas
    manger.)

Activité 3 Que font-ils?

Élève A (sample answers)
a. Elle joue au tennis.
    Elle voyage.
    Il mange un sandwich.
    Il fait une promenade.
    Elle regarde la télé.
b. Elle nage.
    Que fait Jean-Pierre?
    Il joue au foot.
    Que fait Éric?
    Il étudie.
    Que fait Delphine?
    Elle travaille.
    Que fait Marc?
    Il joue au basket.

Élève B (sample answers)
a. Elle joue au tennis.
    Que fait Florence?
    Elle voyage.
    Que fait Jérôme?
    Il mange un sandwich.
    Que fait Philippe?
    Il fait une promenade.
    Que fait Stéphanie?
    Elle regarde la télé.
b. Elle nage.
    Il joue au foot.
    Il étudie.
    Elle travaille.
    Il joue au basket.

Unit Test Lessons 5, 6, 7, 8

Form A

Part I. Listening Comprehension

1. The Logical Answer (20 points)

1. a	2. c
3. b	4. c
5. b	6. b
7. a	8. b
9. c	10. b

Part II. Language

2. The Right Choice (12 points)

1. a	2. c
3. b	4. b
5. b	6. b
7. a	8. b
9. a	10. b
11. b	12. c

3. Être or faire? (8 points)

1. êtes	2. faisons
3. sont	4. font

4. The Right Activity (16 points)

1. parlent	2. mange
3. joues	4. regardons

5. écoutez   6. habitez
7. chantes   8. travaillons

5. Non! (12 points)
1. ne voyage pas
2. ne nage pas
3. n'invitons pas
4. ne visitent pas

6. The Right Question (12 points)
1. À qui est-ce que tu parles?
2. Où est-ce que tu travailles?
3. Qu'est-ce que tu écoutes?
4. Quand est-ce que tu organises une boum?

Part III. Written Expression

7. Composition (20 points)
Answers will vary.

Form B

Part I. Listening Comprehension

1. The Logical Answer (20 points)
1. a   2. c
3. b   4. b
5. a   6. a
7. c   8. a
9. b   10. c

Part II. Language

2. The Right Choice (12 points)
1. b   2. a
3. b   4. c
5. b   6. b
7. a   8. c
9. c   10. a
11. c   12. b

3. Être or faire? (8 points)
1. sommes   2. faites
3. sont   4. fais

4. The Right Activity (16 points)
1. parlez   2. mange
3. jouons   4. regardent
5. écoutes   6. habites
7. dansent   8. travaille

5. Non! (12 points)
1. ne téléphone pas
2. ne dîne pas
3. n'étudions pas
4. ne voyagent pas

6. The Right Question (12 points)
1. À qui est-ce que tu téléphones?
2. Qu'est-ce que tu manges?
3. Pourquoi est-ce que tu étudies le japonais?
4. Comment est-ce que tu chantes?

Part III. Written Expression

7. Composition (20 points)
Answers will vary.

Form A/B (Alternate)

Part III. Cultural Awareness

7. Culture (20 points)
1. a   2. b
3. b   4. b
5. a   6. c
7. c   8. c
9. c   10. b

Listening Comprehension Performance Test

A. Conversations
1. d   2. a
3. c   4.

5. d

B. Questions et réponses
6. b   7. b
8. d   9. c
10. a

Reading Comprehension Performance Test

1. c   2. b
3. a   4. c
5. b   6. a
7. b   8. b
9. a   10. c

Writing Performance Test

A. Lettre à Stéphanie

Answers will vary. Sample answers:
Je m'appelle Jill Smith.
J'habite à Louisville.
Je joue au basket.
Jill

B. Préférences

Answers will vary. Sample answers:
Likes:
J'aime manger.
J'aime jouer aux jeux vidéo.
J'aime téléphoner à mon copain.
Dislikes:
Je n'aime pas travailler.
Je n'aime pas chanter.

C. Activités

Answers will vary. Sample answers:
regardons la télé.
jouons pas au foot.
parlons français.
parlons pas anglais.
dansons.
chantons pas.
nageons.
étudions pas.

D. Questions

Où est-ce que tu habites?
Est-ce que tu parles anglais?
Est-ce que tu aimes voyager?
Est-ce que tu veux visiter [Boston] avec moi?

E. Note à Christophe

Je regrette.
Je ne peux pas jouer au tennis avec toi aujourd'hui.
Je dois travailler.
Qu'est-ce que tu fais samedi?
Est-ce que tu veux jouer à deux heures?
Jill

Multiple Choice Test Items

Leçon 5

1. a. parler français
2. c. écouter
3. b. manger
4. b. jouer
5. c. travailler
6. a. parler espagnol
7. a. écouter un CD
8. a. je veux bien
9. b. je regrette
10. a. je veux bien
11. c. dîner au restaurant
12. b. jouer
13. c. écouter
14. a. dîner au restaurant
15. c. travailler
16. c. manger
17. b. manger
18. c. d'accord
19. b. je ne peux pas
20. a. je dois étudier

Leçon 6

1. b. suis
2. b. est
3 a. es
4. a. sommes
5. c. êtes
6. a. vous êtes
7. c. ils
8. b. elles
9. c. est
10. c. nous sommes d'accord
11. b. en classe
12. b. n'est-ce pas
13. a. Non, il est à la maison.
14. c. est
15. c. sont
16. a. nous sommes d'accord
17. c. je ne suis pas curieux
18. c. Ils sont là-bas.
19. b. n'est-ce pas
20. a. nous sommes ici

Leçon 7

1. a. parle
2. b. habites
3. b. organise
4. b. invitent
5. b. j'étudie
6. b. dîne
7. c. habitent
8. a. il parle espagnol
9. c. nous chantons bien
10. b. écoutent
11. b. voyageons
12. b. étudier
13. c. je n'aime pas danser
14. c. je n'aime pas
15. b. téléphone
16. a. étudier
17. a. rarement
18. c. ils ne jouent pas au football
19. c. voyager
20. b. danser

Leçon 8

1. c. Où
2. a. Comment
3. a. Pourquoi
4. c. À quelle heure
5. a. Quand
6. b. Parce que
7. a. Qui
8. b. Avec qui
9. a. À qui
10. b. Avec qui
11. b. fais
12. b. qui
13. c. Qu'est-ce que
14. b. Qu'est-ce qu'
15. b. est-il
16. a. voyagez-vous
17. c. font
18. a. faites
19. b. faisons
20. a. fais

Comprehensive Test 1
(Units 1, 2, 3)

Form A

Part I. Listening Comprehension (25 points)

1. Loto! (5 points)

1. c.	2. b
3. a	4. b
5. a	

2. Quelle heure est-il? (5 points)

6. a	7. b
8. a	9. b
10. b	

3. Invitations (5 points)

11. a	12. b
13. c	14. b
15. c	

4. La réponse logique (10 points)

16. a	17. b
18. b	19. c
20. b	21. c
22. a	23. b
24. b	25. c

Part II. Language and Communication (40 points)

5. Au café (5 points)

26. b	27. a
28. c	29. b
30. a or b	

6. L'été (5 points)

31. c	32. c
33. a	34. d
35. b	

7. Ma copine Sylvie (5 points)

36. b	37. c
38. b	39. a
40. c	

8. Une interview (5 points)

41. d	42. a
43. e	44. a
45. c	

9. L'intrus (7 points)

46. b	47. b
48. b	49. c
50. d	51. b
52. b	

10. Allô! (8 points)

53. d	54. a
55. b	56. e
57. d	58. c
59. a	60. b

11. Situations (5 points)

61. c	62. a
63. c	64. a
65. b	

Part III. Reading Comprehension (20 points)

12. Quatre annonces (9 points)

66. a	67. d
68. b	69. a
70. b	71. d
72. d	73. c
74. c	

13. Une lettre de Christine (5 points)

75. b	76. a
77. a	78. b
79. b	

14. À la télé (6 points)

80. b	81. a
82. c	83. c
84. c	85. c

Part IV. Cultural Awareness (15 points)

15. Méli-mélo culturel (15 points)

86. b	87. a
88. b	89. a
90. b	91. a
92. b	93. a
94. a	95. b
96. a	97. b
98. b	99. a
100. b	

Comprehensive Test 1
(Units 1, 2, 3)

Form B

Part I. Listening Comprehension (25 points)

1. Loto! (5 points)

1. c	2. c
3. b	4. b
5. c	

2. Quelle heure est-il? (5 points)

6. b	7. a
8. b	9. a
10. a	

3. Invitations (5 points)

11. b	12. a
13. c	14. b
15. c	

4. La réponse logique (10 points)

16. c	17. a
18. a	19. b
20. c	21. b
22. a	23. b
24. c	25. a

Part II. Language and Communication (40 points)

5. Au café (5 points)

26. c	27. b
28. b	29. a
30. c	

6. L'été (5 points)

31. c	32. a
33. b	34. d
35. b	

7. Ma copine Sylvie (5 points)

36. b	37. c
38. a	39. c
40. b	

8. Une interview (5 points)

41. b	42. d
43. b	44. a
45. c	

9. L'intrus (7 points)

46. b	47. c
48. a	49. c
50. a	51. c
52. a	

10. Allô! (8 points)

53. e	54. d
55. b	56. c
57. d	58. a
59. c	60. b

11. Situations (5 points)

61. b	62. c
63. a	64. b
65. b	

Part III. Reading Comprehension (20 points)

12. Quatre annonces (9 points)

66. d	67. b
68. c	69. b
70. c	71. c
72. b	73. a
74. a	

13. Une lettre de Christine (5 points)

75. a	76. a
77. b	78. a
79. a	

14. À la télé (6 points)

80. a	81. c or a
82. b	83. a
84. b	85. a

Part IV. Cultural Awareness

15. Méli-mélo culturel (15 points)

86. b	87. a
88. b	89. a
90. b	91. b
92. b	93. b
94. a	95. a
96. b	97. b
98. a	99. b
100. a